D1156688

OXEN, WOMEN, OR CITIZENS?

Number 143
OXEN, WOMEN, AND CITIZENS?
Slaves in the System of the Mishnah

by
Paul Virgil McCraken Flesher

OXEN, WOMEN, OR CITIZENS?
Slaves in the System of the Mishnah

by
Paul Virgil McCraken Flesher

Scholars Press
Atlanta, Georgia

OXEN, WOMEN, OR CITIZENS?
Slaves in the System of the Mishnah

Library of Congress Cataloging in Publication Data

Flesher, Paul V.
  Oxen, women or citizens?

  (Brown Judaic studies ; no. 143)
  Bibliography: p.
  Includes index.
  1. Slavery in rabbinical literature. 2. Mishnah--
Criticism, interpretation, etc. I. Title. II. Series.
HT921.F64   1988   296.1'2306   87-37670
ISBN 1-55540-212-7 (alk. paper)

Printed in the United States of America
on acid-free paper

For My Parents

Virgil Henry Flesher

&

Ellen May Flesher

Table of Contents

Part One: Slaves in Scripture and in the System of the Mishnah

    The Problem
    The Hebrew Indentured Servant
    The Foreign Slave
    Conclusion

    Classification and Hierarchy: The World of the Mishnah
    Slaves in the Mishnah
    Bondmen and Freedmen
    Classification: The Mishnah's Categories of Slavery
    The Mishnah's Categories of Women:
        Sexuality and the Householder's Control
    Sons and Householders
    Hebrew Indentured Servants and Canaanite Slaves in the Mishnah
    Conclusion

Part Two: The Mishnah's System of Slaves

    Reason and Action
    Merely Physical Acts and Bodily Conditions
    Caste Status and Kinship Ties
    Conclusion

Part Three: The Mishnah's System of Slavery

Preface

The framers of the Mishnah, a second-century A.D., Jewish law code, distinguish between slavery and freedom by showing how slavery alters the central components of human freedom — will and action. Slavery gives the master the power to control some of the slave's abilities and denies the slave free use of the others. The slave thus constitutes a tool for his owner, a human tool. As a human being, the slave possesses the potential to exercise all human powers through action, reason, and will. Because the slave is a tool, however, his powers are overridden and controlled by his master, who turns them to his own purpose. The householder accomplishes this feat through his faculty of will; the master's will replaces that of his slave. A slave can thus effectively perform only his master's dictates, not his own inclinations. Furthermore, since the actions performed by both the master's own body and the slave ultimately stem from the master's decisions of will, the Mishnah's sages liken the slave to his master's body, specifically, his hand. Since the master supplies the power of will for both, the slave's actions become the master's actions. The framers thus identify the slave with his master on both mental and physical levels. In other legal and religious systems, the slave may possess similar features of slavery, but for the Mishnah, these attributes comprise part of its statement of the system as a whole.

This description of slavery in the Mishnah's system and the study that produced it do not comprise the first scholarly investigation into slavery in ancient Judaism. Although slavery in the Mishnah *per se* has never been studied, many scholars have written about slavery in rabbinic literature (for example, Ephraim Urbach, Solomon Zeitlin, Joachim Jeremias, Abraham Geiger, Boaz Cohen and others).[1] Two things are new in my work. First, I emphasize treating a rabbinic text, the Mishnah, as a system unto itself. Second I take a component of that system, the slave, and use it as a means to delineate that system. I hold that the Mishnah presents a consistent and coherent portrayal of Israelite society, a portrait so cogent that the system as a whole must be explicated in order to fully grasp its scheme of slavery. The reverse also holds true, for the system makes its statement through what it says about slavery.

---

[1] See, in the Bibliography, Bamberger; Cohen, "Bondage;" Cohn; Geiger; Jeremias; Wacholder; Urbach; Zeitlin; and Zucrow.

Still more important, the framers of the system introduce the theme of slavery to make points about the system that they could make through no other topic. In particular, the focus on slavery helps to delineate the Mishnah's concept of freedom.

Like Plato's *Republic*, the Mishnah portrays the best world that its authors could imagine. Although the *Republic* is philosophy and the Mishnah is a law code, both constitute products of systematic thought. There are two important attributes to the Mishnah's character as systemic thought.[2] First, as a system, the Mishnah constitutes a code of law, which its framers have carefully designed according to set principles. These editors arranged its laws to make particular points about subjects of their choice. The points fit together into an overarching, intellectual scheme that joins them and makes them into a unified and coherent view of the world. Second, the Mishnah authorities have not constructed the Mishnah to present or reflect actual practice or historical reality, but to depict an imaginary and utopian world. We know this because the world they describe focuses on institutions and activities that had not existed for more than one hundred and thirty years. For the Mishnah's authorities, the world they present exists only in their imagination. Of course, a few rules in the Mishnah may reflect laws that had been followed in real life some hundred and thirty years earlier, but they are formulated the same as other regulations and so are indistinguishable from the rest of the Mishnah. Thus, the depiction of slavery that this book undertakes to describe is one that stems from systematic thought about Israelite society, not from historical reality.

To further explain the distinction between my approach and that contained in previous studies, let me contrast my work to that of an important scholar of rabbinic literature, Ephraim Urbach. I choose his work as representative both because he is the foremost scholar in this field and because he has done the largest study of slavery. I shall point out several problems in Urbach's work which my study of slavery is designed to avoid. All the critiques I make of his investigation apply to all other studies of slavery in rabbinic Judaism.

First of all, Urbach misunderstands the nature of the Mishnah as a law code. Urbach views the Mishnah, as he views the other legal writings in the rabbinic literature, as a mere collection of laws. The texts, for him, comprise merely *ad hoc* collections lacking any systemic coherence or unity in themselves. Individual laws thus form the focus of Urbach's investigation; the document in which a law appears is irrelevant. The notion that the Mishnah forms a cogent statement plays no role in Urbach's approach to the text. This atomistic picture of the Mishnah's nature brings about two results. First, Urbach holds that each sentence is distinct from all other sentences and therefore each individual law can be dated on its own, without reference to the text in which it appears. Urbach assigns dates to individual laws that are generations or even centuries prior to the

[2] For a more detailed discussion, see the Introduction.

composition of the text in which they appear. He uses, for instance, laws from the Mishnah (ca. 200 A.D.), the Palestinian Talmud (ca. 450 A.D.), and the Babylonian Talmud (ca. 600 A.D.) as evidence for rules and social practice prior to 70 A.D.[3] He even goes so far as to draw upon mishnaic regulations as evidence for laws and practices in the pre-Maccabean period, more than 400 years earlier![4] Moreover, he does this without providing any clear argument in support of his claims. Urbach in fact uses the same methods developed in the *Wissenschaft des Judentums* in the first half of the nineteenth century. This approach was used extensively by Heinrich Graetz in his doctoral dissertation, completed in 1845. Ismar Schorsch evaluates Graetz' work in a comment that likewise applies to Urbach.

> The method of dating on the basis of ideological similarity and historical reasoning . . . was not terribly refined. It often was arbitrary and hypothetical, with similarities accepted as influence and speculation replacing facts.[5]

Second, the other outcome is that Urbach uses all laws bearing on the same issue to explain that issue, no matter the date or provenance of the text in which they occur. Thus, he can use as evidence the Mishnah, a document edited in Palestine at the end of second century A.D., alongside the Babylonian Talmud, compiled by Jews in Babylonia in the sixth century. In fact, in one paragraph about selling daughters into slavery, Urbach draws upon the Mishnah, the Tosefta, Sifra, the gaonic Tractate on Slaves (a collection of laws compiled *sometime* after ca. 650 A.D.), the Babylonian Talmud, and Nachmanides (a medieval talmudist from Spain).[6] In light of advances in the methodology of writing history since Graetz, Urbach's methods are simply untenable.

The title of Urbach's work, "The Laws Regarding Slavery As a Source for Social History of the Period of the Second Temple, the Mishnah and Talmud" reveals further problems with his approach. Urbach not only misunderstands the Mishnah's systemic nature as a law code, but also the nature of law, for he uses "laws" as evidence for "social history." Urbach holds that laws provide direct evidence of social practice, that is, they are descriptive. He thinks that when a law says that people should do a certain action in a particular situation, people actually did that action. This is simply wrong-headed, for law is by nature prescriptive. A law states a form of behavior that people should do, not what

---

[3] See, for instance, Urbach, pp. 33-34.

[4] See Urbach, pp. 9-31, esp. p. 31.

[5] Ismar Schorsch, "Ideology and History in the Age of Emancipation," in *The Structure of Jewish History and Other Essays,* by Heinrich Graetz, translated and edited by Ismar Schorsch, (New York: JTSA, 1975), p. 37.

[6] Urbach, pp. 16-17.

they actually do.[7] No direct link necessarily exists between the behavior
envisioned by a law and the behavior practiced by members of the community
for which the law was composed. It is not even valid to assume, without further
evidence, that the law was actually made known to the members of this
community. This point has long been recognized by schools of philosophy of
law, such as analytical positivism, and by schools of jurisprudence, such as the
historical and sociological.[8] Urbach's attempt to use laws as evidence of actual,
historical practice is therefore misguided.[9]

In the few cases in which Urbach actually treats an individual law as
prescriptive rather than descriptive, he still views the law as evidence of actual
practice. He holds that the law forms a corrective for a historical situation.
Urbach seeks, in this case, to discover the particular situation behind the law.
For most mishnaic rules, this is not possible. But if the problem that a law is
designed to correct is not clear from the law itself, Urbach supplies one from his
imagination. Take the following example in which Urbach quotes a mishnaic
law (M. Sotah 3:8) and then interprets it. I give the whole of his interpretation.

> "A man may sell his daughter, but a woman may not sell her daughter":
> the main intention of this *pronunciamento* was, apparently, to prevent
> widows who had been left without adequate means of support from
> evading their obligations to their daughters in this manner.[10]

Urbach's explication of the passage has no basis in the passage itself and is
therefore imaginary. The passage talks in general about women with daughters,
without focusing on any particular category. This is clear from the quote and is
reinforced by the context of this passage within the Mishnah. There it forms
part of a list in which the powers of men are compared to the powers of women.
The point of the list is to show that men have much broader social powers than
women. Despite this unambiguous meaning, Urbach states — without offering

---

[7] This point is well articulated by Hans Kelson, who considers laws as "normative
ought-propositions," that is to say, statements of what people "ought" to do. See
Kelson, pp. 37-38, 58-59, 120.

[8] Members of all three schools understand the distinction between the statement
of a law and its practice. Representatives of the school of analytical positivism,
such as Hans Kelson and H. L. A. Hart, hold that a legal system is an intellectual
creation which ultimately depends on the cooperation of the people governed in
order to work. Members of the school of historical jurisprudence, which peaked in
the nineteenth century under Savigny, clearly understood the dynamic relationship
between legal concepts and social activity. Sociological jurisprudence as well
focuses on the distinction between law as positive ("official") law and the
behavior of the people. See the example of Ehrlich.

[9] Urbach occasionally nods in the direction of this issue, saying that there may
be a difference between laws that are practiced and "hypothetical" laws. See pp. 5
and 8. But the distinction does not inform the method by which he conducts his
study.

[10] Urbach, p. 16.

any support — that the passage refers to widows, and to destitute widows in particular. What Urbach infers as the *actual* social situation that this law is designed to correct thus exists only in Urbach's imagination. In the following study, however, the problems that Urbach encounters in his study fall away when we treat the Mishnah as a document that presents a cogent system.

The underlying presupposition that informs all Urbach's judgments is his concept of the relationship between the document he examines and the world to which he thinks it gives evidence. His concept derives from the philological/historical method developed in the early nineteenth century by historians such as Leopold Ranke. Urbach assumes that there are two components in interpretation — the text and the (historical) context. His task then is to study the text and to describe the historical situation which it reveals. For Urbach, the document provides direct evidence about reality; a single step separates the text from history.

In the past few decades, literary criticism has moved beyond this position to recognize that reality and the text are not directly linked. Instead a layer exists between between the two. In the study of narrative documents, this layer has been called the "narrative world."[11] A narrative world comprises the world presented by the text. It stands between reality and the text and is thus related to, but never identical with, the real world. The situation imagined in a novel, for instance, forms a narrative world. The author populates that world with characters and organizes it with plot, setting and so on. The work may be set in the past, as with Walter Scott's *Ivanhoe*, or in the contemporary world, like Charles Dickens' *Hard Times*. In either case, because of its fictive elements, the narrative world forms a layer distinct from the real world.

The same observation applies to literature usually considered non-fiction — such as news reports and historical writing. Hayden White has shown that historical narratives do not present reality, but the writer's perception of reality.[12] Elements of fiction thus lie even in the most exacting studies of the past and reports of current events. They present a narrative world removed from the real world, not the real world itself. Of course, this narrative world in some way represents the real world and thus can serve as a basis for reconstructing it, but that constitutes a further stage of analysis.

Like narrative works, the Mishnah points to a literary world distinct from reality. Since the Mishnah constitutes a law code, rather than a narrative, I call this layer the "systemic world," or more simply, the "system." The Mishnah's system — like a narrative world — contains many fictive elements. Since these are combined and interwoven with non-fictional information (if there is any) in a

[11] I take my understanding of this concept from Norman Petersen. He uses the idea of narrative world to study Paul's letter to Philemon and the place of slaves in that world. See Petersen.

[12] See White, "Interpretion" and White, *Metahistory*.

manner that obliterates the distinction between them, we must, for the purposes
of this study, treat the whole system as imaginary. The distance between the
Mishnah's system and the reality which it purports to depict is emphasized by
situation it presents, namely, Judaism as practiced in the Temple, an institution
which, at the time of the Mishnah's publication, had not existed for more than
130 years. This distance inspires the idea that the Mishnah's framers attempted
to depict a utopia.

The existence of a layer — the Mishnah's system — between the text of the
Mishnah and historical reality (whatever it was) reveals the inadequacy of
philology for studying the Mishnah. The presuppositions concerning the
relationship between text and context, between language and history, render it
incapable of addressing the Mishnah's systemic character. Philology thus forms
an inadequate tool for the accurate analysis of the Mishnah. If Ephraim E.
Urbach, one of the most renowned philologian-historians of Rabbinic Judaism,
cannot provide a convincing analysis, then such an investigation lies beyond the
reach of philology.[13]

We must turn instead to other methods to make sense of the Mishnah and
its concept of slavery. The study at hand constitutes an investigation of the
Mishnah's concept of slavery using systemic analysis. It attempts to reconstruct
the Mishnah's systemic world insofar as it is relevant to the analysis of slavery.
Ultimately, I claim to describe the slave's place in the Mishnah's system, not in
any historical setting. Of course, just as a narrative world can serve as the basis
for reconstructing history, so the Mishnah's system can provide the foundation
for such an exercise. But that task lies beyond the scope of this book.

---

[13] The review of Eilberg-Schwartz by Robert Brody of the Hebrew University (*The
Journal of Religion*, January 1988, vol. 68, #1, pp. 140-1) reveals the
philological study of rabbinic texts in disarray. Although Brody acknowledges
that Eilberg-Schwartz attempts to apply new methods to the study of the Mishnah
(which he implies is a worthwhile goal), he views the insights resulting from the
new methods as mistakes! In the end, he states "new methodological
sophistication must build on a foundation of careful and competent philology."
Such a remark reveals that Brody misses the point; new methods are developed
because old one(s) are inadequate. The new is intended to replace the old, not be a
mere addition.

Acknowledgments

This book began as a doctoral dissertation at Brown University under the guidance of Jacob Neusner. Throughout the years I have known him, Professor Neusner has unstintingly given his time, his attention, his wisdom and his insight. He has carefully and painstakingly analyzed my work, testing my arguments and reasoning, always requiring my best. Moreover, without his pioneering work, there might be no religious study of Judaism, no university-based, academic field in which I could work.

Wendell S. Dietrich, also of Brown, brought me outside the bounds of late antiquity to the world of modern philosophy and theology. There, he showed me how to recognize and analyze a system of thought, skills that have played a central role in the writing of this book. And because no graduate student can survive without a supportive graduate adviser or department chair, Ernest S. Frerichs (as both) bears considerable responsibility for my progress thus far.

My debts are not confined to Brown; Marvin Fox (Brandeis University) and Eugene D. Genovese (University of Rochester) read my work with painstaking care, provided insightful comments and prevented inadvertant errors on my part. William Scott Green (University of Rochester) has been a teacher and advisor since the earliest days of my undergraduate career. I thank him for the interest in his discipline he gave to a rather callow youth and for the encouragement he regularly gives me to pursue that interest.

This work took its initial shape in Professor Neusner's graduate seminar. It reflects the generous attention of Louis Newman (Carleton College), Roger Brooks (University of Notre Dame), Judith Romney Wegner (Williams College) and Howard Eilberg-Schwartz (Temple University). Professors Brooks and Eilberg-Schwartz also read and critiqued the entire work in draft stage. James Bowley and Ed Wright each read an early draft and made helpful remarks and corrections.

The work could not have been completed without financial support, in the form of grants, stipends and fellowships, from the following institutions: Brown University, the Max Richter Foundation, the Charlotte W. Newcombe Foundation, the Feder Fund for Judaic Studies and the Foundation for Future Generations.

This book owes much to friends, as well as colleagues. Although I cannot possibly list them all, I want to acknowledge a few important ones: Annette Boulay, Professor J. Stanley Lemons and Nancy Lemons, and Professor Michael McGehee and Jerilyn McGehee.

The one person whose influence permeates this study is Caroline McCracken-Flesher — my intellectual companion, close friend and wife. In discussions at every stage of this book, she has brought to bear her formidable talents as a scholar, helping to hone my ideas and sharpen their presentation. She has contributed her considerable editorial skills to help make the arguments of this book clear and the sentences understandable. Her constant companionship has made the life we share an experience of discovery and a constant source of joy.

Finally, I dedicate this book to my parents, Virgil H. and Ellen M. Flesher. From my childhood, they have encouraged me to explore new worlds and to consider new ideas. They have trained me to think for myself, to make my own judgments and decisions, and then to act on them. I am ever grateful for the preparation they gave me and for their continuing support.

Introduction

This study asks what, in the system of the Mishnah, makes a slave a slave? We want to discover what makes the slave distinct from — yet like — the other important categories in this second-century Jewish law code. How does he compare to oxen, women and full citizens? The answer takes shape within the same principles that organize the Mishnah as a whole. Since, as I shall explain, the Mishnah's central feature is its taxonomic organization of the world into a hierarchical structure of categories, the slave — like the other three categories — is defined primarily by his place in this structure. The question of the slave's position will become clear in response to two questions: first, how does he fit into the classificatory structure as a classified object; second, how does he affect the classification of other objects with the same structure? The answers to both questions are found in the slave's location within the householder's interaction with Temple cult.

First, the slave's position within the Mishnah's classification of the world results from his relationship to a citizen, otherwise known as a householder. This is because the classification of the slave stems not from any natural features, but from the power of his master. Although the Mishnah's framers view the slave as physically, mentally and spiritually equivalent to his master, the master has supreme power over the slave. Israelite society — through the institution of the Temple cult — recognizes the master's power relationship to his slave and uses it to classify the slave within the Mishnah's structure of the world. By condoning the householder's act of enslavement and accepting the slave on the master's terms, the Temple reinforces the slave's position within the system as an object classified by other human beings.

Second, the slave furthermore possesses the capacity to classify objects, just like a citizen-householder. But the master's power over the slave gives him the capacity to determine the effectiveness of his slave's acts of classification. A slave's actions approved by his master are recognized by the Temple cult as effective, even when they apply to the classification of sacred objects. A householder, for example, determines when his slave may consecrate grain as tithe for the Temple priests. The slave can perform the act of consecration with or without his master's permission, but the grain enters the status of holy tithe only when the master allows. The fact that the master's wishes determine the Temple cult's reaction shows how the classificatory relationship between master and slave determines the slave's position in the social world. Let us take a moment to unpack the relationships among slave, householder and society.

The Mishnah's authorities divide Israelite society into four categories of people: householders, minor sons, women (both minor and adult) and slaves.[1] Even at this most fundamental level, an important distinction appears between the categories of free persons and slaves. The Mishnah's framers define householders, minor sons, and women by their natural, inherent characteristics, but they define slaves by external factors. This point becomes clear from the definitive characteristics of each category. Householders possess two main features: they are male and they have the full power of reason. The Mishnah's framers differentiate minor sons by their lack of reason and distinguish women by gender. The Mishnah's sages define slaves, by contrast, as persons subject to a householder's full control. The slave's inherent features — which the framers recognize as the same as those of free people — have no bearing on his classification.[2]

This definition of the slave as the product of a relationship has important ramifications for our study of slavery in the Mishnah. First, to understand what it means for the slave to stand subject to his master's power, we must investigate the householder and determine what type of power he possesses and how that power functions. Human power, as defined in this document, comprises an individual's capacity to produce legal effects, usually through his actions. Sages conceive a householder's power over his slave, in this light, as the power to prevent his slave's actions from bearing legal effects. Second, any attempt to understand the slave must also investigate society's sanction of the master's power over his slave, for the Mishnah portrays this power in social, not personal, terms. The master does not prevent the slave from acting — a personalized form of power. Instead, he prevents the slave's acts from bearing legal effects within the context of Israelite society. Although as a general rule, the master renders void all his slave's activities, when the master chooses, he can

---

[1] This is the most fundamental scale. There are, of course, other scales that divide the people Israel into other categories; for example, the caste system separates people into castes such as priests, Levites, Israelites, and so on. We will deal extensively with this issue in Chapter Four.

[2] The classification of slaves by their subjugation to a master creates problems of terminology for us as participants in a society with a historically-high consciousness of gender distinctions. The Mishnah's framers make few gender distinctions with regard to slaves, because gender is only of secondary concern in comparison to the taxonomic criterion of the householder's control. So when the framers speaks of slaves, they in general mean both male and female. Only in matters of cultic purity does the criterion of gender take precedent over considerations of the master's power. See the discussion of this issue in Chapters Three and Four. Therefore, since there is no gender-neutral pronoun in the English language that can be applied to human beings, I shall refer to the slave as "he," even though most of the time the slave under discussion could be male or female.

make individual acts of his slave bear legal consequences. It is society's recognition and support of the master-slave relationship that enables the master to possess this form of socially effective power over his slave. Third, this form of Israelite society, and the portrayal of the master and slave within it, appears solely in the Mishnah.[3] That means the portrayal of society itself arises out of the Mishnah's formal and topical concerns. To understand the Mishnah's slave, therefore, we can adopt only one approach to the analysis of slavery in the Mishnah. We must begin with the whole — the Mishnah itself — and work inward through its portrayal of Israelite society and the householder to arrive finally at the slave himself.

In the Mishnah, the portrayal of Israelite society is expressed in the form of a law code. That is to say, the Mishnah constitutes a systematic exposition of law depicting a single, systematized view of society and the world within which it exists. By a systematic exposition of law, I mean that the Mishnah's framers have subjected their document to a rigorous process of editing, one involving the three stages: selection, organization, and reformulation. By a single systematized view of society, I mean that the Mishnah's sages present a uniform portrayal of Israelite society as a system, not as an irregular picture containing contradictory elements. Both claims require further elaboration, so let us unpack each in turn.

Selection constitutes the first stage in the construction of the Mishnah as a systematic exposition of law. The Mishnah's redactors have chosen a core of legal material from a period of legislation lasting more than one hundred and thirty years. During this period, from the destruction of the Israelite Temple at Jerusalem in 70 A.D. to the publication of the Mishnah about 200 A.D., a Jewish religious elite existed. The authorities of this group promulgated rulings on both civil and religious law. These legal opinions were not produced in any consistent fashion, but were formulated in response to issues that arose over the course of time. They probably stemmed from many different sources, some perhaps from pressing social problems of the day and others from questions asked by students. These legal dicta were thus composed in an irregular and unsystematic fashion, with no attempt to address any one topic or set of problems in an organized manner.

So when we turn to the editing of the Mishnah, we find that its framers began their work by selecting a limited number of dicta from the legal products of this period. Since the criteria used in this selection process are the same as that used for the second stage of the Mishnah's editing — namely, its

---

[3] The Mishnah designs its categories of slavery independent of Scripture, as we shall see in Chapter Two. In fact, it is the only rabbinic text to do so. All later rabbinic texts derive their categories of slaves from Scripture. This holds true, for example, for Sifra, Sifré to Deuteronomy, the Mekhilta, the Palestinian Talmud, the Babylonian Talmud, the geonic tractate on Slaves, and even for Maimonides in his *Mishneh Torah*.

organization — we shall describe the two stages together. The selection and organization of topics in the Mishnah stems from the two categories upon which its framers center their discussion. The first category comprises a social institution, the Temple cult, the second a class of human beings, the householder. These two categories and their interaction form the focus of interest for the Mishnah's framers. This becomes apparent from the topical organization of the Mishnah into six divisions. Four of these focus on matters central to the Temple cult: 1) Agriculture, which describes the agricultural tithes due to the Temple and other agricultural regulations stemming from the Temple cult; 2) Appointed Times, which discusses the festivals connected with the Temple cult; 3) Holy Things, which describes sacrifices and other forms of Temple cult worship; and 4) Purities, which details the purity regulations governing the Israelites in their everyday life and in their worship at the Temple. The other two divisions focus on matters of interest to householders: 5) the division of Women focuses on relations between men and women (marriage, divorce, and so forth), while the 6) division of Damages depicts laws governing relations between householders, namely, civil law and criminal law.

The differentiation of divisions into tractates provides further evidence of the importance of the householder and the Temple cult as criteria for selection and organization. Each of the tractates in the division of Appointed Times, for example, focuses on aspects of different cultic festivals, while those in the division of Damages center on issues of relations among householders. Within each tractate, furthermore, different subtopics conform to this pattern of selection. For example, the subtopics of the different tractates in the division of Women primarily deal with relationships between householders and women, but only rarely with relationships among women or between women and children. Similarly, subtopics in the division of Holy Things tend to describe matters concerning the householder in the Temple cult while generally ignoring the role of women and minors. Evidently, the Mishnah's framers selected laws and organized them according to the categories of Temple cult and householder.

The third stage in making an *ad hoc* collection of individual laws into a systematic exposition is reformulation, that is, making uniform the wording and language of the different dicta. The form of the legal rulings in the Mishnah derives from the nature of its publication. The Mishnah was promulgated orally; it was not originally written down but taught to professional memorizers. To aid their task, the Mishnah's framers composed the Mishnah to facilitate memorization. Each form used a minimal number of words and attempted to convey as much information as possible. Recent research has shown that each of the Mishnah's laws in fact conforms to one of six different patterns.[4] The

---

[4] For a discussion of these forms, see Jacob Neusner, "Form and Meaning: Mishnah's System and Mishnah's Language," in *JAAR*, 45, 1(1977) 27-45 and *Ancient Israel After Catastrophe: The Religious World View of the Mishnah*, (Charlottesville, VA: UPV, 1983), esp. pp. 36-7.

nature of individual forms is not significant to our study; the important point is that this limited repertoire of forms imposes a uniform appearance on the laws. It means that all legal dicta look the same; no formal difference exists between rulings made a hundred years prior to the editing of the Mishnah and those composed, say, the previous week. It further means that no saying by a named authority appears in *ipsissima verba* or even in the form in which it was transmitted. Every ruling has been altered to meet the Mishnah's formal requirements. Thus, through selection, organization and reformulation, the Mishnah's framers transform a collection of unrelated rulings into a systematic exposition of law.[5]

The ramifications of this three-stage process of editing become apparent when we turn our attention from the literary characteristics of the Mishnah as a law code to the society that code depicts. When we ask what society the Mishnah portrays, we realize that the Mishnah presents an imaginary one. At the time of publication, no Israelite Temple had existed for more than a century. The Mishnah's framers neither had first-hand experience of Israelite society under a Temple, nor did they know anyone who had. Since the Mishnah's framers performed the selection, organization and reformulation with out any comparison to an existing Temple, the Mishnah perforce contains their *image* of the Temple and Israelite society, not some faithful recording of the real thing. Of course, the framers may have had some accurate information about the Temple, but this data appears within the framework of their imaginary conception.

The Mishnah presents this imaginary picture of Israelite society from a systematic and uniform perspective. Its framers have cast the individual laws — whatever their origins — into a document that depicts their own internally consistent understanding of the world. Let me give a brief and unnuanced picture of this world view — to be worked out in greater detail in the remainder of the book. This view's primary feature is that the world has been set out in a specific order, one in which everything has its proper place. People, animals, plants, buildings, chattels, and so on all have an assigned place within this world. The sages construct this organization by the principles of taxonomy. First, the framers design an abstract system of categories. Second, the objects, animals and people that make up the world are classified and placed into these categories. Each category has a place in the taxonomically based hierarchy of

---

[5] The editorial activities of the Mishnah's framers remove the content of their work from its original relation to "historical reality." They shape the material according to their own interests and points of emphases. This activity brings on results similar to those described by Hayden White with regard to modern historians. He argues that writers of history or editors of historical material present their work according to literary forms that stem from the literary conventions of the age, not from the historical data themselves. Similarly, the Mishnah's framers arrange the Mishnah according to their own literary criteria — criteria that are not necessarily derived from the nature of their data. See White, "Interpretation" and White, *Metahistory*.

the Mishnah's world. This fact in turn reveals the relationships of different categories to each other; they do not exist as a jumbled, disorganized collection of entities. This hierarchical organization is accomplished through the taxonomic relationship of genus and species. The genus is a large class of objects that can be divided into a number of subgroups — called species. Human beings, for instance, constitute a genus and can be divided into the species of men, women, minor sons and slaves. This hierarchy is recursive. A category that functions as a species on one level can serve as a genus on another. In the genus of human beings, for example, women comprise a species, but in the genus of women, women are the genus which can be subdivided into different species of women. In this way, then, taxonomy constitutes the means by which the Mishnah's framers order their world.

The framers organize the Mishnah's classificatory system along the lines established by the two criteria of selection previously discussed, namely, the householder and the Temple cult. On the one hand, many of the important categories relate in some way to the proper conduct of the Temple cult. For example, the main categories in the Division of Agriculture — the different tithes and agricultural offerings — are important to the cult. The same applies to the festivals of the Division of Appointed Times and the sacrifices described in the Division of Holy Things. On the other hand, some important categories focus on householders and their relationships to other people, such as those in the divisions of Women and of Damages. Furthermore, some items are classified by both criteria of selection. Human beings, for instance, are classified in relationship to the householder and at the same time receive a position in Israelite society through the Temple-based caste system. Similarly, the different states of purity and impurity relate both to human beings and to the Temple. The Mishnah's classificatory system thus focuses on the specific issues of householders and the Temple cult.

It is important to emphasize that while the classificatory system is static, the objects it classifies are not. The Mishnah's world is always in flux, with objects, people, and so forth constantly being classified and reclassified. This classification is done in two ways, through the purposive actions and intentions of householders — and other human beings — and through accidents and other events beyond the control of human beings. People are classified and change classification, for instance, through purposive actions such as marriage and divorce, sale and manumission. Similarly, a householder's act of consecration can change a goat from a mere farm animal into a sanctified creature destined to be a sacrifice to God. Furthermore, a farmer's act of harvesting grapes changes them from plants to crops required to be tithed. By contrast, any grapes that accidently fall to the ground during harvest pass from the farmer's ownership and enter the classification of food for the poor. The Mishnah thus portrays a classification system that is fixed and static, but one in which objects are moved from category to category.

This latter issue constitutes the main concern of the Mishnah's sages. They wish to ensure the proper classification and reclassification of the objects of their world. They want to make clear when an object belongs to one category and when it transfers to another. They accomplish these goals by attempting to clarify the classification of objects that are interstitial or whose status is ambiguous. The framers thus never spell out, in a systematic manner, the system of categories into which they organize the world. Instead, they assume this organized system and concentrate on making clear when objects belong to one category and when to another.

This brings us back to our study of slaves. We began by claiming that slaves conform to the overall system of the Mishnah. How do we demonstrate that claim? The key to understanding the slave's position in the classification system is comparison, specifically, comparison of the category of slave to equivalent categories. An equivalent category is one that constitutes a species of the same genus. The most important equivalent categories are those mentioned in the title: oxen, women and citizens. The Mishnah's framers treat each category as equivalent to the slave in a different genus. Oxen and slaves belong to the genus of property, women and slaves belong to the genus of subordinate human beings, and citizens and slaves belong to the overall genus of human beings. Since they belong to different genera, each of these categories points to a different facet of the slave. By comparing the slave to each category and discovering their similarities, we can determine the characteristics of the genus to which they both belong. By discovering their differences, we will know what makes the slave a distinctive category within that genus.

The citizen, whom we call the householder, forms the most important category to which the slave can be compared. This is because he constitutes the normative category of human beings. This category sets the standard of humanity and comprises the epitome of the human being. When we study the slave within the context of the genus of human beings, therefore, the primary comparison must be to the householder. The extent to which the slave is like the householder reveals the extent to which he constitutes a normal human being. The slave's differences from the householder indicate the differences slavery causes.

Women also comprise a category within the genus of human beings, but they represent a lower level than the householder. Since the householder constitutes the normative standard, women represent the secondary categories of human beings. By comparing women with slaves, we can evaluate the attributes of the unfree category of slaves in light of the features of free, yet secondary, categories.

Oxen, the third category, represent the genus of property. The Mishnah's framers treat the slave within the property system as well as that of human beings. By comparing slaves to oxen and other categories of property, we can evaluate their position in this system. The characteristics that slaves share with the other categories show the extent to which they belong to the genus of property. The differences that distinguish them within this genus reveal the distinctive qualities that make the slave a separate species of property.

The ultimate category to which the slave must be compared, however, lies not outside the system of slavery but within, namely, the ex-slave or freedman. In the Mishnah's system, the freedman is defined as a slave who has been released from his subjugation to a householder. He now constitutes a free man (or woman), but one whose past stems not from individual human beings but from slavery. By comparing the slave with the ex-slave, therefore, we can discover the lasting effects of slavery and the definitive nature of the slave's subjugation to a householder. We can furthermore see how the Mishnah uses social conventions to define slavery as a category of human beings and does not rely on the slave's natural inherent characteristics to do so.

I have divided this study of slavery in the system of the Mishnah into three sections. Part One investigates the Mishnah's view of the portrayal of slavery in the Hebrew Scriptures, which is the only document that the Mishnah's framers view as authoritative. Throughout the Mishnah, Scripture serves to define issues and problems and to supply facts for their solution. Our interest is to discover whether the Mishnah's framers use Scripture as the basis for their own system of slavery. To provide a point of comparison, Chapter One examines Scripture's presentation of slavery and Chapter Two describes the system of slavery in the Mishnah and compares that system with the portrayal of slavery in Scripture.

Part Two focuses on the details of the Mishnah's system of slavery. Chapter Three examines the slave's relationship to his master and the way in which that relationship defines the slave's characteristics. Chapter Four then investigates the bondman's place in Israelite society — specifically, within the Temple cult. Chapter Five focuses on the ex-slave and attempts to determine his place in the cult. Special emphasis is given here to studying how his past as a slave affects his present status.

Chapter Six, the only one in Part Three, broadens the focus of the investigation from the concrete categories of slave and freedman to the abstract concept of slavery. By placing the characterization of slavery in comparison to a delineation of the Mishnah's idea of freedom, we can see how these abstract concepts conform to the categories of householder and slave from which they derive.

Finally, the reader should also examine the Annotated Bibliography at the end of the book. In it, I evaluate other investigations of slavery in light of the approach developed here. In this way, I attempt to show how this study relates to the scholarly research on slavery in different cultures and time periods.

Part One

Slaves in Scripture and in the System of the Mishnah

Chapter One

The Concept of Slavery in Scripture

Our analysis of slavery in the system of the Mishnah must begin with the realization that its authorities did not create their work in a vacuum; they built on the foundation of Scripture. For the Mishnah's framers, Scripture was God's revelation to the people Israel and, as such, constituted an unchallengeable source of facts. Sages used these facts in their construction of the Mishnah, taking for granted that Scripture provided accurate information about God's view of the world. To fully understand the Mishnah's portrayal of slavery, therefore, we need to distinguish the ideas about slaves that the framers took from Scripture. This exercise serves two purposes. First, Scripture's concept of slavery can function as a control to help us determine ideas introduced into Israelite culture by the Mishnah's framers. After delineating Scripture's perception, we can use it to identify concepts in the Mishnah that stem from Scripture and to distinguish them from those original to the Mishnah. Mishnaic ideas that do not derive from Scripture constitute, by definition, the framers' distinct contribution to the topic.[1] Second, once we have distinguished these two sources of Scripture and the Mishnah's sages, we can evaluate their relative importance. Sages may have borrowed Scripture's depiction of slavery whole and made only minor elaborations of their own. Alternatively, they may have designed their own system of slavery and occasionally incorporated Scriptural facts into it. Thus, discovering Scripture's concept of slavery constitutes the first step for an analysis of the Mishnah's system of slavery.

To understand the ideas with which the Mishnah's framers began, we must read Scripture as they read it. Although we cannot claim to see into the framers' minds and determine exactly how they viewed Scripture, we know one principle that guided their understanding of Scripture. The Mishnah's sages analyzed

---

[1] When I state that the contribution of the Mishnah's authorities is whatever does not stem from Scripture, I refer only to the history of Israelite culture and society. Other cultures may have done things the same way the Mishnah does. But by definition these stand outside the realm of Israelite history. Thus in the Mishnah, that which does not derive from Scripture can be assumed to originate, for all practical purposes, with its authorities.

Scripture and its picture of slavery as a unified whole, not as a collection of disparate elements written at different times in various places for diverse reasons. The Mishnah's framers were of course unaware of modern scholarship's concern with the prehistory of the biblical text, which disregards the importance of the final, redacted form of Scripture as a locus for interpretation. They could not have imagined, for example, that the Pentateuch was put together out of earlier sources.[2] Instead, they regarded the final form of Scripture as the sole context for interpretation and hence treated all information about slavery as part of a homogeneous source evidencing one conception of slavery. Thus we too must view Scripture as a single unit.

Even though the Mishnah's authorities viewed Scripture as a unified whole, they did not necessarily consider all its sections of equal value for their purposes. This fact holds true for pericopae about slaves. Slaves appear throughout the Hebrew Scriptures; words signifying slaves occur in patriarchal myths, law codes, historical narratives, prophetic revelations and even wisdom literature. Despite this, Mishnaic pericopae reflect slavery only as portrayed by the legal sections of the Pentateuch. Never once do the framers refer to even its narrative portions, let alone material found elsewhere in the Hebrew Scriptures. This fact becomes clear when we look at the Pentateuch through the eyes of source criticism. Among the many sources and proto-sources in the Pentateuch, scholars have identified three major law codes: the Covenant Code (Ex. 20:22-23:33), the Holiness Code (Lev. 17-26), and the Deuteronomic source (Deut. 12-26).[3] Of the Scriptural passages concerning slavery to which the Mishnah refers, all but one of them occur in one of these three codes. With regard to slavery in Scripture, therefore, the Mishnah's authorities focused their attention on the pentateuchal laws.

The Pentateuch's legal sections distinguish two types of slaves, those who are Israelites and those who are not. Although neither category receives extensive treatment, each of the three codes briefly describes the Hebrew slave:[4]

---

[2] The Mishnah's sages knew knothing about the modern, source-critical analysis of the Pentateuch and its division of the text into the four sources of J, E, D, and P. The idea that the Pentateuch contains different codes of law, such as the Covenant Code and the Holiness Code, was likewise foreign to them.

[3] I am aware that scholars of the Old Testament disagree about the exact verses that make up the different codes. The disputes do not affect our study, for the passages concerning slaves belong to undisputed sections of these laws. For convenience, I have followed Eissfeldt, p. 143.

[4] Ex. 22:2 mentions the case of a convicted thief who lacks the money to make restitution for the goods he stole. Scripture requires that he be sold into slavery to pay the compensation. It is unclear from the passage whether the sold thief enters the category of "Hebrew indentured servant." On the one hand, he is an Israelite and so could be eligible to be sold as a Hebrew servant. On the other hand, he has committed a crime, and hence may be unworthy of the privileged treatment

the Covenant Code in Ex. 21:2-6, the Holiness Code in Lev. 25:39-43, and the Deuteronomic recasting of the Exodus passage in Deut. 15:12-18.[5] Only the Holiness Code provides such an explicit discussion of foreign slaves (Lev. 25:44-46). Both the Holiness Code and the Covenant Code, however, provide further information about them in other passages: Ex. 21:20-21, 26-27, 32, and Lev. 22:11. In addition, a legal portion of the Priestly source mentions the enslaved foreigner (Ex. 12:43-44).

In the vast majority of the Scriptural passages ignored by the Mishnah's authorities, the word "slave" is used as a linguistic expression to indicate the subordination of one person to another.[6] At the most basic level, Scripture simply uses this term to refer to a man's slaves.[7] In addition, "slave" can also designate a king's subjects or individual members of the people Israel in their relationship to their God, Yahweh.[8] Frequently a person uses the word "slave" when he talks to his superior. If the speaker wants to show deference to another — such as a king or God — he refers to himself as a slave.[9] Because of this broad usage, such passages usually contain little information about the social classification of slaves.

A few passages involving slaves, however, provide a great deal of information about slavery, but sages ignore all of them. For instance, the Mishnah contains no reference to Genesis 24, in which Abraham sends a trusted slave to find a suitable wife for his son Isaac. In performing his task, the slave acts like a free person; for instance, he decides which girl would be a good wife. Furthermore, the girl's family treat the slave as a free person by hosting him in

---

accorded to Hebrew servant. The resolution of this question either way has no effect on our thesis.

[5] It is theoretically possible that Jeremiah 34:8-22 should be included here, but its material is so close to that of Deut. 15 that we can make no clear distinction between the two passages.

[6] I would estimate that this applies to some 150 to 200 uses of the word "slave" in Scripture. See also the discussion of this matter in van der Ploeg, pp. 84-86.

[7] See, for example, Gen. 24, 26:25, II Sam. 19:18, Prov. 29:21.

[8] Let me list a few examples: Gen. 50:7, Ex. 12:30, Josh. 1:1, Judg. 2:8, I Sam. 19:1, II Kings 19:5, Ps. 132:10, Jer. 21:7.

[9] For instance, Gen. 42:12, Josh. 9:8, I Sam. 3:9, 23:11, I Kings 8:23-36, Is. 36:11, Ps. 19:13, 109:28, Dan. 1:12.

their house.[10] From this story, the Mishnah's sages draw no conclusions about the high social position to which slaves can aspire.[11]

Several other Scriptural pericopae contain information about slavery ignored by the Mishnah's authorities. Both II Kings 4:1 and Nehemiah 5:7 & 10, for example, explicitly mention the enslavement of Israelites who have fallen into debt.[12] No mention of debt slavery, by contrast, occurs in the Mishnah. Similarly, the Mishnah does not even allude to the possibility of a slave owning other slaves, although in II Samuel 9:10, Ziva, a slave of King Saul, owned twenty slaves himself. Furthermore, Joshua 8:3-27 describes how the Israelites reduced the Gibeonites to a perpetual class of slaves. As we shall see, such a class of slaves — one defined by membership in a particular ethnic group — does not appear in the Mishnah. These examples illustrate how the Mishnah's authorities ignore information about slavery that is not located in the Pentateuch's legal passages. To discover the description of slaves the framers found in Scripture, therefore, we must restrict our analysis to the Pentateuch's legal material.

That the Scriptural sources of the Mishnah's scheme of slavery are located in the Pentateuchal laws should not surprise any student of the Mishnah; for throughout the Mishnah, its fundamental concepts that derive from Scripture stem from the Pentateuchal laws. This point holds true not only for slaves, but also for every category of persons in the Mishnah. Whenever the Mishnah's framers mention a Scriptural passage or concept in relation to a class of people, that passage or concept stems from the legal sections of the Pentateuch. The studies of both H. Albeck and J. Neusner have demonstrated this point.[13] Their

---

[10] The opposite point about the position of slaves is made in Genesis 22, which contains the story of Abraham's attempted sacrifice of his son Isaac. In it, Abraham takes slaves with him on his journey, but leaves them behind with the baggage when the main event is about to take place. No passage in the Mishnah reflects this episode or explicitly concludes that slaves should not take part in a family's activities.

[11] Not even the Mishnah's stories about Tabi, the slave of Gamaliel, show any interest in raising slaves, as a general class, above a lowly position. In M. Ber. 2:7, sages relate Gamaliel's mourning the death of Tabi. The point of the story is that this constitutes an exception to the general rule that people should not mourn for slaves. Similarly, in M. Suk. 2:1, the Mishnah's framers make the point that Tabi is not considered like an Israelite and is thus exempt from the religious duties of the Festival of Booths. True, in the latter story, Gamaliel calls Tabi a "Disciple of the Sages" (תלמיד חכם). But this is merely a rhetorical device used to show that Tabi knows a particular law.

[12] Amos 2:6 and 8:6 might also refer to debt slavery, but they contain no explicit mention of debt. Compare Urbach, p. 4.

[13] H. Albeck (*Mishnah*, see the introductions to each tractate) and J. Neusner (*Evidence*, pp. 329-351) have shown that when the Mishnah depends on Scripture, it chooses the legal material of the Pentateuch. Since their work covers the entire Mishnah, we can assume, initially anyway, that when the Mishnah's framers use

work identifies all the Scriptural pericopae used by the framers; none of them stem from outside these legal passages.

This brief survey of Scriptural passages about slaves shows the significance of the framers' use of the Pentateuchal laws. They select areas of Scripture that claim to constitute rules given by Yahweh, while ignoring pericopae that reveal human practices, such as the cases just mentioned concerning Abraham's trusted slave and Ziva, King Saul's slave. Thus, the Mishnah's framers draw only on "divine legislation" and do not recognize human precedent, even when included in Scripture. For the system of the Mishnah, divine legislation constitutes the only authoritative Scriptural source of law.[14]

This point brings us to the next step of our investigation. Since the Mishnah's authorities obviously treat the Pentateuch's legal material as having a unity that distinguishes it from the rest of Scripture, do they likewise perceive a unity in that material's portrayal of slaves? Do sages discern an overall concept of slavery evidenced by these laws or do they simply use individual laws about slaves in isolation from each other? We must answer this question in two stages. First, in this chapter we shall explicate the portrayal of slavery presented by the Pentateuch's legal material. Second, in the following chapter we shall compare this concept of slavery to that presented in the Mishnah. In this way, we can determine whether the framers adopt Scripture's idea of slavery or whether they design their own. We now turn to the first stage of our investigation.

The Problem

The problem before us is to construct a description of slavery in the Pentateuch that goes beyond the mere paraphrase of a few rules to a coherent picture of the slave. We need to discover not just Scripture's laws of slavery, but the image of the slave about which Scripture legislates. Given the paucity of Pentateuchal rulings on slaves, this picture perforce remains incomplete. But even an unfinished description will provide a helpful comparison for our study of the Mishnah, because the Mishnah's authorities worked from the same text.

If we place Scripture's slaves into the larger context of Israelite society, we can flesh out some of the gaps in its depiction of slavery. The main unit of the Israelite community, the household, provides the focal point of this context. Each household possesses a specific structure; an adult male — the householder

---

Scripture in their discussion of slavery, they will choose from the pentateuchal laws.

[14] M. Avot supports this point by revealing that the rabbis living a generation after the completion of the Mishnah held this view. According to M. Avot, the rulings presented by individual rabbinical figures in the Mishnah were originally given to Moses by Yahweh on Mt. Sinai. Instead of writing down these laws, Moses orally transmitted them to his successors. The rabbis behind the Mishnah, according to Avot, are the final link in this oral transmission of law. Thus, for the Mishnah's framers, Yahweh constitutes the sole authoritative source of law.

— stands at its head, while woman and children occupy lower, dependent positions. In addition, the position of these groups in the household corresponds to their capacity to participate in Israelite society at large. The householder possesses the most extensive rights of participation, although his dependents have fewer participatory rights. These differences can best be explained by representing them on a sliding scale. Such a scale reveals the relative social positions of the different categories of people. Both Hebrew slaves and foreign slaves possess a place in the household. By using the information about them provided by Scripture, we can determine their position in the household relative to these categories. By first describing where free persons belong on this social scale, we can then place slaves in relation to them.

The householder occupies the top position on this scale. He constitutes an autonomous individual because he possesses his own social position. This position stems originally from his family ties, specifically those to his father and mother, and is determined at the time of his conception.[15] Throughout a male's life, this status remains the same; it is unaffected by marriage, divorce, death, or other changes to his kinship ties. This enables him, in his own right, to participate fully in the community's activities. The next point of the scale is occupied by the householder's wives, his dependents. Wives participate in Israelite society through their marital relationship. They derive caste status and family ties from their spouses and not from their own family background. For example, a priest's daughter enjoys the caste privileges of a priest as long as she remains in her father's household. But, if she marries an Israelite, she loses those privileges and assumes those of her husband. Thus, women depend on the male head of the household to determine their position in society. At the bottom of the scale stands mere animate property. Here there is no issue of caste status, nor of any other form of status. Scripture does not imagine, for example, that a cow or goat could be a member of the priestly caste. Furthermore, there is no question of autonomy at this level. All forms of property are subject to the whims of their owners. Only in a few cases does Scripture place limits on the owners capacity to use his property as he chooses. The question now facing us is to determine where on this scale Scripture's two classes of slaves stand. Do the characteristics of each category make them more like a householder, a wife, or a cow?

Scripture's basic theory of society, which underlies the scale just outlined, plays an important role in determining the status of slaves. The central myth of the Pentateuch is that all Israelites, "the children of Israel," are descended from the patriarch Israel (Jacob). Scripture portrays the people Israel as an extended family in which each person is related through kinship ties to everyone else. The converse also holds true; anyone who does not descend from Jacob does not

---

[15] In the Pentateuch, if a man and woman possess compatible castes, their offspring take the father's caste.

fully belong to the people Israel. Although foreigners who reside among Israelites can join the community in both religious and commercial activities, Scripture does not treat them as part of Israel, but as a distinct group alongside.[16]   Clearly, a person's ancestry constitutes the criterion for membership in Israelite society.

This concept of the people Israel likewise separates slaves into two categories; Lev. 25:39-46 explicitly distinguishes those who were born Israelites from those who were born outsiders. The Hebrew slave is in reality a long-term servant. He keeps most of his autonomy, being bound to his master only by an agreement to work for him. Thus, he retains the potential for participation in Israelite society. This type of slave we shall call an "indentured servant." By contrast, slaves who originate outside Israelite society have a much lower position on the scale. Scripture places them somewhere between dependents, such as wives, and mere property. On the one hand, as we shall see, these slaves participate in religious activities as their masters' dependents. On the other hand, they are their masters' property and lack many rights enjoyed by other dependents.[17]

---

[16] Scripture classifies the foreigner living within topographical boundaries of the Israelite community as a sojourner (גר). The Pentateuch frequently emphasizes that he should be treated as if he were an Israelite, particularly in matters of commerce and justice. See for example Lev. 19:34. If the sojourner undergoes circumcision, he becomes nearly equivalent to a native and is permitted, even required, to participate in cultic activies. See Ex. 12:43-50, Lev. 17:8ff, Num. 15:14-16, and so on, Scripture at all times retains the distinction between the born-Israelite and the sojourner; thus emphasizing that the sojourner's lack of Israelite ancestry prevents him from becoming a full member of the people Israel. The sojourner, therefore, comprises the exception that proves the rule. See the discussions in Pope, Schreiner, and Kellermann.

[17] People familiar with other descriptions of slavery in the Pentateuch will at this stage think that I have left out a category, the female slave — known in Hebrew as the שפחה, or the אמה. Actually, this person is a concubine, as is clear from the description in Ex. 21:7-11, and not merely a slave as is commonly assumed. The use of the female slave as a sex object is likewise reflected in Lev. 19:20-22, where Scripture imposes a fine for having sex with someone else's concubine. The Mishnah's framers also recognize the sexual use of the concubine, for in the few passages where they mention this category (e.g., M. Bek. 1:7), she is treated as a concubine and not merely as a slave. This solves the problem raised by Lemche ("Slave") who noted that Exodus pericope does not describe a general category of female slave. Paul, "Exod. 21:10" and Mendelsohn, "Sale," argue the two sides of this issue in relation to Nuzi law. Patrick (p. 71) emphasizes the status of the אמה as a concubine. Note, however, that in Deut. 15:12-18, the female slave is treated not as a concubine, but simply as the female version of the male slave.   As we shall see, the Mishnah's authorities combine both characterizations into one. The Mishnah treats the female slave like a male slave, with the added attribute of sexual use.

The immediate task before us is to analyze Scripture and spell out the social status held by these two types of slaves.[18] Then, in the next chapter, we shall turn to the Mishnah and determine how its framers used the Pentateuch's concept of slavery. We now start by examining the Hebrew indentured servant.

The Hebrew Indentured Servant

Exodus calls the Israelite who sells himself to his fellow a "Hebrew slave." However, when we examine this "slave's" identity, we find that the Pentateuch recognizes him as an autonomous individual. His status stems from his own family ties, not from his relationship to his master. He thus bears little resemblance to a chattel-slave, but constitutes an "indentured servant." This term is appropriate, for the Hebrew indentured servant shares two important characteristics with his seventeenth-century, Common-law namesake.[19] He contracts out his labor for a specified period of time (six years or until the next Jubilee year),[20] and while serving, he retains the family and social ties he possessed prior to entering servitude.[21] Our investigation first focuses on Scripture's denial of the indentured servant's slavehood, and then proceeds to examine his autonomous standing. We shall see that he is autonomous because he derives his status from his own family background, rather than assuming his master's position, as would a dependent.

Scripture in effect denies that the Hebrew indentured servant is really a slave at all. Both Deuteronomy and Leviticus speak of him as a "brother" and a

---

[18] Silver (pp. 68-72) fails to see how the racial background of slaves affects their standing in society. While he sees the differences in how Hebrew servants and foreign slaves become enslaved, he does not perceive that the terms of their bondage also differ.

[19] The best general discussion of the English practice of sending indentured servants to the American colonies is Smith, *Bondage*, esp. pp. 3-25. Several other scholars understand the Hebrew slave as an indentured servant. See for example Patrick, p. 70.

[20] Obviously, this does not mean a modern contract with all its terms set forth in the document. Falk (pp. 92-95) demonstrates that Scripture has no "law of contract" in the modern sense. Rather, the terms are set by customary law. Scripture, in its discussion of the Hebrew servant, describes this standard practice.

[21] As we shall see in the following discussion, Lev. 25:39-43 makes a point of emphasizing that the Hebrew indentured servant has the same kinship ties and rights at the end of his period of servitude that he had prior to its beginning. If he enters as a married man, he leaves as a married man. Ex. 21:1-3 reiterates this point. Ex. 21:4-6 makes the same point with regard to the single man who becomes an indentured servant. An unmarried man whose master gives him a "slave-wife" during his servitude may not retain her as a wife when he leaves. He enters single and he must leave single. If he wishes to remain "married" he must become a permanent slave.

"Hebrew," but never call him "slave."[22] Indeed, the term "Hebrew slave" is used only once in Scripture, in Ex. 21:2. Furthermore, Lev. 25:39 explicitly forbids the master to treat the purchased Hebrew as a slave. In this way, Scripture rejects the notion that one Israelite can be regarded as another Israelite's property.

Scripture confirms that the indentured servant ranks above slavery by showing that he possesses the characteristics of an autonomous individual. That is, the indentured servant's social status derives from his family background. Since he retains the ties to his family of origin, he likewise keeps the same status. Indeed, Lev. 25:41 specifies that when the servant has completed his indenture, he returns to his family.

> [When the Hebrew indentured servant has served his time] then he shall go out from you, he and his children with him and go back to his own family and return to the possession of his fathers.

Lev. 25:41

This verse indicates two significant points about the Hebrew servant's relationship to his family of origin. First, the servant retains his family ties through his period of servitude. These ties determine the servant's place in the community. By keeping his acknowledged position as a member of his father's family, the Hebrew servant retains the caste status determined by his family background and thus remains a member of Israelite society.

Second, by stating that the Hebrew indentured servant returns to "the possession of his fathers," Scripture further demonstrates that the servant retains his rights as his father's heir. The term "possession of his fathers" refers to the land assigned to each family when Israel entered the land of Canaan. According to Scripture, this land must remain in the family and cannot be permanently sold or given to an outsider. The servant's retention of the right to inherit this property demonstrates that not only does he remain a member of his family, but his standing within the family remains unchanged.

Having shown that the indentured servant retains his own family connections, let us now turn to the other side of this issue and show that he does not become a member of his master's household, and hence cannot assume the

---

[22] The term brother is not often used in the legal material in the Pentateuch. But when it is used, it serves to emphasize the dichotomy between Israel and the nations. Two examples will make this clear. When Deut. 17:15 lays down the law concerning who may become a king, it emphasizes that the king must be a Hebrew. He must be chosen "from among your brethren" and goes on to specify that Israel "May not put a foreigner over you, who is not your brother." Similarly, Deut. 23:20-21 states that a Hebrew may lend money and charge interest to a foreigner, but "to your brother you shall not lend upon interest." In this way, it is clear that when Scripture uses the term "brother," it emphasizes the distinction between Israelite and foreigner. Thus, when Scripture refers to the Hebrew slave as "brother," it indicates that the slave is a member of Israelite society.

latter's status. Scripture limits the period of the indenture to six years, after which the servant goes free. After this period, however, the servant may voluntarily become his master's permanent slave. A special rite of passage is required to transfer him from temporary servitude to permanent slavery. This very fact testifies to the indentured servant's autonomous identity, for the rite's purpose is to sever ties with his family of origin and bring him into his master's household. Ex. 21:2-6 describes this ceremony:

> ...in the seventh [year], he [i.e., the Hebrew indentured servant] shall go out free, for nothing.... But if [he] plainly says, "I love my master, my wife, and my children; I will not go out free," Then his master shall bring him to God, and shall bring him to the door, or unto the doorpost; and he shall bore his ear through with an awl; and he shall serve him for life.

Ex. 21:2, 5-6[23]

In what way does this rite reveal the independence of the indentured servant from his master? The ceremony of piercing the servant's ear at the threshold of the master's house symbolizes the servant's transition from outside to inside the household.[24] Before the piercing, the servant is an autonomous individual. Afterwards, he derives his identity solely from membership in the master's household. By having his ear pierced, then, the indentured servant gives up his independent status, enters the purview of the householder, and becomes the latter's dependent.[25] The rite thus symbolizes the servant's surrender of his previous familial identity and his adoption of the master's.

If the indentured servant is not property but an autonomous individual, then what is his relationship to his master? Scripture answers the question by invoking the metaphor of the hired worker and the sojourner (Lev. 25:40). Like them, the Hebrew servant is bound to the Israelite householder by a contract of labor, which is the sole tie between himself and his master. Similar to the hired man and the sojourner, he retains his own autonomous standing in Israelite society. The tie of labor does not suffice to bring him under the full authority of the master or to make him a member of the latter's household. The householder

---

[23] Many scholars, including Paul and Lemche (Lemche, "Slave"), hold that Exodus 21:2-6 stems from Kirkuk or Nuzi law. If this is so, they claim, then the "Hebrew" of "Hebrew slave" reflects not a person of Israelite race, but rather a member of a social class, that of a poor class of workers. See Gray for an in-depth discussion of this problem and further bibliography. Of course, the prehistory of the Exodus passages was unknown to the Mishnah's framers and so our study need not address this problem.

[24] See Draffkorn, p. 223.

[25] See Paul's discussion (p. 50) in which he argues that this ceremony permanently attaches the Hebrew servent to the household. See also Falk, "Exodus," pp. 86-88 and Patrick, pp. 70-71.

has no power to dictate the Hebrew servant's activity beyond the agreed tasks. The servant thus remains independent of the householder.

One characteristic of the Hebrew indentured servant appears to contradict this image of him as an autonomous individual, namely, that Scripture assumes that he enters servitude through sale. For instance, Ex. 21:2 begins, "If you acquire (תקנה) a Hebrew slave," while Lev. 25:39 says, "If your brother should become poor with you and sell (נמכר) himself to you." Does this fact alter our picture of the servant as autonomous? No, for as our argument has made clear, the Hebrew indentured servant sells not his person, but his labor.[26] Thus, the Israelite who sells himself does not become his master's property. Even after the transaction he remains an autonomous member of Israelite society. Therefore, the "sale" seems to function more like the execution of a contract. Even though the enslaved Israelite must work for his master over an extended period of time, his social standing remains that of a free man.

The Foreign Slave

The foreigner who becomes enslaved to an Israelite occupies a low position on the Israelite social scale. We locate him between his master's dependents, such as his wives and children, and the master's property. We arrive at this placement in two ways. First, although the foreign slave's tie to his master constitutes a property relationship, Scripture grants the slave a caste position determined like the status of other dependents. The tension this engenders leads us to place him on the scale between dependent and property. Second, another set of data from Scripture justifies this placement by explicitly treating him as an intermediate category. For example, the penalty for killing one's own slave falls somewhere between the punishment for killing a free man, and the impunity with which one may slaughter one's own sheep (Ex. 21:12, 20-21). Let us now turn to Scripture and describe the position of the foreign slave in more detail.

Lev. 25:44-46 presents the foreign slave as property. This passage forms Scripture's only explicit statement concerning the status of the foreign slave. Scripture juxtaposes it with a discussion of the Hebrew indentured servant, thereby emphasizing the distinction between the two.

> As for your male and female slaves whom you may have: you may buy male and female slaves from among the nations that are round about you. You may also buy from among the strangers who sojourn with you and their families that are with you, who have been born in your land: and they may be your property. You may bequeath them to your sons after you, to inherit as a possession forever.

> Lev. 25:44-46

---

[26] See van der Ploeg, p. 81 and Chamberlayne, p. 58.

How does this passage characterize the foreign slave as property? First, Israelites purchase slaves from foreigners. From the Israelite's viewpoint, this transaction constitutes a transfer of property. Second, whereas Hebrew servants are acquired by an agreement that treats master and servant as having equal power to enter into contract, no such equality exists with regard to the foreign slave. The foreign slave becomes part of his master's estate and, should his master die, falls to the son as inheritance. This picture of the foreign slave as the one who is permanently unfree — one whose slavery has no limits — clearly indicates his status as property.

In contrast to this treatment as property, Scripture also treats the foreign slave as a dependent member of his master's household and determines his status accordingly. This becomes clear in two aspects. First, Scripture requires the master to break the slave's ties to his former society and kin and to bring him into the Israelite community. This is done by circumcising the slave. After circumcision, the foreign slave is treated like a member of Israelite society and can take part in cultic observances. This process is illustrated in the following passage where we see that the foreign slave may partake of the Passover sacrifice prepared by his master.

> This is the ordinance of the Passover: no foreigner shall eat of it, but every [foreign] slave that is acquired with money may eat of it after you have circumcised him.
>
> Ex. 12:43-44

This requirement points out the clear distinction drawn by Scripture between insider and outsider to Israelite society. Since the foreign slave is a gentile, Scripture initially denies him the right to eat the Paschal sacrifice. By contrast, once he becomes a member of an Israelite's household, he may partake. This is because through circumcision, he becomes his master's dependent. He loses his biological family and ethnic ties and instead assumes those of his master. He no longer occupies the status of an outsider, but becomes a dependent member of his master's household in particular, and of Israelite society in general.[27]

The second aspect of the foreign slave's position as a dependent is provided by the privilege of a priest's slave to join in eating priestly rations (Lev. 22:11). Here, the slave not only becomes an Israelite but also takes on his master's caste status. By living with a family, the slave becomes incorporated into the household.[28] This is particularly true for a priest's slave. Since priests serve as

---

[27] Since Passover celebrates the redemption of the people Israel from slavery, the slave's participation is highly ironic. His celebration of the release of Israel from the condition in which he himself remains demonstrates that his ties to his master's household, and thus to Israelite society, are stronger than his bond of servitude.

[28] It is unclear in the passage whether the foreign slave is circumcised. In accord with Gen. 17:12-13, I hold that he is. That passage makes clear that without

the main functionaries of the Israelite cult, they possess the right to consume priestly rations brought to them as offerings by Israelites. It is significant that the slave, like the priest's family, shares in this privilege.

> And if a priest acquires a [foreign slave] as his acquisition of money, [the slave] may eat of it [i.e., priestly rations]

Lev. 22:11[29]

The fact that the foreign slave takes on his master's caste status and therefore may eat priestly rations clearly makes his position analogous to a priest's dependent. Priestly rations are holy produce and hence must be consumed in a state of cultic purity. In allowing the priest's slave this privilege, Scripture implies that the foreign slave has joined the family, and, like its other members, can attain such purity. By taking this for granted, Scripture further indicates that the slave, as a dependent, takes on the master's caste status. The foreign slave is neither outcaste nor untouchable.

We now see that Scripture treats the foreign slave sometimes as a dependent and sometimes as property. We claimed above that the combination of these two positions placed the foreign slave between these two categories on our scale. But how do we know that such a conclusion is warranted? Perhaps Scripture simply expresses two contradictory views of the status of the foreign slave. But this is not the case, for Scripture's treatment of the killing of a foreign slave shows that there is indeed a hybrid view of the foreign slave. A slave's killer incurs a penalty less than one who kills a free person, but more than for one who destroys property. For example, Ex. 21:20-21 presents a situation in which a master beats his slave and the slave subsequently dies:

> He who strikes a [free] man who [subsequently] dies shall surely be put to death. ...and when a man strikes his male [foreign] slave or his female [foreign] slave with a rod so that the slave dies under his hand, he shall be punished (נקם ינקם). But if the slave survives a day or two [and then dies] he is not to be punished; for the slave is his money (כי כספו הוא).

Ex. 21:12, 20-21[30]

---

circumcision, the slave would still be outside Israel and therefore ineligible to eat priestly rations.

[29] It is clear that here in Lev. 22:11, as well as in Ex. 21:20-21, Scripture speaks of the foreign slave. Although it does not explicitly mention foreign slave, it does identify the slave with the "money" (כסף) (of his master. This identification is made only with the slave of foreign origins. Gen 17:13-14 and Ex. 12:43-44, which deal explictly with foreign slaves, both refer to the slave as his master's "money." This is the same identification that occurs in Lev. 22:11 (and also in Ex. 21:20-21), therefore we know that Scripture discusses foreign slaves in this passage.

[30] As we saw in a previous footnote, Ex. 21:20-21 refers to a foreign slave because Scripture identifies him as his master's "money." There are two other

In this situation, the foreign slave has none of the rights of a free Israelite. The killing of a free Israelite is requited by the execution of his killer. With the foreign slave, however, the worst judgment the killer could receive is a nebulous, undefined punishment.[31] Indeed, unless the slave dies on day one, the master will go unpunished. The difference between the cases at verses 20 and 21, according to David Daube, lies in the master's intention in administering the beating.[32] Daube argues that if the slave dies immediately, Scripture presumes that his master intentionally beat him to death. But if the slave dies a few days later, Scripture treats the death as accidental. Thus, a householder incurs no liability for the manslaughter of his foreign slave. He is culpable only if he has intentionally murdered him. The foreign slave has a greater right to life than livestock, however, for a householder may slaughter his ox with impunity. Scripture does not grant animals a right to life, but rather considers the slaughter of animals, such as sheep and goats, normal practice. Therefore, the foreign slave stands lower than a dependent person on the social scale, but retains some

---

passages here in Ex. 21 (vss. 26-27 and vs. 32) for which we must address the question of whether they refer to Hebrew slaves or foreign slaves. Ex. 21:32 obviously treats the slave as the property of his master. Furthermore, from its context in vss. 28-32, we can see that Scripture regards the slave as lacking all family ties. Since, from the picture of the Hebrew slave that we have derived from Scripture's explicit discussion of his status and rights, the slave here in vs. 32 cannot be a Hebrew. Therefore, Ex. 21:32 concerns the goring of a foreign slave.

Ex. 21:26-27 is not as clear-cut. Taken by itself, we could argue that it refers to the Hebrew slave. Many scholars, such as Mendelsohn, Paul and Falk, have argued that this passage treats the slave with great concern for his humanity and for the protection of his person. They therefore conclude that vss. 26-27 refer to the Hebrew slave. If, along with the Talmud, we consider the passages in their formal context — that is, with vss. 23-25 — we could argue that the passage concerns the foreign slave. Since the slave cannot have equal retribution against his master, as free men can have against their assailant (vss. 23-25), Ex. 21:26-27 treats the slave as property with only limited rights to protection. Therefore, this passage would refer to the foreign slave. Personally, I think that the latter explanation is correct, but both interpretations fit with our portrayal of Scripture's system of slavery.

[31] The fact that the master's "punishment" here is not death is clear from formal criteria. Vss. 20-21 stand at the end of a list that begins at verse 12. For each misdeed on the list, Scripture explicitly requires the death penalty (vss. 12-17). For the last two items (vss. 18-19 and 20-21), however, Scripture specifies different penalties. The juxtaposition of the two lists clearly indicates that Scripture could have chosen to require the death of the tortfeasor but did not. As Brevard Childs states: "Such an interpretation cannot be maintained [that is, that punishment mentioned is the death penalty]. The formula 'he will be punished' is strikingly vague and cannot be identified with the death penalty *per se* . . . any doubt as to whether a different standard from that used for the free citizen was applied to slaves is removed by the final motivation clause." (Childs, *Exodus*, p. 471, brackets mine).

[32] Daube, "Causation," pp. 247-249.

rights that place him above mere property, the latter position being a status with no rights whatsoever.

Conclusion

Having determined that Scripture locates the Hebrew indentured servant and the foreign slave at different levels of Israelite society, one question remains. Why does Scripture assign them to those specific places? The answer lies in the source of social status in general, namely, a person's genealogical background. Birth into Israel supplies two things necessary for participation in that society: overall membership in the extended family of Israel and a defined niche in that society. By being born into a particular Israelite family, one acquires a specific caste status and the rights associated with it. However, even though birth guarantees that a person belongs to Israel, the capacity to assume the rights that accompany one's status is contingent upon two other factors: age and gender. To assume the rights of full participation in the community, an Israelite must be the proper age (adult) and the right gender (male). If these two conditions are not satisfied — that is, if the person is a minor or a woman — then the person may function only as the dependent of an adult male.

These concerns obviously come into play when Scripture determines the status of the Hebrew indentured servant, for the servant fulfills all three requirements; he was born an Israelite, he is an adult, and he is male. The issue for the Hebrew indentured servant is whether servitude, like the wrong age or gender, hinders a person's enjoyment of his full rights. As we saw above, servitude does not have this effect on his status. The indentured servant sells only his labor and not his person, thereby retaining his place in Israelite society. Working for another Israelite, even for an extended period of time, does not affect his status or rights. The Hebrew indentured servant remains an adult, male Israelite after entering servitude and therefore is autonomous.

The foreign slave, by contrast, lacks the essential requirement for membership and status in Israelite society, namely, Israelite birth. This fact gives rise to the question, how can the foreign slave participate in Israelite society without being a descendant of Jacob? The problem is this: since the slave originates outside the people Israel, by definition he should be totally excluded from them. But since he belongs to an Israelite householder, he lives and works within the Israelite community. Scripture solves this dilemma by providing another means for determining membership and status — the two attributes normally defined by birth. The foreign slave attains membership in the family of Israel by undergoing circumcision, the rite routinely performed on every newborn male to bring him into the Covenant between God and Israel and to identify him as an Israelite. By subjecting the slave to this rite, he is "born again" as an Israelite. Membership supplied by circumcision, however, only attaches the foreign slave to Israelite society; he must still be given a specific place in society. As we have seen, the status of the foreign slave is determined by the bond between him and his master. This tie locates him in Israelite society as his master's dependent and defines his caste status and other society attributes. In this way, the slave's bond to his master serves as a surrogate kinship tie to define his position in Israelite society.

We have now delineated the concept of slavery presented in the Pentateuch's legal sections. Scripture's theory of Israelite society as an extended family divides slaves into two groups, those who are Israelites — and therefore constitute indentured servants — and those who are foreigners — and thus rank as chattel slaves. The different genealogical background of each type of slave requires Scripture to determine their social position in different ways. The Hebrew indentured servant is born an Israelite and thus his own ancestry determines his social position. The foreign slave, by contrast, originates outside Israel and hence cannot claim a place in Israelite society in his own right. Instead, the slave enters Israelite society through circumcision, although his relationship to his master determines his specific social position. This, then, constitutes the outline of slavery presented in the Pentateuch's legal material.

With this understanding of Scripture's portrayal of slaves in hand, we can now analyze the Mishnah's theory of slavery. Initially, we want to discover the relationship between the two texts' depictions of slaves. Although this chapter has served largely as preparation for such a study, one aspect of this relationship between the two texts is already clear; the Mishnah's framers use pericopae found only in the Pentateuchal laws. As we saw above, this is because sages draw information from Scriptural passages that claim the status of divine legislation and ignore those that merely describe the actions of men. Thus, the Mishnah's use of Scripture focuses on instruction from God, not on human precedent. In the next stage of our investigation, we must determine how the Mishnah's sages use these passages. The central question is whether sages continue their reverence for God's strictures when they spell out their own system of slavery. That is to say, we want to know whether they attempt to carry forward the divine scheme of slavery they found in Scripture or whether they design their own system of slavery to which Scripture supplies facts but does not dictate the overall shape of the system.

Chapter Two

Slavery in the System of the Mishnah

Descriptions of slavery in different cultures frequently sound alike. The following sentences could easily describe slavery in many societies:

> A slave is a human being who constitutes owned property, a position that places him squarely under his master's power. A slave's master can force him to perform tasks of the master's bidding. If the slave balks, the master can beat him with impunity. To make matters worse, the slave depends on that same master for food, clothing, and shelter.

This description fits slaves in a number of societies, possibly referring to slaves in Greece in the fourth century B.C., Scandinavia under the Vikings, or the nineteenth-century American South.[1] But such a concentration on shared traits hides the distinctive attributes of each society's concept of slavery. For despite general similarities, slavery does differ from culture to culture. Furthermore, the reasons for that difference stem from the cultures themselves. Slaves derive their distinctive characteristics from the particular attributes of the society in which they are located. To take an extreme illustration, slaves in the nineteenth-century American South differed strikingly from slaves in second-century Rome, and this difference stemmed from factors particular to each society. In America, some slaveholders justified slavery by arguing that members of the Negro race — their sole source of slaves — were slaves by nature.[2] Because of this attitude, slaves were given little opportunity to hold money or property, for this

---

[1] Patterson's monumental work makes it plain that all these traits are not always found in every slave system. However, they are as widespread as I claim. See Patterson, *Social Death*, pp. 17-27. For Greece, see for example, M. I. Finley, "Was Greek Civilization based on Slave Labour?" in Finley, *Greece* and J. Vogt, "Slavery and the Ideal of Man in Classical Greece" in Vogt. For the Vikings, see Williams. For slavery in the American South, see Stampp and the many works by Eugene Genovese.

[2] This is Stampp's point, Genovese argues against it. The idea that people are slaves by nature has had distinguished adherents from the earliest times, such as Aristotle (*Politics*, I 5&6). This justification is of course nonsense and based on false premises, but until recently it was a formidable and persuasive argument. For a fuller discussion of this matter, see Stampp, pp. 6-14.

right belonged to free men. In addition, slaveholders rarely freed their black slaves; after all, they reasoned, blacks were born to be slaves. In Rome, by contrast, no such idea of natural slavery existed; race played no part in its system of slavery. Indeed, the Romans took slaves from all peoples; they enslaved members of the various "barbarian" tribes and nations as well as Greeks, whom the Romans recognized as having a culture superior to their own. Thus, although they considered the institution of slavery as normal, they viewed no one people as inherently slavish. As a result, wealthy masters permitted favored slaves to administer money, property, or even other slaves. Furthermore, they frequently manumitted these slaves, expecting that the freedmen would be more beneficial to them in liberty than in bondage. As this example illustrates, the distinct characteristics of a slavery system reflect the cultural setting in which it exists. The opposite also holds true; because a concept of slavery stems from its host culture, that concept serves as an indicator for the broad traits of that culture.

Similarly, since the system of the Mishnah imparts particular features to its scheme of slavery, the treatment of slaves in turn points to the general characteristics of the Mishnah and the culture it presents. Throughout this study of slavery in the system of the Mishnah, therefore, there will be an interplay between the characteristics of slaves and the framers' organization of Israelite society. This causes two practical effects on our study. On the one hand, when we analyze the Mishnah's presentation of slavery, it will tell us how the system of the Mishnah depicts the larger society as well as its portrayal of slavery. This is because the Mishnah's sages treat all categories of society according to the same principles. The principles of organization that apply to slaves likewise apply to other people within the Mishnaic depiction of Israelite society. On the other hand, to discover the central point from which to begin our analysis of slavery, we must describe the fundamental principles that organize the Mishnah's world. By showing how these principles place human beings within that world, we can determine the starting point for our analysis of slavery.

Classification and Hierarchy: The World of the Mishnah

The Mishnah's authorities construct their world and therefore its system of slavery through the process of classification. Their central concern is to assign everything in the world to its proper place. This procedure contains two stages, namely, the specification of categories and the assigning of individual objects to those categories. To begin with, the Mishnah's framers delineate the central categories into which they organize their world. They classify different types of plants, animals, buildings, clothing and even human beings. The initial step is simply to provide a name for each category, or in other words to identify it as a category separate from other categories. The next step of this process is to delineate the significant characteristics of each category. This constitutes the focus of the classificatory exercise, for objects in the Mishnah's system possess no inherent characteristics. Instead, they derive their important features from the categories to which they belong. Take, for example, a goat that has been designated as a sin offering. Its primary characteristic is not its "goat-ness." Instead, as a sacrifice, its central feature is its holiness. Concomitantly, sages spell out the laws that govern the use of members of each classification. Such laws derive from a category's significant attributes. These regulations usually delineate the manner in which the members of a category should be used and the results if they are not used correctly. Because the aforementioned goat is a sacrifice, the laws governing its use stipulate that it must be offered on the Temple altar. The goat may not be sold, given away or eaten. Through this example, we can see how classification determines the significant features of an object. These features in turn constitute the basis for laws governing the use of the object.

Once the categories have been set forth, the objects that populate the Mishnah's world must be placed in them. The Mishnah's authorities accomplish this task by two means, namely, through "nature" or through the actions of human beings. This is because all the Mishnah's this-worldly categories belong either to the natural realm or the human realm. All objects initially belong to a category assigned to them by the natural order of the world. Within the realm of nature, therefore, each inhabitant possesses its proper position and remains there; no alterations in an object's fundamental classification take place. For example, at birth each individual goat belongs to the general category of goat. Many elements of the Mishnah's world belong to a single category and remain in that category throughout their existence. A rock, for example, is always a rock. Some things, however, belong to or pass through a limited succession of predetermined categories. These categories usually correspond to changes in an element's nature during the course of its lifetime. For example, animals are born, grow old and die. Grain sprouts, matures and then withers. Although each stage constitutes a separate classification, no fundamental changes ever occur in the underlying character of the animal or the grain. The realm of nature, therefore, presents a static picture in which all changes are predetermined. It constitutes a permanent system of categories which is both self-perpetuating and cyclical. As a taxonomic system it can continue forever without interference from human beings.

Human beings do interfere, however. They constitute the second means — in addition to nature — by which objects are placed into different categories.[3] They can take an object originally classified by nature as a member of one category and place it into a second. The first category belongs to the realm of nature while the second constitutes part of the human realm. Furthermore, once an item enters the human realm it can be classified and reclassified many times.

---

[3] The role of human beings in classification has been extensively spelled out by Eilberg-Schwartz, pp. 95-180.

Each time an object's classification is changed, its significant characteristics are altered and likewise the laws governing its use. For example, take the case of harvested grain from which priestly rations have not yet been removed. Such produce, although clearly intended to be used as food, may not actually be eaten. However, by separating the priestly rations from the bulk of the grain, a householder radically alters the classification — and therefore the significant characteristics — of the produce. The separated produce has become sanctified and must ultimately be eaten by the priests. The householder's action has likewise changed the classification of the bulk of the grain. It is now food and can be eaten or sold without restriction. So we see that human beings are the active agents of classification in the Mishnah's system.

While all human beings have the power to alter the classification of objects in the world around them, they do not all exercise the same degree of power. Certain categories of people have a greater capacity to affect their environment than others. This observation brings us closer to the focus of this study, slavery. For as we shall see, the slave's capacity to classify objects both derives from and points to his place in the Mishnah's world. Before we examine that issue, however, let us first study the more general distinctions sages make among people. This will in turn help us to pinpoint the position of slaves in relation to other social categories.

The most fundamental division of human beings in the Mishnah separates them into two groups, Israelites and non-Israelites. Israelites can change the classification of objects in a wide range of categories. Foreigners, by contrast, can affect items in a much smaller selection. To take one probative illustration, Israelites can designate animals to be sin offerings and guilt offerings, but foreigners cannot.[4]

The reason for this difference of power is clear. Israelites, as a social group, stand at the center of the Mishnah's world, and therefore comprise the only significant community of people in the Mishnah's system. Because of this, the framers design the Mishnah's categories in relation to the people Israel. In other words, to say that certain categories belong to the human realm is too general; such categories belong to the Israelite realm of humanity. This relation between Israelites and these categories works in two directions. On the one hand, Israelites can determine the classification of objects in their world. On the other

---

[4] The difference between Israelites and foreigners here is important. Sin and guilt offerings are required from Israelites when they transgress various rules. Such offerings help maintain an individual's proper place in the Temple cult and thereby maintain his relationship to God. The cult thus takes cognizance of an Israelite's misdeeds. The misdeeds of a foreigner are not even noticed, indicating that he has no relationship to the Israelite Temple cult. The two classes of offerings that a foreigner may bring — free-will offerings and vow offerings — constitute unsolicited gifts and do not mediate a relationship between the giver and the cult. See M. Sheq. 1:5, which depends on Lev. 22:18.

hand, the laws governing the use of items in different categories apply primarily to Israelites. To illustrate, an Israelite can choose whether to classify a particular portion of grain as priestly rations. If he does so, that grain must be taken to the Temple and given to a priest. Neither the Israelite who sanctified it nor any other person may interfere with the achievement of that goal.

Foreigners, by contrast, remain outside the focus of the system of the Mishnah and thus stand beyond its system of classification.[5] This becomes apparent in two ways. First, many of the Mishnah's central categories are irrelevant to non-Israelites. The rules accompanying such classes apply to Israelites but not to foreigners. The sabbath day, for example, is holy to Israelites and they may not work on it. Foreigners, by contrast, are not required to rest on the sabbath. Second, non-Israelites lack the power to place objects into certain categories. This should not be surprising; since some classifications are irrelevant to them, they cannot assign things to those categories. Food illustrates this point well. Sages define meat strictly in terms of Israelites. Only when an Israelite slaughters an animal — a cow for example — does its meat enter the category of food. When a non-Israelite slaughters a cow, its meat becomes carrion (M. Hul. 1:1). Carrion does not enter the Israelite classification of food permitted to Israelites, even though it can be eaten by foreigners. So we see that Israelites have the greater power to affect the classification of their world because the Mishnah's authorities order the world for their benefit. Foreigners, by contrast, have much less power because they stand outside of that world.

Within Israelite society itself, people possess different capacities to affect the classification of objects. To understand how this works, we need to understand how the framers organize Israelite society. For sages, the householder constitutes society's central category and the household forms its fundamental building block.[6] The framers see Israelite society as a composite of households, as we shall see, not as the extended family portrayed in Scripture. Therefore, the organizing criterion for this society is whether a person belongs to a household, or — as the Mishnah's authorities would formulate it — whether a person comes under a householder's control. The free adult male Israelite forms the head of the household. Concomitantly, he possesses the greatest power to affect the classification of objects in the world around him. Other members of the household — such as wives, children, and as we shall see in a moment, slaves — possess a lesser capacity to affect the classificatory system. This lower degree of power derives from one of two causes. First, a person simply may lack the full power of a householder. For example, the minor, because of his young age, lacks the capacity of reason. He therefore cannot use reason to affect

---

[5] At this time, Gary Porton is preparing a study of the foreigner in the Mishnah and the Tosefta.

[6] The importance of the householder as a category for the Mishnah is extensively discussed by Jacob Neusner in Neusner, *Evidence*, pp. 230-241, 250-256.

the classification of objects. Second, wives, as we shall see, possess the same amount of personal power as their husbands, but they cannot freely exercise that power. Instead, householders control their wives' effective exercise of power. An Israelite's position in a household, therefore, indicates the extent of his power to affect the classification of objects around them.

The reason for this discussion of the Mishnah's organization of its world has been to discover place of the slave within it. In the Mishnah's main system of slavery, since slaves are human beings, the taxonomical arrangement has provided two places.[7] First, like other human beings, slaves comprise objects to be classified, to be placed into their proper categories. Second, since they belong to the genus of human being, they have the power to dictate the classification of objects in the world around them. Let us look at each aspect more closely. First, slaves constitute categories of Israelite society. Like other social categories, the position of slaves is determined by the criterion of the household. Since slaves are owned by Israelite householders, they belong to Israelite households. This factor of the household divides the system of slavery into two categories. The first category comprises the bondman.[8] He constitutes the property of an Israelite householder and thus occupies the lowest position in a household.[9] The second category is the freedman. He was once a bondman, but has now been freed from the power of his master. In fact, the freedman himself now belongs to the classification of householder. Later in this chapter we shall study these two groups in greater detail. At this point, we are attempting to provide a description of the system of which these slaves form a part and the principles governing its organization.

As human beings, bondmen and freedmen also possess the power to effect the classification of objects. Since the bondman constitutes the property of a householder, his power is channeled for his master's use. The framers attempt to portray the bondman as a living tool, a tool capable of classifying objects. The important characteristic of tools, for this analogy, is that the tool is effective when it is being used. When not in use, the tool lacks the capacity to do anything. So, when the bondman performs a task for his master — that is, "he

---

[7] The Mishnah contains 129 passages that discuss slaves. They are listed in the Appendix. Of these, 123 represent the *main* system of slavery which uses the categories of bondman and freedman. See the discussion in the section, "Slaves in the Mishnah." The remaining six pericopae carry forward the scheme of slavery found in the Pentateuch. We shall analyze these later in this chapter.

[8] I recognize that the words bondman and freedman are marked with respect to gender; linguistically, they both refer to males. It is common usage within the study of slavery to use these words as collective nouns indicating members of both sexes.

[9] Boaz Cohen (in Cohen, "Bondage") holds that the term "bondman" implies some sort of indentured servitude and does not refer to a slave. For the purposes of this study, I use the term "bondman" to identify the Mishnah's main category of slavery. The Mishnah's bondman is a slave, and not an indentured servant.

is being used" — the framers treat the bondman's actions as effective. When the bondman is not working for his master, the framers attempt to ensure that his actions have no effect on the classification of objects in his environment. As we shall see in Chapters Three and Four, the framers are only partially successful in accomplishing this; the bondman's human nature prevents his being treated merely as an inert tool. The freedman, by contrast, can exercise his power of classification to the normal limits governing householders. Since he constitutes a householder himself, no other person can restrict his affect on the classification of his environment. We shall detail the systemic characteristics of the freedman in Chapter Five.

Before we begin our description of the Mishnah's categories of slavery, we must address one more theoretical issue, namely, how do the framers rank bondmen and freedmen in the Mishnah's hierarchy of Israelite society? Specifically, we want to know how sages rank these categories in relation to the social divisions of householders, women and minors. To accomplish this study, we shall temporarily set aside the freedman and concentrate on determining the bondman's place. Once that task has been accomplished, we shall return to the freedman and ascertain his position.

The Mishnah's authorities distinguish the four main categories of Israelite society — householders, women, minor sons and bondmen — in a two-stage process. First, they establish the Israelite householder as the central category of Israelite society. They then define the other three categories in opposition to him. In the system of the Mishnah, the householder sets the standard of humanity. He represents the ideal human being, for he has both the full potential of a human being and the capacity to use that potential fully. To restate this point in terms of the Mishnah's system of classification, the householder both possesses the full power to classify the objects around him and can exercise that power to the fullest degree. The Mishnah's framers define the other three types of people as counterparts to the householder; each class stands in opposition to or negation of one of his particular qualities. Age distinguishes the minor son from the householder.[10] Since householders are adult, minor sons are not adult. The minor son thus stands in opposition to the normal position of the householder. In terms of gender, women take the role of opposition; the householder is male, women are female. Bondmen, finally, oppose the householder in terms of freedom. The householder is free, as this is understood in the Mishnah's system (see Chapter Six). The bondman, by contrast, is subject to the full control of his master. As we can see, then, each category is defined by the negation of a particular attribute of the householder. We can restate these categories in terms of themselves; each category is like the householder except where its defining attribute makes them different. Women,

---

[10] Minor daughters are classed, as we shall see, in the category of women. Their immaturity constitutes a secondary, although significant, issue.

for example, are like householders except where their sexual differences cause a distinction. The bondman, similarly, possesses the same characteristics as the householder except where his position as property makes him different. To the Mishnah's authorities, therefore, all categories of people possess the same characteristics as the householder, except where the defining attribute of that category differentiates it.

The Mishnah's framers rank these different classes of people by the same principle they use to distinguish them. That is to say, they rank each category in relation to the householder.[11] This rank is shown by the extent to which the characteristics of a particular category are like those of the householder. The more attributes a category shares with the householder, the higher the category is ranked; the more a class of people differs from the householder, the lower that class's position. The rank of a category of people therefore stems, first, from the opposition of that category to the category of householders and, second, from the amount of difference between that category and the householder.

This means of determining hierarchy has important ramifications for ranking different types of people relative to one another. The problem can best be understood through an example. The Mishnah's framers rank women in opposition to householders, but they do not rank them with respect to bondmen or minor sons. It is very difficult accurately to determine the rank of one category in relation to the others. This is because each category's rank relative to the householder stems from different factors. The minor son derives his rank from his young age, the woman from her gender, the bondman from his lack of freedom. Each factor allows the members of a category to do certain things and forbids them from doing others. Since the criteria differ among the categories, each class of people can do some things that the others cannot do and is restricted from doing certain deeds that the other classes can. For instance, bondmen constitute the sole category of people that also comprise owned property. In this regard, then, they clearly stand below Israelite women and minor sons. But bondmen can perform certain actions that free women can and that minor sons cannot. Women and bondmen can bear witness to a person's death before a court of law (M. Yeb. 16:7), for example, while minors cannot.[12] So, although the ranks of each type of person are clear in relation to the householder, they cannot be accurately specified relative to each other. Therefore, it will be helpful for us to compare the category of bondman with those of women and minor sons because we know the defining feature of each category. This comparison will

---

[11] This is similar to Louis Dumont's description of the hierarchy of castes in the Indian caste system. See Dumont, pp. 239-246. For his more general discussion of the matter, see Dumont, pp. 65-91.

[12] M. Yebamoth chapters 15 and 16 discuss those who can give evidence about the death of a woman's husband. Minors are never once mentioned. This is because minors lack the power of reason and hence are considered to be untrustworthy as witnesses.

not result, however, in a social scale with each category occupying a specific point.

When we turn our attention to the category of freedmen, we discover that sages define it according to the above principle. That is to say, the framers delineate the category of freedman in opposition to another category. But for the freedman, the householder does not constitute the defining category. Instead, sages define the freedman in opposition to the bondman. For the freedman, the bondman — not the householder — comprises the central category that defines the "normal" condition of human beings. Within the Mishnah's system of slavery, therefore, it is normal to be enslaved; the class of free persons comprises the secondary category.

As free persons, members of the category of freedmen also belong to the main categories of Israelite society. The specific category is determined by the freedman's age and gender. If the freedman is an adult male, he enters the classification of householder; if he is underage he becomes a minor. Finally, freedwomen enter one of the categories of free women. But freedmen and freedwomen are not identical with people who have never been enslaved. The fact that they or their ancestors were slaves causes certain differences. As we shall show in a moment, the freedman, like the bondman, is cut off from his past and therefore has no ancestors. Such differences help indicate that the category of freedmen originates in distinction to the bondman and not in opposition to the householder. The place of the freedman in the Mishnah's portrayal of Israelite society, therefore, stems from the same criteria that determine the rank of other free persons. But the differences between freedmen and other free people reveal the category's position in the Mishnah's scheme of slavery.

Slaves in the Mishnah

Before we continue to describe the Mishnah's system of slavery, we need to characterize the evidence on which the explication is based. The Mishnah contains 129 passages that mention slaves.[13] Some of these passages distinguish between two explicit categories of slaves, Hebrew slaves and Canaanite slaves, while other passages make no such distinction. In past scholarship, this difference between the two types of passages was not treated as significant. When a scholar or commentator referred to a passage that did not specify whether the slave was Hebrew or Canaanite, he simply made a decision one way or the other. The category he chose was usually posited in accord with the issue under discussion, rather than deduced and argued on the basis of analysis. It is not surprising then that different writers have treated the same passage as referring to different categories of slaves. This state of matters

---

[13] These passages are listed in the Appendix.

obviously provides an unstable foundation on which to undertake a study of slaves in the Mishnah.

The tenuousness of this approach becomes more apparent when we count the number of passages belonging to each group, an exercise never before undertaken. The results show that only six passages refer to the distinction Hebrew/Canaanite. The other 123 make no mention of the slave's ethnic background.[14] That means that previous scholarship has used the six passages — without question — to define the categories for the other 123. Given the lopsidedness of these figures, this position hardly seems defensible. Instead, I argue, the evidence points to two separate schemes of slavery, even at this elementary level. Indeed, as I shall demonstrate momentarily, when we analyze the 123 passages without the assumption of ethnic-based categories, we discover that the slavery categories found are those of bondman and freedman. Furthermore, the categories are determined by the factor of the householder's control — that is, by the taxonomic criterion which also functions to delineate the other categories of human beings in Israelite society. The Scriptural distinction of native and foreigner does not define the categories of slavery in the Mishnah's main system of slavery. That is not to say that this scheme of slavery does not use Scripture — it does — but that Scripture's categories of slaves are not used as the basis for the Mishnah's categories, except for the six just noted. Thus, the Mishnah contains two systems of slavery, the main system of bondman and freedman found in 123 passages, and a secondary scheme of Hebrew and Canaanite slaves that carries forward Scripture's categories of slaves found in six passages. The Mishnah's main system of slavery constitutes this book's central focus and we shall continue with our analysis of it now. At the end of the chapter, we shall briefly examine the six passages that portray Hebrew and Canaanite slaves.

Bondmen and Freedmen

The Mishnah's bondman fits the common definition of slavery; he is a human being who belongs to the status of property. For example, the master can treat his bondman more or less as he wishes and can force the bondman to perform almost any task.[15] The bondman has little legal capacity to resist or refuse. For instance, a householder can change his slave's residence and ownership by selling him (see for example M. Ket. 8:5), he may separate a child from its slave-mother (M. BM 8:4) and even control the slave's sexual activity (M. Tem. 6:2). The purpose of this study, however, is to go beyond common generalities to discover the specifics of the humanity/ property combination —

---

[14] See the Appendix for the two lists.

[15] The Mishnah's framers place a few limitations on the master's power over his slave. See, for example, M. Naz. 9:1, Git. 4:6, BQ 3:10 (which follows Ex. 21:26-27), and BQ 8:3.

that is, of slavery — in the Mishnah's system. We want to answer the question, what effect does the status of property have on a human being? In brief, the Mishnah's framers recognize the bondman as a complete human being, but as one whose status as property prevents him from achieving his full potential. Sages do not portray him as a sub-human "monster," that is, as something lacking the full rudiments of humanity.[16] To explain in detail how the humanity and property join in the category of the bondman, we need to grasp the framers' understanding of these two concepts. To accomplish this, let us briefly look forward to the results of the studies in Chapter Three.

The Mishnah's framers conceive the nature of humanity as consisting of three forms of personal power. All normal, adult human beings possess the potential to exercise these types of power. We shall call these (1) the power exercised through acts requiring reason, (2) the power exercised through merely physical acts and bodily conditions, and (3) the power exercised through relationships. The purpose of each form of power is to cause legal effects; thus, until such an effect takes place, power has not been exercised. This notion implies the existence of two levels of effects, physical and legal. Power is exercised only when a physical effect brings on a legal one. For instance, if a person breaks a pot, he causes a physical effect. His breaking of the pot becomes an act of power only if it furthermore causes legal effects (which it would in most circumstances). The concept of humanity in the Mishnah, therefore, centers on the capacity to cause legal effects through personal power.

The three types of power cause legal effects in different ways. First, any action that can be accompanied by the exercise of reason or intention falls into the classification of acts requiring reason. These make up the majority of actions performed by an adult. Legal effects result from such actions in most cases. Second, merely physical acts and bodily conditions irrevocably and, as we shall see, necessarily bring on legal effects. If a merely physical act is performed — such as intercourse — or a particular bodily condition is discovered — such as cultic impurity or disease — certain legal ramifications necessarily ensue. Third, the power exercised through relationships controls a person's status both within the household and in Israelite society at large. The relationships in question consist of primarily kinship ties. They link members of a household and thus define the duties, rights and privileges an individual has with respect to other members. If a person has a father and a mother, for example, he has certain duties and rights with regard to them and vice versa. Relationships furthermore determine status in the Israelite community. For example, a woman's caste status — whether she belongs to the caste of the priests, the Levites or the Israelites — is determined by her relationship to her father or to her husband.

---

[16] As does Aristotle, for example, in his *Politics*, I 5&6.

Having identified the characteristics of humanity for the Mishnah's system, let us now briefly describe how the status of property affects the bondman's capacity to exercise these forms of personal power. Simply put, the status of property gives the owner the capacity to control his slave. We shall call this ability "the householder's control." The householder can control two types of his bondman's personal power. First, the householder can, in effect, turn on and off his bondman's power of acts requiring reason. That is, he can make the bondman's acts requiring reason bear legal effects or prevent them from bearing legal effects. When the acts are effective, the bondman usually acts as his master's agent. The acts bear legal ramifications for the master, not for the slave personally. In only a few cases can a bondman act for himself.[17] When the master does not authorize his bondman deeds, the bondman's acts requiring reason bear no legal effects. Second, the master prevents the bondman from holding any relationships apart from the property relationship between his slave and himself. In other words, he cancels all the bondman's previous kinship ties, if any, and prevents him from forming new ones. In this way, the bondman has no duties, rights or privileges that are outside his master's control. Therefore, although the bondman has the potential to cause legal effects through these two forms of power, his master controls his capacity to do so.

Only one form of personal power held by a bondman stands outside his master's control, that of merely physical acts and bodily conditions. The reason for this will be more fully explained in Chapter Three. For the moment, it will suffice to note that since this is a power over which the bondman himself has no control, neither does his master. In sum, the master's capacity to control two forms of his bondman's personal power and his inability to control the third is what I term "full householder's control."

The freedman, by definition, no longer falls under a householder's control.[18] This holds true for all types of control. An ex-master can neither dictate a freedman's activity, prevent the legal effects of his acts, nor influence the freedman's status in Israelite society. Since the property-relationship between the master and slave has been broken, the master's power over his ex-slave has ceased. Now, unlike the bondman, the freedman's own social characteristics determine his status and accompanying rights within Israelite society. A freedman who could eat priestly rations while enslaved, for example, now lacks that right. It is important to understand the underlying principles here. An adult, male freedman automatically becomes a householder himself. Israelite society ranks householders according to their own caste — with priests, Levites

---

[17] Such as when he takes a Nazirite oath that his master permits him to keep.

[18] The Mishnah passages that mention the freedman are: Bek. 8:1; Bikk. 1:5; BQ 5:4, 8:4; Ed. 5:6; Git. 4:4, 4:6; Hor. 3:8; Ket. 1:2, 1:4, 3:1, 3:2; MS 5:14; Naz. 9:1; Peah 3:8; Qid. 4:1, 4:7; RH 1:7; Sheq. 1:3, 1:6; Ter. 8:1; Yeb. 2:8, 8:2, 11:2 and Zab. 2:1. The Mishnah also mentions a person who is half enslaved and half free in Ed. 1:13, Git. 4:5 and Pes. 8:1.

and Israelites occupying the top three positions. Sages place freedmen in a caste all to themselves and do not combine them with another category, such as that of Israelite. Thus, an ex-slave's caste status is determined by his previous slavehood, not his former master's status. The following ranking of the different castes makes this point clear.[19]

A. A priest takes precedence over a Levite,
B. a Levite takes precedence over an Israelite,
C. an Israelite takes precedence over a *mamzer* [i.e., a person born of parents who lack the legal right to marry each other],
D. a *mamzer* takes precedence over a *netin* [i.e., a member of a class of people connected with the Temple who are not allowed to marry Israelites],
E. a *netin* takes precedence over a proselyte,
F. a proselyte takes precedence over a freedman [lit., a freed slave].

M. Hor. 3:8[20]

The freedman clearly belongs to a separate caste within Israelite society (F). His own characteristics determine his caste position, and the householder to whom he was formerly subject has no influence. Furthermore, sages here obviously consider freedmen part of their scheme of slavery because the defining feature of his caste status is his former enslavement.

The status of freedmen as a separate caste in the Mishnah has important ramifications concerning slavery's effect on social identity. For the Mishnah's framers, slavery cancels out the bondman's — and therefore the freedman's — previous identity. Indeed, it obliterates all traces of the bondman's former identity. No clue remains to indicate even his ancestral background, not even to reveal whether he was originally an Israelite or a foreigner. The Mishnah's framers ignore the distinction of Scripture, which differentiates between Israelite and foreigner, and instead uses the ethnically neutral terms, bondman (עבד) and freedman (עבד משחרר). As we mentioned above, of the 129 Mishnah passages that discuss slaves, 123 of them speak of bondman or freedman; only six use Scripture's criteria of Israelite and foreigner.[21] So let me state the point with

---

[19] The end of M. Hor. 3:8 introduces the importance of knowing the Law as an alternative means for ranking these categories. However, this factor does not alter this criterion for distinguishing the categories.

[20] The Mishnah contains two lists that rank the castes of Israelite society. Although the categories in the two lists are the same, the ranks of some of them differ. This can be easily explained. The context of M. Hor. 3:8 makes it clear that its list centers on the issue of who should be redeemed first if captured by an enemy. The second list (M. Qid. 4:1), which we shall deal with in Chapter Four, ranks its items according to their status in the Temple cult.

[21] See the discussion of these passages later in this chapter.

emphasis: *once someone becomes a bondman, slavery constitutes his defining feature; the Mishnah provides no indication of his previous ethnic identity.*[22]

If the bondman was originally a foreigner, his enslavement has cut him off from his former life and social identity. Then, should his master later liberate him, sages consider him a member of the Israelite community. This means that the freedman is not accorded the identity he had prior to enslavement — that is, outsider — but he is identified by his position as a former slave. Similarly, if the bondman was originally an Israelite, enslavement affects him just as it affects the enslaved gentile; it cuts him off from his membership and position in his former society. Thus, if he should become manumitted, his prior enslavement would determine his place in Israelite society, not his status before enslavement.[23] Evidently, whether freedmen spring from Israelite or foreign stock — and the Mishnah's system does not reveal which — their former position as slaves defines the most important aspect of their present social standing, namely, their caste status.

This equal treatment of slaves and freedmen from both backgrounds is astonishing, for it joins two incompatible categories of people. Throughout the Mishnah — and throughout all forms of Judaism in antiquity — there was a radical separation between Israelites and non-Israelites. Indeed, this separation formed the basis for Scripture's scheme of slavery. This twofold division of humankind stemmed from the myth that God chose the people Israel to be his people. In doing so, he set them apart from the other nations. In the words of Exodus 19:5-6, "You [Israel] shall be my own possession among all peoples; for all the earth is mine, and you shall be to me a kingdom of priests and a holy nation." Thus, the Mishnah's framers' placement of both Israelite and gentile into the same categories of bondmen and freedmen — a process that destroys their previous identity and makes them alike — demands explanation. This explanation must be postponed, however, until we have examined in detail how the Mishnah classifies the different categories of its social world. Once we understand how the classification of bondmen and freedmen compares with that of women and minor sons — that is, at the end of our study — we will possess the information necessary to explain the homogenizing effect of slavery.

---

[22] I spent several months trying to devise a way to argue that bondman was either of Israelite or non-Israelite stock. Every attempt ultimately met with failure.

[23] We know that this is a real possibility when we observe other societies that enslave their own members. Those cultures — such as Egyptian (under the Pharaohs), Russian (Twelfth Century), Korean (Koryo and Yi dynasties), and Chinese at various times — which reduce indigenous members to chattel slavery, and not just indenturedness, erase the identities of such people. These people lose their prior position in society and become merely slaves. See Patterson, *Social Death*, pp. 41-45.

Classification: The Mishnah's Categories of Slavery

The categories of bondman and freedman together make up the Mishnah's system of slavery. We have shown, in general terms, that the bondman comprises a householder who lacks freedom and the freedman constitutes a bondman who has been freed. To understand this scheme of slavery as the Mishnah portrays it, however, we must go beyond generalities and attempt to discover the fundamental factors by which sages delineate the two categories. In other words, we must discern how the Mishnah's framers define what we have called freedom so that it distinguishes the category of bondman from that of freedman. For sages, as we shall see, this definition focuses on the householder; he does not exercise such power over a freedman. To understand how the framers use this fact as a criterion of classification, we must briefly discuss, on a theoretical level, the process of classification.

Classification, according to Carl Hempel, "divides a given set or class of objects into subclasses."[24] In other words, classification arranges an internally undifferentiated collection of items into subgroups or categories whose members share common features. Logically, this is a two-step process. When confronted with unclassified objects, a person first decides upon the characteristic to be used for classification. This we shall call the criterion of classification, or the taxonomic criterion. Then, on the basis of this criterion, he separates the objects into different categories. Imagine, for example, a person who has never seen fruit in his life discovering a bowl of bananas, oranges and peaches. How would he categorize them? He could choose to use shape as the criterion of classification. This would result in two categories, one consisting of the bananas, the other of peaches and oranges, since they both are round. Conversely, he might pick the criterion of color. This time he would place oranges by themselves, but put the bananas with the peaches because both are yellow. Finally, if he differentiated according to taste, he would distinguish three kinds of fruit, since each has a distinct flavor. We can see that the criterion one chooses to organize categories decides the contents of those categories.

Our problem is the reverse of that just described. The Mishnah's bondmen and freedmen are not an undifferentiated group still waiting to be classified — as was the fruit — but people already sorted into specific categories. Our problem, then, is to determine the decisions sages made when they constructed these categories and the concerns that influenced their choice of the taxonomic criterion. We can answer these questions by analyzing the scheme of slavery in the reverse of the logical order of classification. The first task, which we have just completed, is to determine the Mishnah's categories of slavery. The Mishnah's authorities, as we well know, divide their scheme of slavery into bondmen and freedmen. Next, we must discern the feature of slavery that serves as the criterion of classification for these categories. Since we posited above that

---

[24] See Hempel, p. 137.

the taxonomic criterion is whether the slave falls under a householder's control, we must now demonstrate this claim. The third step of analysis requires us to determine why sages chose this particular characteristic for the criterion of classification. We want to know the larger interests that guided their decision. This information will enable us to discern the relationship between the scheme of slavery and the Mishnah's larger system. Since we have already determined the Mishnah's categories of slavery, we now turn to the second stage of investigation, determining the criterion of classification.

Finding which characteristic of slavery the Mishnah's framers chose as their criterion of classification is not a straightforward matter. Although the categories are based on this characteristic, other characteristics obscure our attempt to identify it. Let me explain. Logically speaking, sages first chose a particular characteristic of slavery for their taxonomic criterion and then distinguished their categories of slavery accordingly.[25] When we analyze their system, by contrast, we begin with the categories. The members of one category share many characteristics that are absent in the other category. We must discover which of these serves as the criterion of classification.[26] The example of the fruit portrays our difficulty. Imagine that a person puts apples and tomatoes in the same category; how can we determine whether he grouped them together because they were both round, or because they were both red? This constitutes the analytical problem facing us.

In a complex classificatory system like the Mishnah's scheme of slavery, we can solve this problem with a two step approach. First, the Mishnah divides its scheme into two categories — bondmen and freedmen. In a bipartite scheme like this one, the taxonomic criterion is present in the members of one category and absent among those in the other.[27] Thus, we begin by finding the characteristics common to members of each category but absent in the other. In

---

[25] I use the term "logically" for a reason. We do not know how the Mishnah's framers actually put together their system, all we have is the completed system. When I say that the framers logically did things in this way or that, I do not mean to imply that I know the order that they used in reality. In fact, for all we known they may have taken a prior system and modified it.

[26] Of course, there is no theoretical reason why a set of characteristics cannot constitute the criterion of classification instead of just one characteristic. This set could determine the categories in one of two ways. First, we could treat it as a unit and distinguish categories according to whether the whole set was present. Second, we could use the set to distinguish among several categories, depending upon whether one characteristic of the set was present or not. For example, suppose we had several categories, distinguished by characteristics A, B and C. Category one might have all three attributes, A, B and C; Category two might have just A and B; while category three might have only features B and C. For a further explanation of the use of sets of characteristics, see Jevons, pp. 692-694. The Mishnah's framers do not use sets of characteristics in distinguishing their categories of slavery.

[27] See Hempel p. 151 and Jevons, pp. 694-698.

this way, we can determine the features distinct to each, although we still do not know which of them served as the criterion of classification. Second, the taxonomic criterion dictates many of the characteristics and features of the categories. Therefore, we first must discover the attribute that will explain most, if not all, other attributes of each category. This feature constitutes the criterion of classification. We can double check our results by comparing the categories. If their criteria are the opposite or the negation of each other, then we have accurately determined the criterion of classification.

Sages distinguish bondmen and freedmen on the basis of whether they are subject to a householder's control. This characteristic, as we posited above, provides the impetus for the framers' concerns in most of the pericopae that deal with slavery. Specifically, of the 123 passages concerning the bondman and the freedman, 104 of them turn on the question of the householder's control.[28] To

---

[28] I base this statement on the analysis that will unfold in the following chapters. Briefly, the importance of the householder's control over the slaves becomes clear in passages that deal with four different distinctions. The first group of pericopae focus on the bondman as the property of his master. The other three groups focus on the householder's control of the three types of personal power that his bondman may potentially use: the power of acts requiring reason, the power exercised through relationships, and the power of merely physical acts and bodily conditions. I shall explain these forms of power in Chapter Three.

The first group of passages which shows that the issue of bondmen and freedmen is the householder's control focuses on the issue of the bondman as property. This includes issues of ownership as well as modes of transfer such as sale. See the discussions of these passages later in this study: Git. 2:3 (Chapter 3), 4:4 (Chapter 5); and BB 3:1 (3), 4:7 (3). The following passages about the bondman also focus on the issue of the slave as property, but I do not deal with them directly in my investigation: Peah 3:8; Shebi. 8:8; MS 1:7; Bikk. 3:12; MQ 2:4; Ket. 3:7, 3:9, 8:5; Sot. 3:8; Git. 1:4, 1:5, 1:6, 4:6; BQ 3:10, 4:5, 8:1, 9:2; BM 1:7, 4:9, 8:4a, 8:4b; BB 5:1, 10:7; Shebu. 5:5, 6:5; Zab. 2:3; San. 11:1; Bek. 8:7, 8:8; and Arak. 3:1, 3:3, 6:5.

The second collection of pericopae focuses on the householder's control over the bondman's personal power of acts requiring reason, or on the fact that the freedman is released from such control. The passages I discuss in following chapters are: Ter. 3:4 (Chapters 3, 4), 8:1 (Chapters 2, 5); MS 5:14 (5); Bikk. 1:5b (4); Pes. 8:1b (5), 8:2 (3, 4), 8:7 (4); Sheq. 1:3 (4, 5), 1:5 (4), 1:6 (4,5); Suk. 2:8 (4), 2:1 (4); Hag. 1:1 (4); Naz. 9:1 (3, 5); BQ 8:4 (3, 5); BM 8:3 (3), 7:6 (3); and Zeb. 3:1 (4). Passages falling into this classification not discussed in this study are: Ber. 3:3, 7:2; Ter. 7:3; Pes. 7:2, 8:1a; Suk. 3:10; RH 1:7, 1:8; Ket. 2:9, 5:5; Sot. 1:6; Git. 4:5a, 7:4; Shebu. 4:12, 5:5; Ed. 1:13a; Men. 9:8; and Arak. 1:1.

The third group of passages centers on the householder's control over the bondman's power exercised through relationships and the freedman's freedom from that type of control. I directly address the following pericopae in this study: Yeb. 2:5 (Chapter 3), 7:2 (Chapter 3), 7:5 (Chapter 3), 8:2 (5), 11:2 (3, 5); Git. 9:2 (3); Qid. 3:12 (3), 3:13 (5), 4:1 (5), 4:7 (5); BQ 5:4 (5); and Hor. 3:8 (2, 5). I do not address the following passages of this classification in the study: Bikk. 1:5a; Yeb. 7:1, 7:3, 8:1, 11:5; Git. 4:5b; Ed. 1:13b; Zeb. 5:6, 5:7; and Bek. 1:7.

explain this in detail requires concepts and distinctions that I have not yet introduced; so rather than discuss these passages now, we shall unpack this issue in due course.

For the moment, a single example can illustrate the centrality of the householder's control in determining the Mishnah's categories of slavery. The privilege of a priest's bondman to eat priestly rations provides a telling instance concerning a householder's control of his bondman. In the following passage, both aspects of the householder's control — physical and social — come into play.

> A. [In the case of a priest's] bondman who was eating priestly rations and [messengers] came and said to him
>   (1) "Your master has died,"[29] or,
>   (2) "He has sold you to an Israelite [i.e., a non-priest]," or,
>   (3) "He has given you as a gift [to a non-priest]," or,
>   (4) "He has freed you."
>   [In each case, the bondman's tie to his priestly master, and thus to the priestly caste, is severed, hence rendering him no longer qualified to eat holy food.]...
> B. Rabbi Eliezer [holds that once the bondman's ownership has changed — whether or not the bondman knows it — he is liable for misuse of priestly rations and therefore] requires [the bondman] to pay the principal and the added fifth. [Eliezer holds that the bondman was ineligible to eat priestly rations at the time in question and so must pay.]
>
> M. Ter. 8:1[30]

The fourth and final group of pericopae focuses on the bondman's power of merely physical acts and bodily conditions. The point of these passages is that the master does not control this power of his bondman. The following passages are discussed in this study: Ker. 1:3 (Chapter 4), Neg. 14:12 (Chapters 3, 4), Yad. 4:7 (3), and Zab. 2:1 (3, 4, 5). These are the passages of this classification that I do not directly discuss: Ket. 1:2, 1:4, 3:1, 3:2; Ed. 5:6; Bek. 8:1; and Tem. 6:2.

29 The Mishnah's framers here assume that a bondman loses his right to eat priestly rations upon the death of his master. But in most cases, when a priestly master dies, his bondmen would pass to the heirs, who would usually be priests. Hence, the bondman would still be enslaved to a priest, and so entitled to eat sanctified food. Nevertheless, it is possible that the heirs may not be priests and therefore unable to confer on the bondman the right to eat priestly rations. The bondman would be liable for the fine as the property of a non-priest.

30 This discussion is actually a dispute between Eliezer and Joshua concerning whether the bondman is culpable for misappropriating priestly rations. Joshua holds that the bondman is not culpable. However, Joshua's position does not contradict our point here, because Joshua actually holds that the bondman's master still controls his status. But in addition, a person's self-perception also helps govern his status. Thus, only when the bondman learns of his actual situation does his status change. This point is further spelled out in Green,

The priestly householder's control of his bondman is evident in two ways. First, in the situation imagined at the start of A, the bondman possesses the privilege of eating priestly rations because his priestly master's caste status extends to him (Lev. 22:11). Second, whether or not the bondman belongs to a priest — the criterion necessary for this privilege — is totally at his priestly master's discretion. The priest may choose at any time to sell him or free him, and in neither case does the bondman have any say in the matter. Thus, the criterion of classification for the bondman is that he stands under a householder's control. Conversely, this passage also shows how the freedman is free from control by householders. We can see this in A4, where the master frees his bondman. Immediately, the bondman becomes a freedman, and more significantly, his master's status no longer governs his own. Thus, he becomes ineligible to eat priestly food. Thus, we see in this example that the criterion of the householder's control distinguishes the categories of bondman and freedman.

The discovery that the framers distinguish bondman and freedman from each other by the criterion of the householder's control is important not only to the Mishnah's scheme of slavery but also to the broad traits of its larger system. For as we argued at the beginning of this chapter, just as the general concerns of the Mishnah's system dictate its categories of slavery, so too those categories point to the broader traits of that system. One aspect of this dialectic is that the Mishnah's framers treat their categories of slavery according to the same guidelines as the other categories within Israelite society. Taking this cue, we can make the following prediction; since the householder's control plays a significant role in defining the Mishnah's categories of slavery, it also plays an important role in defining other categories of Israelite society, such as women and sons. To test this prediction, let us investigate how the Mishnah's framers organize their categories of women.

The Mishnah's Categories of Women: Sexuality and the Householder's Control

Up to this point, we have treated the Mishnah's class of women as if it constituted a single, indivisible category. But when we analyze the six sub-groups into which the Mishnah's authorities divide women — minor daughters, adult daughters, wives, divorcees, widows, and levirate widows — we discover an important point.[31] The Mishnah's framers use the same taxonomic criterion to differentiate the categories of women that they use to distinguish the bondman from the freedman, namely, the householder's control. Indeed, as I shall argue in the course of this book, the householder's control constitutes a systemic

---

Joshua, pp. 57-8, Neusner, *Eliezer*, pp. 61-62 and [Avery-]Peck, *Priestly Gift*, pp. 229-230.

[31] The categories themselves derive from Scripture, but the taxonomic framework which we shall describe in a moment is designed by the Mishnah's framers themselves.

principle that governs many elements in the Mishnah's system. Let us see how this works for women.

Sages divide the six categories of women into three pairs: minor and adult daughters, wives and divorcées, and widows and levirate widows. This has been clearly demonstrated by Judith Romney Wegner in her study, *Chattel or Person? The Status of Women in the Mishnah*.[32] Wegner shows that the Mishnah's authorities consider the primary purpose of a woman's life to be the bearing of children for her husband. They therefore consider wifehood to be the normal state of women. The framers reveal this fact by using the word for wife (אשׁה pl. נשׁים) to refer to women in general. Even though not all women are wives, the double meaning of the term points to the proper place for a woman. This focus on marriage enables sages to distinguish three stages in a woman's life: prior to her marriage, from the moment of her wedding to the death of her husband, and after the death of her husband. These three stages correspond to the three pairs of categories of women. The two types of daughters comprise women not yet married, the wife and the divorcee are those classes of women who have a husband (or ex-husband) still living, and the two categories of widows comprise those whose husbands are dead.[33] We shall now describe these pairs of categories and then show, at the level of taxonomy, how the framers constructed this tripartite scheme.

The minor and the adult daughter comprise the first pair.[34] A girl belongs to the category of minor daughter from birth to the age of twelve and a half. She stands under her father's control. She has no property rights; any income that she earns and any object that she finds goes to him. The father has complete authority to arrange her marriage, either by betrothing her or by selling her as a concubine. A girl enters the category of adult daughter if she is not married at the age of twelve and a half. At this time, she becomes an independent woman

---

[32] This pairing of categories and the general description of them that follows is based on the work of Judith Romney Wegner. Professor Wegner delineated the pairing of categories in her work, I merely place them into the Mishnah's larger taxonomic system. Her study is being published by Oxford University Press as *Chattel or Person? The Status of Women in the Mishnah*. See Wegner, *Women*, especially the section entitled "Mishnah's Taxonomy of Women" in Chapter One. I want to thank Professor Wegner for sharing her manuscript with me prior to its publication.

[33] The category of divorcee is defined at the moment of a woman's separation from her husband. Subsequent changes in the husband's status — for example, he dies — have no effect on the divorcee's classification.

[34] The Mishnah holds that the daughter belongs to an interstitial category for six months instead of passing directly from minor daughter to adult daughter. While in this category, the girl is called a *naarah* (נערה). During this period, she enters into some of the responsibilities and duties of an adult, but she retains some of the restrictions of the minor daughter. See M. Nid. 5:7 and Wegner, *Women*, Chapter Two.

possessing the right to acquire belongings and earnings independent of her father. Furthermore, she arranges her own marriage. The second pair consists of the wife and the divorcee. A wife stands under the control of her husband. In this position, she has more rights than a minor daughter, but not as many as an adult daughter. For example, while she may own property, her husband has the usufruct of it. The divorcee, by contrast, is an independent woman who both owns and controls her own property. Her former husband has no power over her. The widow and the levirate widow constitute the third pair of women. Widows are independent women with rights similar to those of divorcees. But a wife enters the category of widow only if she has borne an heir for her deceased husband. If she has not, she instead becomes a levirate widow and enters the purview of her dead husband's brother.[35] A levirate widow is in a state of limbo. While she may take actions to maintain herself, including dealing in property, her brother-in-law controls her marital status. Sages, following Scripture, expect the brother- in-law to take her as a wife and produce sons in the name of the dead man. But he must choose to do so. If he refuses, then she performs a ceremony releasing herself from his control and becomes a normal widow. But until the dead man's brother decides which option he will take, the levirate widow stands in limbo, with her future under the control of her husband's brother.

Now that we know the categories of women, the next step of our analysis is to discover how sages constructed and organized these categories. Although we know in general terms how sages distinguish the categories, we now must discover the taxonomic criteria by which the Mishnah's framers delineate the classes of women. First, we must discern the taxonomic basis for sages' division of women into three sets of categories. Second, we shall show that, in each pair of categories, the framers actually distinguish one category from the other by the criterion of the householder's control. To visualize the framers' organization of women into three pairs, we can imagine that sages made two distinctions, one dividing the categories into rows and one separating them into columns (see Fig. 1 below). Along the rows, sages differentiate three sets of categories. In the columns, they divide each set into two categories. The basis for distinguishing the three sets of categories in the rows is the women's sexuality. The type of sexuality that defines a woman category stems from the stage of life she is in. Prior to marriage, virginity constitutes the definitive mode of sexuality. For women whose husbands are living, namely wives and divorcees, the type of sexuality in question is their sexual activity. And finally, after the husband's death, the framers evaluate widows according to their productivity, that is, by whether they have borne an heir for their dead husband. We shall further explicate this scheme in a moment.

---

[35] Of course, if the husband has no brothers, she becomes a normal widow.

		Sexuality		
		Virginity	Activity	Productivity
Under a house-holder's control?	Controlled	Minor daughter	Wife	Levirite widow
	Not Controlled	Adult daughter	Divorcee	Widow

Figure 1

In the columns, the criterion of the householder's control, as we said above, distinguishes the two categories in each pair from each other. In each of the three pairs, one category of women stands under a householder's control and the other does not. But the taxonomic criterion distinguishing these categories does not comprise a householder's overall control of a woman. Rather, the criterion is the control of a specific aspect of the woman's person, namely, her sexuality. In other words, sages distinguish these categories by whether the householder controls the sexual function definitive of that category of woman. Sages thus distinguish daughters according to whether or not the father controls their virginity. The minor daughter's father does, but the adult daughter's father does not. Similarly, a wife's husband controls her sexual activity, but a divorcee's ex-husband does not. Finally, the brother-in-law of a levirate widow controls her reproductive capacity since she has failed to produce an heir, but any widow who has borne an heir for her dead husband becomes an independent woman.

According to this scheme, sages distinguish the categories of women by the criterion of whether a householder controls a woman's particular type of sexuality. We can demonstrate its accuracy by focusing on the paired categories of women and asking a simple question: what changes when a woman moves from one category to the other? Specifically, we want to know whether the householder's control of her sexuality changes when her classification changes. In each pair, when a woman switches categories, we should find that a householder relinquishes his control over a woman's particular sexuality. We now turn to examine whether this description applies to the three pairs of women, beginning with the two types of daughters.

The Mishnah's authorities distinguish daughters according to whether a householder controls their virginity. We can show this in two steps. First, virginity constitutes the definitive type of sexuality for daughters prior to their marriage, for the brideprice paid by the husband-to-be is specifically for the girl's virginity. The amount the suitor pays depends upon whether or not his betrothed is a virgin. If she is a virgin, he pays 200 *zuz*; if not, then he pays only 100 *zuz* (M. Ket. 1:2, 4). So if a girl has had intercourse, she no longer possesses the requisite type of sexuality for a daughter and thus is literally worth less to a potential husband than a virgin.

Second, a father has the right to acquire redress for the sexual activity of his minor daughter, but not that of his adult daughter. This fact reveals that the framers classify daughters according to whether a householder controls their virginity. Sages treat a minor girl's virginity as the property of her father. Thus, if his minor daughter loses her virginity, he can take measures to recoup his losses. Sages provide two options for him, which they link to stages in the minor daughter's sexual maturity. Before the girl reaches puberty, the father can sell her as a slave. But once she reaches puberty, at age twelve, he can only seek restitution from the violator in the form of a fine. This fine is equivalent to a virgin's brideprice (see Deut. 22:29 and Ex. 22:11). Once the girl reaches maturity at age twelve and a half, however, the father no longer has any control at all over her sexuality.

A. Any situation where [the father has a right to] sell [his daughter, he has no right to collect a] fine [for her violation (Deut. 22:29)].

B. Any situation where [the father has a right to collect a] fine [for his daughter's violation], [he has no right to] sell [her].

C. A [pre-pubescent] daughter [i.e., under the age of twelve years and a day] — [the father] may sell her, but [he has] no [right to collect a] fine.

D. A [pubescent] daughter [i.e., between twelve years and a day and twelve and a half years] — [the father] has [a right to collect a] fine [for her violation], but [he may] not sell her.

E. An adult daughter [i.e., one older than twelve and a half years] — [the father may] not sell her, nor [can he collect a] fine.

M. Ket. 3:8

The right of the father to seek compensation when a man violates his minor daughter shows that the father controls her sexuality (C-D). By contrast, when the girl reaches adulthood (E), the father can no longer take measures to gain restitution; he does not control her virginity. Thus we see that sages distinguish the two categories of daughters by whether a householder controls their virginity.

The householder's control over a woman's sexual activity likewise delimits the second pair of categories, the wife and the divorcee. A householder controls his wife's sexual activity, but a divorcee is free to choose her own sexual partner. This taxonomic criterion becomes evident during a divorce, the point at which a woman moves from the category of wife to the category of divorcee. For sages, a divorce serves to end a householder's control over his wife's sexual activity. The operative language of a divorce document emphasizes this point:

A. The essential formula in the bill of divorce is:

B. "Lo, you are permitted to any man."

M. Git. 9:3

By divorcing his wife, a husband deprives himself of power over her sexual activity. Sages further emphasize this point when they deal with a man who attempts to get around this important clause of a divorce document.

A. He who divorces his wife and says to her, "Lo, you are permitted to any man except so-and-so" —

B. Rabbi Eliezer permits [the divorce to stand because his statements have no bearing on the divorce],

C. Sages forbid [the divorce to stand]....

D. But if [the husband] had written [the phrase at A] in [the writ of divorce itself],

E. even if he had erased it,

F. [the writ is] invalid [and the divorce does not take place].

M. Git. 9:1

The Mishnah's authorities deny the husband any control over his former wife's sexual activity. He cannot forbid her from marrying anyone. Thus, we see here that the framers distinguish the wife from the divorcee on the basis of whether a householder controls their sexual activity. Of course, her sexuality is not the only aspect of the wife that a husband controls, but it is the definitive attribute that determines which of the wife's other characteristics he controls.[36]

Finally, a householder's right to control a levirate widow's reproductive capacity differentiates the levirate widow from the widow. Specifically, sages want to ensure that a widow has produced an heir for her dead husband. If she has, then the husband's death frees her from the control of all householders. If a widow has not borne an heir, then she enters the control of her brother-in-law as a levirate widow. The following passage reveals the criterion of having borne an heir as the central factor for the classification of widows. It deals with the problem of a householder who has performed his duty and married his sister- in-law, only to discover that she carries her dead husband's child.

A. [Concerning a case in which a householder] consummated [his bond] to his dead brother's wife, and [then] it was discovered that she was pregnant [with her dead husband's child] and she gave birth [to a male child] —

B. if the baby is strong [i.e., likely to survive], then he must divorce her and bring a sin-offering [to the Temple, because he has improperly married his brother's wife],

C. if the baby is not strong, they may remain married. [Since it is uncertain whether the child will survive to attain his inheritance, they remain bound by the levirate tie].

M. Yeb. 4:2

The point here is clear, the brother of the dead man controls his sister-in-law only if she has not produced an heir. Sages show the contrast between levirate

---

[36] See the discussion of this issue in Chapter Three of Wegner, *Women.*

widow and the normal widow by discussing a case in which a widow is mistaken for a levirate widow (A-B). In this case the brother lacks the duty and right to marry her in the first place, and their union is expressly forbidden by law (M. Ker. 1:2). By contrast, if the woman actually belongs in the category of levirate widow (C), then the brother-in-law has acted properly in taking control of her sexual function. Thus, the third pair of women centers on the sexuality of bearing an heir. The householder controls the widow's sexual function of fertility if she has not produced an heir, and if she has, then she becomes independent.

The point of this extended discussion of the Mishnah's categories of women has been to test the argument that the Mishnah's classification of slaves reveals principles that govern the classification of other social groups. With regard to the categories of women, this argument certainly holds true, for the Mishnah's framers form both their categories of slavery and their categories of women according to the same taxonomic criterion, namely, the householder's control. Both groups of categories form part of the Mishnah's larger scheme of society and are thus organized by concerns beyond their particular genus. Before we can delve deeper into the significance this fact holds for our study of slavery, we must examine the last major category in the Mishnah's social system, that of minor sons. Minor sons, we recall, constitute one of the three categories of Israelite society that sages delineate in opposition to the classification of householders, the other two categories being those of the bondman and of the overall class of women.[37] To understand how the householder's control serves as an overarching factor in the Mishnah's depiction of Israelite society, therefore, we must study how the householder's power defines the category of minor sons.

Sons and Householders

Sages view the minor son as a potential householder. As with the householder, the central issue concerning the minor is his control over other people. The Mishnaic pericopae depicting the minor focus on the extent of his power over others and his capacity to exercise it. It should not surprise us to discover, therefore, that in terms of classification the minor son and the householder both constitute species of the genus of free, male Israelite. The genus is subdivided according to the power possessed by each species; the adult householder possesses the full complement of power possible in the Mishnaic system, while the minor son does not.

The difference between minor sons and householders becomes clear when we compare the types of control that members of the two categories can exercise. Householders, we recall, possess three types of power, one which takes effect through relationships and two which take effect through action. Minor sons, by contrast, do not possess the capacity to exercise all three classes of power.

---

[37] See the discussion of classification and hierarchy earlier in this chapter.

While they can control other people through a relationship to them and through merely physical acts and bodily conditions, minors lack the capacity to control people through acts requiring reason. Since minors have not yet developed the capacity to reason, sages do not permit them to control other people through acts that require it. Thus, minors may control others only with acts that require mere physical deeds, but adult householders may control by actions that also involve the exercise of reason.

By examining how a son exercises control over a levirate widow at different stages of his life, we can see how these three types of power (relationships, merely physical acts and bodily conditions, and acts requiring reason) distinguish the category of minor sons from that of householders. We begin with control exercised through a relationship. Sages, we recall, require the levirate widow to marry her brother-in-law and produce sons in the dead man's name. This law is predicated on the dead husband having a living brother. If the dead husband has no brothers, then his wife becomes a normal widow. But if her husband has a brother, even if he is only a baby, she becomes a levirate widow. Sages explicitly state this in M. Nid. 5:3, "A suckling [boy] one day old...makes [a woman] liable to [the status of] levirate [widowhood]." In this way, even a baby boy controls the status of his sister-in-law. She remains a levirate widow and is tied to a male (a minor) who lacks the capacity to decide whether to marry her and fulfill his duty or to release her.

When a minor boy reaches the age of nine years and a day, the Mishnah's authorities deem him sexually mature. Since sexual acts require no intention to be effective — sages class them as merely physical actions — a minor's sexual activity has the same consequences as an adult's. Thus, through intercourse, a minor can acquire his dead brother's widow as a wife. Yet, although he may take her as a wife, the minor still lacks the capacity to divorce her. Divorce requires the exercise of his will, which sages do not yet grant to him.

A. A [minor boy] aged nine years and one day who has intercourse with his [sister-in-law who is a] levirate widow —

B. [he has] acquired her [as his wife],

C. and he may not give her a *get* [i.e., divorce her] until he reaches adulthood.

M. Nid. 5:5

Here, we clearly see that the minor can perform physical actions that control others. His act of intercourse makes his sister-in-law his wife, whether or not she wants to be. But he cannot control the levirate widow, now his wife, by an action that requires intention; he cannot divorce her. Similarly, the minor son lacks the capacity to reject her as his wife and to refuse to produce sons for his brother. Thus, until he reaches maturity and gains the power of intention, the levirate widow remains in limbo. Sages make this clear in M. Yeb. 12:4, where they specify the men who can reject a levirate widow and therefore may validly take part in the ceremony of *halitzah*, the Rite of the Removal of the Shoe. This ritual confirms the brother-in-law's rejection of the levirate widow and severs her tie to him.

A. The deaf-mute who has the Rite of the Removal of the Shoe [performed over him by his sister-in-law],

B. the deaf-mute [sister-in-law] who performs the Rite of the Removal of the Shoe,

C. and she who performs the Rite of the Removal of the Shoe over a minor—

D. her act is invalid.

M. Yeb. 12:4

The point at A and C is that the brother-in-law to whom the levirate widow is tied must possess the capacity to decide not to perform his duty. Neither a minor (C) nor a deaf-mute (A) have intention, and thus lack this capacity. Therefore, she cannot perform the requisite rite over them. Thus, while minor sons possess the capacity to control by their actions, they lack the power to control by acts requiring intention. Only adult householders have complete control over other people. Hence the Mishnah's framers distinguish minor sons from householders by the taxonomic criterion of whether or not they possess all means of exercising power.

We have now seen that the category of minor son is distinguished from that of householder by the criterion of the householder's power. Clearly the principle that distinguished the categories of slavery — the taxonomic criterion of the householder's control — also serves to differentiate the categories of minor son and householder. Taking into account that this criterion likewise serves to differentiate the categories of women, we can conclude that the framers set up the Mishnah's categories of Israelite society, including its categories of slavery, according to the same principles. In other words, the Mishnah's depiction of slavery is dictated by issues external to and larger than the matter of slavery, not by the issue of slavery itself. These issues in fact stem from the concerns of the Mishnah's overall system, namely, the portrayal of the householder as the central, definitive category of Israelite society and concomitantly the household as the primary unit of the society. The place of the bondman in the Mishnah is determined by assigning him a location within the household. Thus the Mishnah's framers define its categories of slavery as part of their organization of Israelite society. Now as we mentioned above, not all Mishnah passages mentioning slavery conform to this system. A few derive from an entirely different concept of slavery and thus present an anomaly to the Mishnah's overall system. Let us briefly turn aside from our main investigation and examine this atypical concept of slavery.

Hebrew Indentured Servants and Canaanite Slaves in the Mishnah

Six Mishnaic passages involving slaves portray a scheme of slavery different from that in the rest of the Mishnah.[38] Instead of describing bondmen and freedmen — as does the main scheme of slavery in 123 passages — these six pericopae depict two different categories. The Mishnah's authorities call these categories "Hebrew slaves" and "Canaanite slaves." Sages base these two categories on Scripture's two types of slaves, the Hebrew indentured servant and the foreign slave. Scripture, we recall, differentiates these two types of slaves on the basis of genealogy. Hebrew servants are Israelites who have become indentured servants. They are not permanent slaves. Despite the tie to their master, they stand independent of him. Conversely, foreign slaves are mere chattels. Legally, Scripture grants them a few more rights than other forms of property, but not as many as dependent persons.

The Mishnah's two categories of Hebrew slave and Canaanite slave correspond to the categories of slavery found in the Pentateuch. Two factors point to this conclusion. First, the framers form these categories of slaves according to the same taxonomic criterion used in Scripture, namely, genealogy. The Mishnah's Hebrew slaves are Israelites but its Canaanite slaves are non-Israelites. Second, in these six passages the Mishnah's slaves have the same attributes as those in the Pentateuch. The Mishnah's Hebrew slave is an indentured servant, like that of Scripture, and the Canaanite slave is a chattel slave, like Scripture's foreign slave. We shall now develop each of these points in further detail.

Sages classify the categories of slaves found in these six passages according to the criterion of genealogy. The names they use to designate each category clearly reveal the distinction. On the one hand, the Mishnah talks about "Hebrew slaves," indicating that the slaves are Israelites. In fact, sages have borrowed this designation from Scripture, for this is the very term found in Ex. 21:2 designating the Hebrew indentured servant. On the other hand, the Mishnah uses the term "Canaanite slave" to designate a slave of foreign ancestry. The term does not occur in Scripture, but two connotations of the word "Canaanite" found there readily lend the word to use in denoting a non-Israelite slave. First, the term originally designated a people who lived in the land of Canaan before the Israelites arrived, and, more importantly, later came to be used as a general word for foreigner. Second, Canaan was Noah's grandson whom Noah cursed by condemning both him and his progeny to slavery (Gen. 9:25). In these six passages, the Mishnah's framers, then, have combined these two connotations — the name of a foreign people and the name of a slave-people — into the name denoting the category of nonindigenous slave. Thus in the Mishnah, "Canaanite

---

[38] Again, the six passages are: M. MS 4:4, Erub. 7:6, Qid. 1:2-3, BQ 8:3&5, BM 1:5, Arak. 8:4-5.

slave" designates a slave of foreign origin. Here, then, the Mishnah's framers delimit their categories of slaves by the same taxonomic criterion as Scripture, namely, genealogy.

Now that we have identified the criterion of classification that distinguishes the Mishnah's Hebrew slaves from its Canaanite slaves, we need to determine the features of these slaves. Our special interest lies in discovering whether the Mishnah's categories of slaves possess the same social characteristics as their counterparts in Scripture. Scripture's Hebrew slave, we recall, possessed the characteristics of an indentured servant, and its foreign slave portrayed the features of a chattel slave. To argue that the Mishnah's slaves carry forward Scripture's categories, therefore, we must discover if they share the same characteristics.

To be considered an indentured servant, the Mishnah's Hebrew slave must possess two attributes. First, he must have the capacity to act independently of his master in most areas of his life. This freedom of action ultimately distinguishes servants from slaves. While a slave's master owns the person of his slave, a servant's master does not own him but merely controls ("owns") a facet of his activity, such as his labor. Second, the Mishnah's Hebrew slave must also satisfy the requirement of indenture: he must serve only a specified, limited period of time, that is, his service must be temporary. In this way, the servant retains his connections with the society and his family, and thus ensures his return to full membership in Israelite society upon gaining freedom. As we shall see, the Mishnah's Hebrew slave fulfills both conditions.

The following passage clearly illustrates the first criterion — that the Hebrew slave controls his own person. The case concerns a Hebrew slave who has been injured by a free man, and centers around which categories of damages the tortfeasor must pay and to whom.

A.   He who injures a Hebrew slave is liable [to pay compensation] on all [five counts]. [These five are specified in M. BQ 8:1 as (1) injury, (2) pain, (3) healing, (4) insult, and (5) loss of time. For the first four counts the tortfeasor pays the slave, for the fifth he he pays the master.]

B.   But [a householder] need not pay for the slave's loss of time, if the slave belongs to him, [but he must pay for the other four counts].

M. BQ 8:3

The Hebrew slave controls most facets of his own life. This is evident from the fact that the person who injures him pays four counts of damages to him and only one to his master. Indeed, at B we see that even a Hebrew slave's master must pay him compensation on the four counts when he injures him. Thus the indentured servant, in general, is an autonomous person. The master controls only one aspect of the Hebrew slave, his time, or in other words, his labor.

Hence, as with the indentured servant found in Scripture, the master of a Hebrew slave controls only his slave's labor.

The second characteristic necessary to the indentured servant is that his servitude be temporary and of an established length of time. The following passage sets forth specific, predetermined periods when the servant obtains his liberty.

A.   The Hebrew slave...becomes autonomous (lit. acquires himself, (וקונה את עצמו)

B.   by [serving his master six] years (Ex. 21:2),

C.   by [the arrival of the] Jubilee [year, even if he has not served six years] (Lev. 25:40), or

D.   [in the case of an Israelite who sold himself to a non-Israelite, his relatives may redeem him] by [paying a] reduced [purchase price, pro-rated according to the number of years he has served (Lev. 25:50-51)]....

M. Qid. 1:2

This passage clearly shows that the Hebrew slave serves for a specified, limited period of time. All three methods by which he obtains his freedom indicate that he serves a specified number of years, at the end of which he goes free. B and C, which concern a person in service to an Israelite, indicate the point at which the period of service ends. D refers to the case of a Hebrew in thrall to a non-Israelite who wishes to go free before his term of indenture has been completed. The temporary servitude these modes of emancipation reveal is the central characteristic of indenture and therefore indicates that the Mishnah's Hebrew servant is indeed an indentured servant. In addition, the Mishnah's authorities draw all three methods from Scripture's depiction of the Hebrew indentured servant (Ex. 21:2, Lev. 25:40, 50-51), which clearly identifies the Mishnah's Hebrew indentured servant with that of Scripture.

Having shown that the Mishnah's Hebrew slave is an indentured servant like that of Scripture, we can now turn to its counterpart, the Canaanite slave. To determine whether the Mishnah's Canaanite slave likewise stems from the Pentateuch's portrayal of slavery, we must ascertain if he is a chattel slave. Two attributes in particular mark a chattel slave. First, he stands under the domination of his master with few rights of his own. All contacts with the society around him take place through his master. Second, he constitutes a permanent slave, with no fixed limits to his service. This characteristic can be seen in both the permanent servitude of slaves (as in Lev. 25:44-46), and in the way a slave attains his freedom, that is, only by manumission. Release by manumission presupposes that the slave has no predetermined length of service. His master, of course, could choose to liberate him at any time, but the slave has no reason to expect this at a particular moment. Thus, freedom by manumission applies only to a slave who stands in permanent thrall.

The following passage clearly illustrates the fact that the Canaanite slave stands under his master's power. The situation concerns a free man who injures a Canaanite slave and the issue is whether compensation should be paid.

> A. He who injures a Canaanite slave belonging to others is liable [to pay compensation to the slave's owner] on all [five counts]. [These are specified in M. BQ 8:1 as (1) injury, (2) pain, (3) healing, (4) insult, and (5) loss of time.]...
> B. He who injures his own Canaanite slave is exempt [from paying compensation] on any [count].

M. BQ 8:3, 5

The Canaanite slave receives no personal compensation for any injury he sustains; the money is paid to his master. Unlike the Hebrew indentured servant, the Canaanite slave is viewed as subject to the householder's control. The Mishnah thus treats any injury to the slave as an injury to his master. Hence, if the master injures his own Canaanite slave, he pays nothing, for he has damaged his own property. Like the foreign slave of Scripture, the Canaanite slave is wholly under his master's control and relates to the society only through him.

We can see that the Canaanite slave is a permanent slave from the fact that he goes free only through manumission and not by the end of a specified period of time. The following dispute centers on the procedure for a slave's manumission.

> A. "And the Canaanite slave...becomes autonomous [lit. acquires himself] (1) by money [paid to his master by] others, or (2) by a writ [of emancipation that the slave] himself [receives from the master]," the words of R. Meir.
> B. But sages say, "[A Canaanite slave becomes autonomous] (1) by money that the [slave] himself [gives to his master], or (2) by a writ [of emancipation that the householder gives] to others,
> C. "as long as the money [that the slave gives to his master at B.1] belongs to others."

M. Qid. 1:3

The important point for our study is simply that the Canaanite slave permanently serves his master with no hope of eventual release. Unlike the Hebrew indentured servant who gains his freedom automatically, the Canaanite slave gains his freedom only through the active cooperation of his owner. This means that, like the foreign slave of Scripture, the Canaanite slave is a permanent slave. The Mishnah's Canaanite slave thus fulfills the second criterion for classification as a chattel slave, that of permanent servitude.

It is now clear that the six Mishnah passages that discuss the Hebrew indentured servant and the Canaanite slave carry forward the portrayal of slaves found in the Pentateuch. Just like Scripture's scheme of slavery, these passages differentiate their two categories of slavery by the criterion of genealogy. The slave with native origins becomes an indentured servant while the one of non-native background is merely a chattel slave. Furthermore, these two categories constitute an anomaly to the Mishnah's main system of slavery. For the Mishnah's central portrayal of slavery differentiates its categories by the criterion of the householder's control, dividing them into bondmen and freedmen. In comparison to the Mishnah's main portrayal of slavery, these six passages present a different set of categories organized into a separate system.

The question arises, therefore, what purpose do these six pericopae serve in the Mishnah? The answer is that they all illustrate legal principles that cannot be addressed by the main categories of bondmen and freedmen. Five of them focus on the Canaanite slave's identification with his master.[39] These passages use the Canaanite slave to portray a person whose subservience to a householder deprives him of the capacity to acquire objects for himself; anything he takes or receives belongs to his master, not to him. Thus the Canaanite slave cannot possess or own anything in his own right. For example, M. Qid. 1:3, which we examined above, describes the process of freeing a Canaanite slave. The slave's manumission takes effect when he acquires possession of a writ of manumission from his master. But B's underlying contention is that the Canaanite slave cannot take possession of such a document from his master. Even if the master gives the document to the slave, it still belongs to the master. Therefore, the writ must be given to others who accept it on behalf of the slave. The other four passages likewise use the Canaanite slave to depict a person who cannot possess objects for himself, but only for his superior. M. MS 4:4 shows that any money the slave holds belongs to his master. M. Erub. 7:6 argues that his master cannot give anything to the slave because any object he holds remains in the possession of the master. M. BQ 8:3, 5 reveals that if a householder injures his own Canaanite slave, he pays no damages because the slave, in a legal sense, cannot accept them. Finally, M. BM 1:5 illustrates the point that any object the Canaanite slave finds belongs to his master. In these five passages, therefore, sages demonstrate that the Canaanite slave cannot possess property by himself, anything he acquires belongs to his master.

The Mishnah's main slave category, the bondman, could not have served to illustrate the above principle. As we shall see in Chapters Three and Four, the bondman acts on behalf of his master only when the master grants him specific authorization. A bondman's acquisitions do not automatically belong to his master, but only when the master specifically instructs the bondman to make an acquisition. The bondman therefore cannot serve to illustrate the principle that anything a slave acquires belongs to his master. Thus, sages used the Canaanite slave to portray it.

---

[39] The five passages are M. MS 4:4, Erub. 7:6, Qid. 1:2-3, BQ 8:3&5, and BM 1:5.

In the sixth passage, M. Arak. 8:4-5, the framers likewise use the Canaanite slave to demonstrate a point that does not apply to the bondman. In the Mishnah's main system of slavery, the bondman cannot be put to death or banished from Israelite society. Lev. 27:28-29, however, clearly grants a private individual the right to send some human being under his control to death. He does this by devoting the person to the Temple, the result of which is that the person is put to death. In later rabbinic texts, such as the Babylonian Talmud, this action is mitigated to meaning banishment from the Israelite community.[40] It is unclear whether death or banishment is meant here in the Mishnah. Neither penalty can be applied to a bondman. In M. Arak. 8:4-5 too, therefore, the framers use the Canaanite slave to illustrate a principle that does not apply to the bondman. Since we now understand the place of these anomalous six passages in the Mishnah, we can return to the focus of our study, the Mishnah's main system of slavery.

Conclusion

This chapter's investigation enables us to see the categories of bondman and freedman as a system of slavery nestled within a number of larger systems. These systems fit within each other like concentric circles. The Mishnah's system of slavery fits into the larger system of Israelite society, which in turn has its place in the Mishnah's overall portrayal of the cosmos. To draw together the various studies of this chapter, we shall now briefly work through each system, starting with the largest and working down to the smallest. In this way, as we describe each system, we identify the place of the next one within it. This process ultimately enables us to pinpoint the place of slavery within the Mishnah's system.

The Mishnah's view of the cosmos constitutes its encompassing system. Through it, sages attempt to delineate the place of all things relevant to their concerns. This system contains three main components, two of which we have already described, human beings and the objects that make up the world, such as animals, buildings, and plants. The third component of the cosmic system is God. The inclusion of God may strike the reader as odd, for up to now we have not mentioned the divine. This is because the Mishnah itself rarely refers to God in an explicit manner. A strictly inductive examination of the Mishnah's explicit statements, therefore, does not require, or even permit, the mention of God. But to understand the Mishnah's system, we must include God's unmentioned — but implicit and fundamental — role. For despite the lack of explicit reference, God constitutes the Mishnah's central concern and its primary

---

[40] See discussions of this issue in: Martin Noth, *Leviticus: A Commentary* (Philadelphia: Westminster, 1965) and "Herem" in the *Encyclopedia Judaica* (Jerusalem: Macmillan & Keter, 1971). The latter has a good bibliography on the subject.

organizing category. This becomes clear from the fact that the Temple comprises the Mishnah's explicit focus of attention. The Temple's central position in the Mishnah's system stems from its function as the primary locus for the worship of God, not from any inherent characteristics of its own. Because of this function, four of the Mishnah's six divisions are explicitly devoted to matters pertaining to the functioning of the Temple cult. For example, the Mishnah's sages devote one division to the tithing of crops and livestock necessary for offerings to the Temple cult. In another they delineate the correct mode of preparing and offering sacrifices and in a third, the rules necessary for maintaining cultic purity. The internal evidence of the Mishnah, therefore, points to the framers' overarching concern with the proper worship of God in sanctity. Thus God constitutes a primary component of the Mishnah's system, even though the framers do not explicitly identify him as such.

Since the Mishnah's authorities do not describe outright God's place in their system, we must ascertain his place through means other than the examination of the Mishnah's text. For this purpose, we turn to Scripture. Although this violates our stated methodology of analyzing only the inherent features of the Mishnah, we can justify it because the Mishnah's framers view Scripture as authoritative. In fact, Scripture comprises the only document ever cited in the Mishnah as a source of authority.[41] We are most interested in Scripture's portrayal of the cosmos, which it discusses in two places: Genesis Chapter One (specifically, Gen. 1:1-2:4a) and Genesis Chapter Two (Gen. 2:4b-25).[42] The Mishnah's view of the cosmos can be understood as a conflation of the two versions. We shall describe each in turn and then explain how the Mishnah uses them. Genesis One portrays the cosmos as consisting of two main components, God and the universe. God both creates and classifies this universe and the objects within it. From the outset, Scripture presents God as the sole actor. Chapter One begins with God alone and describes how he methodically creates the universe and the different objects that populate it. By creating an object, God thereby establishes it as a category. The story also presents God as classifying the objects of his creation, that is, as placing objects in these categories. For example, Gen. 1:4-5 reads, "and God separated the light from the darkness. God called the light Day, and the darkness he called Night." This process of naming is an act of classification. God identifies the categories to which light and darkness belong. In the same manner, Genesis One treats human beings merely as objects of the world. God creates and classifies them as he does all other objects. They play no active role in the process of classification. In Genesis One, therefore, creation comprises an act of classification, which in turn identifies God as the sole source of classification.

---

[41] For further discussion of the relationship between the Mishnah and Scripture see Neusner, *Evidence*, pp. 167-229, esp. pp. 221-224.

[42] See Eilberg-Schwartz's discussion of the link between Genesis Two and the Mishnah in his *Intention*, pp. 103-108.

When we turn to Genesis Chapter Two, a different picture emerges. Here Scripture presents a cosmos that contains three main constituents: God, the objects of the world, and human beings, who here possess the status of a separate component. In this role, human beings take over part of the tasks God performed in the earlier story. Although God still creates the world and its objects — that is, he establishes categories of objects — man plays a large role in placing the objects of his world into those categories. For example, Gen. 2:19 reads, "the Lord God formed every beast of the field and every bird of the air, and brought them to the man to see what he would call them; and whatever the man called every living creature, that was its name." Again, by giving names to these creatures, the man — who is the archetypal human being — classifies the animals. And as the story states, these names become the permanent description of the animals. In other words, the classification established by the man determines the place of these creatures within the created world. Thus Genesis Two portrays human beings as active agents of classification, along with God himself.

In the Mishnah, the framers present a view of the cosmos that combines these two stories. The Mishnah's classificatory scheme carries forward that of the stories in Genesis. When the two Genesis stories share certain details, the Mishnah likewise uses them. Where the two stories differ, the Mishnah's system presents both versions. This is clear from the two lower components, namely, the world's objects and human beings. First, in both Genesis stories, the objects that populate its world comprise that which is classified. In the Mishnah, the world's objects likewise are arranged into specific categories. Second, with regard to human beings we discover that Genesis One emphasizes their passive nature — that is, they constitute mere categories like the rest of the world — while Genesis Two portrays man as an active category, who effects the classification of objects around him. The Mishnah combines these two portrayals in its depiction of human beings. For sages, humans constitute both objects to be classified and active, classifying agents.

God's implicit role in the Mishnah likewise follows from these stories in Genesis. In both texts, God is the creator of the world and its categories. There is one important difference, however. The Genesis stories depict the creation of the cosmos, while the Mishnah portrays the result. By focusing on the moment of creation, both Genesis One and Two reveal how the classificatory system was established. Since the system did not come into being on its own but was directly created by God, Scripture's stories explicitly describe God's role. In both Genesis stories, God performs two specific deeds: he creates and establishes the categories of the world and he assigns objects to those categories — a task which in Genesis Two he shares with Adam. When we turn to the Mishnah, by contrast, the system has already been set in place. The Mishnah portrays a world the categories of which have been established and the objects of which have been assigned to them. It should not surprise us, therefore, that the Mishnah does not mention God. Although the creator is necessary at the time of creation, once the system has been set in place, it can function without the intervention of heaven. Self-evidently, therefore, if we could ask the Mishnah's framers who created the classificatory world they describe, they would point to Scripture and answer that God created it. To sages, God constitutes the source of the world they describe and thus he forms the central component of their cosmic system. To summarize, then, the Mishnah reveals a three-tier system of the cosmos: God as the creator of its classificatory system and its ultimate classifier, the world's objects as the items that are classified, and human beings as both passive objects of classification and active agents effecting the classification of other objects.

As we can see, human beings constitute part of the Mishnah's view of the cosmos, and as such they constitute one of its three central components. Furthermore, human beings themselves make up a system of ordered categories. Thus, the Mishnah's authorities differentiate their portrayal of Israelite society into four different classifications: householders, women, minor sons and bondmen. Sages organize these four categories in a particular manner. They identify the householder — the free, adult, male Israelite — as the central, generative category of Israelite society. In the framers' eyes, he sets the standard of humanity. Sages delineate each of the other three categories in opposition to him. In fact, they define each one as the negation or opposite of an important attribute of the householder. Women comprise the opposite of householders in terms of gender; minor sons form the opposite of householders with regard to age. By the same principle, bondmen constitute the opposite of householders with regard to freedom.

Sages further emphasize the householder's position as the central category of Israelite society by granting him power over the other social categories. The householder possesses the power to limit or prevent members of other categories from exercising their power of classification. In fact, the framers use the householder's power as a taxonomic criterion to distinguish species within a genus. Within a genus, certain categories of people belong under a householder's power while others do not. This power, for example, serves to differentiate the genus of free, Israelite males into the categories of minor son and householder as well as to distinguish the categories within the three pairs of women. Most significant for our study, however, is the fact that within the Mishnah's system of slavery, the householder's power differentiates the bondman from the freedman.

Within the system of slavery, the framers define the freedman in opposition to the bondman. Just as the bondman comprises the opposite of the householder's freedom, so the freedman is the opposite of the bondman's unfree condition. In the Mishnah's system, however, what we call "freedom" means being free from the control of a single individual, specifically, from the power of a householder. Thus, the taxonomic criterion of the householder's control defines the bondman as a human being subject to the full power of a householder. The freedman, by contrast, constitutes a bondman who is free from the control of householders. To recapitulate this in terms of the Mishnah's two larger systems, the bondman is a human being whose capacity to classify objects in his world is controlled by his master. The freedman is a person who was once subject — or whose ancestors were subject — to such control, but who may now freely exercise his power of classification. The next stage in our study of the Mishnah's system of slavery, therefore, shall be to understand the nature of this classificatory power, the householder's control over the bondman's exercise of his power, and the freedman's freedom from that control.

Part Two

The Mishnah's System of Slaves

Chapter Three

Slave and Master

The Mishnah's authorities define the bondman in the same way they define livestock and furniture. That is, they identify him as property, as the private possession of an Israelite. Just as an ox or a bed belongs to a householder, so the bondman constitutes the property of his master. Yet the bondman differs from other categories of property in one significant way; as we saw in Chapter Two, he constitutes a category within the system of human beings as well as in that of property. If the bondman belongs in each system, should not the Mishnah contain two definitions for him, one in each system? This is not the case. The framers constructed these two systems so that they share a single definition of the bondman. In both the systems of human beings and of property, the bondman constitutes a human being subject to a householder's full control. In the system of humanity, sages use the bondman's total subjection to his master's power to distinguish him from other categories of human beings. In the system of property, by contrast, they use his humanity to distinguish him from other classes of property. Within the systems of human beings and of property, therefore, the bondman conforms to the same definition; he is a human being standing under a householder's full power. These two systems share this definition because they actually intersect at the category of the bondman. This intersection is not accidental, for it results from the relation of each system to the Mishnah's overall portrayal of the cosmos. When we understand how the systems of humanity and of property fit into the Mishnah's depiction of the cosmos, we shall then know why the Mishnah's main system of slavery contains only one definition of the bondman.

The Mishnah's cosmos, which we described in the previous chapter, contains a triadic and a dualistic structure. The triad comprises God, human beings, and the objects that make up the world — inanimate objects and living creatures. Its dualistic structure stems from the role that these three components fulfil, as either classifiers or classified objects. Two components — God and human beings — carry out the role of classification, for they possess the power to place objects into categories. These we shall call "agents of classification." The second role — that of being classified — is likewise played by two components, the objects of the world and, once again, human beings. The convergence of the dual and triadic structures is represented by the following diagram (Figure 2).

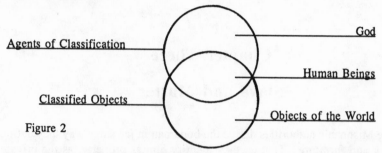

Agents of Classification

God

Human Beings

Classified Objects

Objects of the World

Figure 2

Each circle stands for a part of the dual structure, one for the agents of classification and the other for classified objects. The triadic structure is represented by the three enclosed areas of the intersecting circles. God is an agent of classification who is neither classified nor classifiable. By contrast, the objects of the world are classified but cannot perform classification. Each component — God and the world's objects — plays a single role and therefore remains isolated in its specific areas. Human beings, however, occupy the intersected area of the two circles, for they constitute both agents of classification and objects that have been classified.

In point of fact, classified objects can be divided according to the source of their classification, God or human beings (see Figure 3). As we saw in Chapter Two, objects that have been classified by God belong to the realm of nature, while those classified by humankind belong to the human realm. A wild beast, for example, is part of the realm of nature, but a bed belongs to the human realm. The important point for our study is that the bondman, like the other categories of human beings, belongs to the realm of humanity. This is because the actions of human beings — those of the householder in particular — classify a person as a bondman. The householder classifies the bondman in a straightforward manner, namely, by bringing the bondman under his full power. Thus the bondman as a human being belongs to the objects classified by human beings. To see him as property, however, we must examine how the householder accomplishes the classification of the bondman.

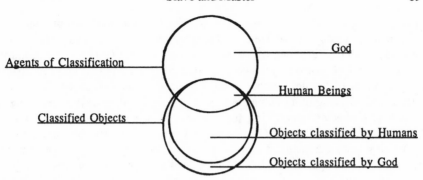

Figure 3

The bondman, as we have observed, belongs to the system of property that constitutes a subdivision of the objects classified by human beings. The framers distinguish property from nonproperty by the following definition; property stands under the full control of a householder. Any object not under a householder's full control falls outside the classification of property. Most objects over which a householder can exercise his power of classification are property. Among these are, for example, the householder's own livestock and crops, pots, utensils, tools, furniture, and clothing, as well as his house, farm buildings and land. Sages classify the bondman as property along with these categories. All other categories of human beings, by contrast, fall outside the system of property. Although householders are responsible for placing people within these categories — for example, they can classify women and sons — they do not own the people they categorize. The following diagram (Figure 4) shows how the system of property comprises a subset of the objects classified by human beings. Note that the circle representing property is located partially over the area representing human beings and partially over the area of nonhuman objects. The part over humanity indicates the location of the bondman.

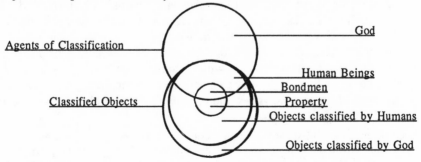

Figure 4

Thus, the category of bondman constitutes the point at which the systems of property and humanity intersect. Although the two systems share no other category, here they fit perfectly. The definition of the bondman provides the explanation for this fit. As we saw, the definition consists of two parts: (1) the bondman is a human being, (2) he stands subject to a householder's full control. To identify the bondman within each system, the framers put different emphases on each part of the definition. In the system of humanity, sages specify the genus as consisting of all human beings (1). They then divide this genus into a number of species, identifying the species "bondman" as a person under a householder's full control (2). In the system of property, by contrast, the framers specify the genus as all objects that are subject to a householder's full power (2). The species are then distinguished as each different type of object. Thus, the bondman is distinguished from the others by the fact that he is human (1). In each system, the criterion that defines the general characteristics of one system serves to distinguish the bondman as a distinct category in the other. In other words, the factor that includes the bondman in the system of humanity — that he is a human being — makes him a distinct category within the system of property. Likewise, the factor which makes the bondman part of the system of property — that he stands under a householder's full control — distinguishes him as a separate category within the system of humanity.

We can test this description by examining how it explains the bondman in specific cases within each system. This has already been accomplished for the system of humanity in the previous chapter. There we showed how the householder's control — the defining criterion of property — differentiates the bondman from other categories of humans. We must now consider how the criterion of the bondman's humanity distinguishes him from other categories of property. To accomplish this task, we must describe the principles that govern the system of property. Once we delineate these principles, we shall use them to show, first, how the bondman belongs to the system of property and, second, to indicate how he constitutes a separate category within it.

The key to understanding the bondman as property is to analyze how sages portray what we have termed "full householder's control." The householder's control consists of two aspects: the householder can force an object — a cow for example — to do what he wants, and he must prevent it from doing what he does not want. Thus, on the one hand, sages grant the householder the power to use his property as he wishes — within limits of course.[1] The owner is permitted to use a living animal or an inanimate object to further his own ends. He can hitch his ox to a plowshare and prepare his field for planting[2] or he can

---

[1] Of course, the Mishnah's system, copying from Scripture, places a few restrictions on the householder's use of his animate and inanimate property, such as the rule of rest on the Sabbath (Ex. 21). See also M. Hul. 5:1-5 (based on Lev. 22:28); Deut. 22:8, 10; and Deut. 25:4.

[2] Again, the Mishnah, following the Hebrew Scriptures, places certain restrictions on the householder's general capacity to do these things. For example, during every seventh year, he is not allowed to plant any crops at all (See M. Sheviit).

store something in his pot or cupboard. On the other hand, the householder must use his power to prevent his property from injuring other people or causing damage to their property. If the owner fails to prevent such injury or damage, he himself becomes liable to make restitution. For example, when a farmer is not using his ox, he should tie it up. If he does not and the ox then wanders into a neighbor's field and ruins it, the ox's owner is liable. Similarly, if a householder leaves a pot in the street and someone falls over it and injures himself, the householder becomes liable. To have full control over an item of property, therefore, means to possess both the power to use it and the responsibility to prevent it from causing injury or damage.

When we turn to specific objects of property, such as a cow or a bed, and ask how the householder exercises his control over them, we discover an important fact. Sages view each category as a composite of features, not as a seamless, uniform object. When different kinds of property share the same feature, the framers treat those items the same with regard to that feature. For example, sages spell out a procedure for selling property that, with minor variations, applies to all types of property subject to sale. They do not construct a different manner of sale for each type of property. Thus, the sale of a bed and the sale of a cow each take place according to the same rules. Conversely, when a form of property has certain distinctive features — that is, characteristics it does not share with other types of property — the Mishnah's authorities treat it differently only with regard to those particular attributes. These peculiar features do not alter how sages treat the qualities it has in common with other forms of property. In our example of the cow and the bed, a cow possesses the characteristic of movement, which the bed lacks. Sages therefore develop rules to govern the cow's power of movement. Since the bed lacks the feature of movement, these rules apply only to the cow and not to the bed. More importantly, these rules do not affect how sages treat the characteristic the cow shares with the bed, namely, being subject to sale. Thus, in the Mishnah's system of property, sages promulgate rules governing characteristics and then apply them to the types of property that share those characteristics.

The most important of these rules are those that govern a householder's exercise of power over his property. Thus, when the framers describe the householder's power over an object, they delineate his control over each particular feature, not his power over the item as a whole. This manner of describing property enables the Mishnah's framers to be economical in delineating the householder's power. When features are shared among a number of different categories, the framers delineate a single set of rules to govern the householder's exercise of power over that feature. Only when an object has an attribute distinctive to it do the framers describe the householder's control over a single category, but even then, they do this only for the distinctive feature. In this way, sages can describe the householder's power over a vast number of categories by delineating how that power applies to a much smaller number of shared features. The framers' focus on interchangeable features is evident from M. BQ 1:4, in which sages discuss the capacity of livestock to damage the property of other people. This passage describes the harm caused by the features of the "tooth" (that is, the mouth) and the "foot."

A. The tooth [of an animal] is an attested danger [that is, it is always ready to cause damage] in that it eats anything that is suited for it.
B. The foot [of an animal] is an attested danger in that it may break [anything] that is in the path where it walks.

M. BQ 1:4

The Mishnah's framers clearly specify the dangers posed by the features of the tooth and the foot which are possessed by animals. Animals are expected to eat any edible material within their reach, and are likewise expected to kick anything in the path on which they walk. But sages never mention a specific animal to whom these features are attached, for they refer to all animals that possess these features.[3] Furthermore, by stating that each of these features constitutes an "attested danger," the framers indicate how the householder's control applies to them. Usually, a householder must pay only half-damages for damage caused by his livestock. But in the case of destruction or injury caused by a feature that is an attested danger, the owner must pay full compensation. This is because the householder knows that his animals can do harm with these features at any time and therefore he must take extra care to prevent such damage at all times.

The final important aspect of these features is that they are modular. This means that a feature's presence in or absence from a description usually has no bearing on the presence of other features in that description and their rules governing the householder's control over them. An animal's possession of a foot, for example, indicates nothing about whether it has a tooth. In some cases, however, one feature will override another feature or change its nature. For example, the ox possesses horns and can become an attested danger with regard to goring. The cow likewise possesses horns, but it is not an attested danger with regard to goring. This is because the two animals have different temperaments. The cow's docility overrides the possibility that her horns might make her dangerous like the "ornery" ox. In such cases, the feature of temperament combines with the physical attribute of possessing horns to determine whether the animal possesses the attribute of goring. In the system of property, therefore, sages treat each category as a composite of modular features.

---

[3] In some instances, sages discuss an animal instead of a feature. In doing so, however, they usually are implicitly referring to a specific feature of that animal. This is true for the description of the ox in M. BQ 1:4 and 2:3. Although sages speak explicitly of the ox, they actually are discussing the ox's feature of goring. This works as a reverse synecdoche in which sages discuss goring by referring explicitly to the ox, because goring is a feature distinctive to oxen.

While no one feature requires the presence of any other, two features — such as horns and temperament — may combine to make up a third.

When we turn to the bondman, we find that the Mishnah's framers portray him within the principles of their system of property. He forms a collection of features, each being controlled by his master according to a specific set of rules. The features that the bondman shares with other types of property are controlled according to the same rules that apply to them. For attributes that are distinctive to the bondman, the framers delineate specific sets of rules to govern his master's control. For example, the bondman is subject to sale, a characteristic he shares with nearly all forms of property.[4] The householder exercises his control over the sale of his bondman in the same way he controls that of other objects of property. By contrast, the bondman possesses the power to reason. Since no other form of property possesses this capacity, the framers develop special rules to guide the householder in his exercise of power over it. Furthermore, the bondman's capacity to reason causes important differences between him and other types of property. Like the cow's docility, the bondman's reason affects the features he possesses — such as his capacity of action — and thereby alters how the householder controls those features.

Both parts of this description of the bondman as property — his master's control of his similarities with other types of property and the control over his differences from those same categories — require further examination. We shall study each in turn. To investigate how the householder controls his bondman with regard to features that the bondman shares with other types of property, we shall study three examples of the transfer of the bondman. The feature of transfer provides important insight into the householder's exercise of control over a bondman because transfer constitutes the exchange of power, that is, the relinquishing of control by one party and its acquisition by another. At the beginning and ending of a householder's power over a bondman, that power becomes clearly revealed. By discovering how, for this feature, the householder controls his bondman as he would other types of property, we will understand how the basic principles of the system of property apply to the bondman.

The first passage deals with a method of acquisition called usucaption. A householder gains control over a bondman by usucaption according to the same procedure applicable to other types of property. Usucaption takes place when a householder has uninterrupted possession of an item of property for a specified period of time and has used it openly and with public knowledge for that time. In other words, to acquire the item, the householder acts as if he already has full power over the item in question. If no one challenges the householder's right to

---

[4] In general, a householder can sell his bondman according to the same rules that apply to the sale of other forms of property, as we shall see momentarily. There are a few exceptions to this rule, such as M. Git. 4:6, which states that a bondman cannot be sold outside the land of Israel.

exercise his control during this period, then at the end of the time, the object enters the householder's permanent control. This mode applies only to individual items of property and not to an indeterminant group of objects — such as a flock of sheep — for it must be clear that the householder has controlled the particular item for the necessary length of time. The following passage lists bondmen as one type of property that can be acquired in this manner.

A. [With regard to] acquisition through usucaption [of the following items]: (1) houses, (2) cisterns, (3) ditches, (4) caverns, (5) dove-cots, (6) bath-houses, (7) olive-presses, (8) irrigated fields, (9) bondmen, (10) any [plant] that bears fruit perenially —

B. possession of them for three years continuously (lit. from day to day) [establishes title to them].

M. BB 3:1

Sages here treat the bondman like the other forms of property (A) and give no recognition of his nature as a human being. By including him in this list of property, they show that in their minds there is no substantive difference in the way a householder acquires power over, say, a house and the way in which he acquires control over a bondman. Thus, with regard to usucaption, the householder controls the bondman like other types of property.

Householders can also transfer a group of bondmen without paying individual attention to each one. In fact, a man can acquire power over bondmen as part of a larger purchase without ever being specifically told that he is doing so. This point becomes clear with regard to the sale of a town.[5] Towns are sold whole, without an itemized property-list. At issue for sages is what types of property are included in such a general sale. The town's real property usually constitutes the focus of this type of transaction. But if the seller indicates that the deal includes movable property, then bondmen are also sold.

A. He who sells a town (עיר) has sold [without specification] (1) the houses, (2) the cisterns, (3) the ditches, (4) the caverns, (5) the bath-houses, (6) the dove-cots, (7) the olive-presses and (8) the irrigated fields.

B. But [he has] not [sold] the movable property [that is in the city].

C. However, [if] at the time [of the sale the seller] had said to [the buyer], "[I am selling you] it [i.e., the town] and all that is in it,"

D. even if cattle and bondmen were in it —

E. lo, all [the movable goods, including the bondmen,] have been sold.

M. BB 4:7

---

5 The framers probably use the term "town" to refer not to a town or village *per se*, but to a large agricultural estate such as a Roman *latifundia*.

Again, the main point for our study is that the sale agreement treats bondmen just like the other types of property included in the sale. The seller does not even have to specify that bondmen are part of the sale, he merely needs to state that he is selling everything that is in the town. In sages' eyes, the bondman's humanity grants him no special status as property and is not even important enough to require a specific mention. Hence, once again we see that when the bondman and the other property share the same characteristics the householder gains power over the bondman in the same manner as other types of property.

The two passages just discussed treat the transfer of power over a bondman as a property transaction. Power over a bondman can also be transferred as an incidental effect of a more important transaction. In the passage below, a woman acquires control over a bondman because her divorce decree is written upon him. The bondman is in fact analogous to a piece of parchment. Let me explain how this transaction works. When a man divorces his wife, he must give her a writ of divorce, usually written on a piece of parchment or leather. But the law does not specify the material on which it should be written and so we find sages discussing what other things may serve as writing material. In this passage, they decide that living things, such as slaves, cattle and leaves, may serve. If the husband writes the divorce decree on his bondman, he must give his wife the bondman in order properly to carry out the divorce procedure.

A. They may write [a writ of divorce] on any [type of material]:
B. upon an olive leaf,
C. or upon a cow's horn — and [the husband] must give [his wife] the cow—
D. [or] upon a bondman's hand — and [the husband] must give [his wife] the bondman.
E. Rabbi Yose of Galilee says, "They do not write on a thing that has in it the breath of life."

M. Git. 2:3

At A-D, the Mishnah's framers again treat the bondman like the other types of property under consideration. Although we would not usually consider a bondman to be a suitable substitute for paper, since sages do so here, they can equate him with the cow and the leaf. Control over the bondman is transferred just like the power over the cow or the leaf. The contrary opinion at E likewise evaluates the bondman as a type of property. By focusing on the common feature of being alive, Yose's view ignores the bondman's human characteristics and treats him analogous to a cow. He holds that the householder may not relinquish his control over bondmen and cattle in this manner. Thus, once again we see that when a bondman shares features with other forms of property, the householder controls him, with respect to those features, just like the other types of property. The bondman's humanity makes no difference.

In sum, we see that when the bondman shares a feature with other types of property — the characteristic of transfer, for example — the householder controls him, with regard to that feature, like the other types of property. Since the householder exercises this power over all categories of property, we see that the framers consider the bondman just another form of property. Thus, the category of bondman fits into the system of property as well as that of humanity.

This brings us to the central and final question concerning the bondman within the system of property, namely, how does the bondman's humanity mark him as a separate category within the system of property? By answering this question, we will show how the Mishnah's single definition of the bondman — as a human being subject to a householder's full control — serves to distinguish him as a category within both the system of human beings and the system of property. The distinctively human attribute that differentiates the bondman from other objects of property is the capacity to effect classification, which livestock cannot do. Like other human beings, the bondman possesses the power to place objects into different categories. This power of classification, however, is not sufficient in and of itself for investigating the bondman as a human being, for it forms part of a more encompassing human power, the power to cause legal effects. To be sure, the power to classify constitutes the ultimate legal effect. Indeed, in the Mishnah's system, it is impossible to alter an object more than to reclassify it. But most exercises of power do not classify objects but simply cause legal effects against them. It is this overall power to cause legal effects, then, that distinguishes human beings in the Mishnah. To show how the framers identify the bondman as a human being within the system of property, therefore, we must examine the bondman's power to cause legal effects.

Two considerations guide our analysis. First, as we saw above, sages' portrayal of human power can be divided into three types: acts requiring reason, merely physical acts and bodily conditions, and relationships. We shall examine the bondman's capacity to cause legal effects using each form of power. Second, we must study how the householder exercises control over each type of power. In this way, we can see how the bondman's human exercise of power still fits into the rules governing the system of property.

We can demonstrate how the bondman possesses each of these three types of power by simply examining his ability to produce legal effects through them. Only an exercise of power that results in legal consequences reveals that the bondman has that particular type of power. For example, suppose a slave states a vow. If his statement causes him to be bound to the conditions of that vow, then he possesses the power to take the vow. But if he does not become subject to the vow's stipulations, then he lacks that power. Additionally, we can evaluate the householder's control in the same manner. If the householder can dictate when the bondman's acts create legal effects and when they do not, then the master controls his bondman's exercise of that type of power. In the example of the vow, if the bondman can bind himself by a vow, then he has that power. But if his master can cancel the vow, then the master can control his slave's power. Thus, by investigating the bondman's capacity to produce legal effects, we can determine whether he possesses the three types of power held by human beings and how the householder controls that power.

Reason and Action

The Mishnah's authorities recognize one feature of the bondman's humanity by granting him the power to perform acts that require the exercise of reason.[6] This fact is highly significant because sages portray the capacity to perform such deeds as a key power of adult householders. By granting the adult bondman such power, the framers show that they consider him equivalent to a householder in this important respect. Before we develop this point further, let me spell out what I mean by "acts that require the exercise of reason." These are deeds that have legal consequences only if the performer has the capacity of reason. That is, in order for the act to be considered legally effective, it must be performed by someone with the mental capacity to understand the act's implications. In sages' view, an adult Israelite meets these conditions. When such actions are performed by a person lacking the necessary mental ability — such as a minor — those acts have no recognized legal effect or standing. For example, if a householder injures his neighbor, he must pay compensation. The householder is culpable because he possesses reason and therefore understands the implications of his action. In contrast, if the householder's minor son — who lacks reason — injures the same neighbor, no compensation is paid. This is because the minor does not understand the ramifications of his deeds. Of course, there is some sort of physical effect, but that is of no legal consequence. To continue our example, even if the neighbor has been physically hurt, the child bears no legal culpability because he lacks the requisite mental capacity.

To return to our opening point, sages grant the adult bondman the same capacity to perform acts requiring reason as an adult householder. However, they complicate matters by denying him free use of his power; the bondman can achieve the intended purpose of an act only when his master allows. That is, the householder defines when his slave's deeds bear legal consequences. When the bondman acts with his master's authorization, the deed has legal effects. But if he acts without his master's permission, then sages consider the act not to have happened legally and it therefore bears no legal consequences.

To show that the householder controls the legal effectiveness of those acts of his bondman requiring reason, two points must be demonstrated. We must first prove that the adult bondman actually possesses the capacity of reason. The second step is to demonstrate that the householder dictates when his bondman's reasoned acts are legally effective. This latter demonstration requires two stages. When the householder allows his bondman to perform an act requiring reason,

---

[6] Reason constitutes part of the same mental faculty as will. Here we shall focus on the capacity of reason; in Chapter Six, we shall center our attention on the power of will.

we must show that his actions have legal ramifications. We must also show the converse point, that a bondman's reasoned act, unsanctioned by his master, bears no legal consequences. Let us begin by showing that the bondman possesses reason.

Proof that bondmen possess the power of reason appears in a case where a householder rents out his bondman's labor. The householder can commit his adult bondman to do certain acts because the bondman has the requisite mental capacity to carry them out. The passage at hand concerns day laborers who are hired to harvest a farmer's crops. While working, they are permitted to snack on the produce. If they choose, however, the laborers may forego this right in exchange for higher wages. A householder may agree to such an arrangement on behalf of his bondman and other members of his household who possess reason and therefore can control their eating habits, but not for those that lack this capacity.

A. A man may make an agreement [with a farmer to not exercise his right of snacking from the crop while he is harvesting it] on behalf of himself, his adult son or daughter,

B. his adult bondman or bondwoman,

C. or his wife,

D. because they have reason (דעה) [and can therefore keep the terms of the agreement].

E. But he may not make [such an] agreement on behalf of his minor son or daughter,

F. or on behalf of his minor bondman and bondwoman,

G. or on behalf of his beast,

H. because these have no reason [and therefore cannot keep the terms of the agreement].

M. BM 7:6

The point here is clear, the adult bondman possesses reason, just like an adult Israelite (A-D). Sages show this in two ways. First, they explicitly state that the bondman possesses the capacity of reason (D). Second, they also reveal this capacity by contrasting the adult bondman (and the other adults) with the minor children — both free and slave — who lack this capacity (E-H). Clearly, the Mishnah's framers accord adult bondmen the same mental capacity as adult Israelites.

Having shown that sages grant the bondman reason, we must now discover the circumstances in which sages recognize his use of it. In terms of our two-point scheme, we want to know whether the householder determines when those acts of his bondman that require reason have legal consequences and when they do not. As we shall see, such deeds have legal consequences when a householder authorizes his bondman to act as his agent. Since agents act in place of another person, the consequences of a bondman's deeds apply to the master and not to the bondman himself. Conversely, when the householder does not grant his bondman permission to perform an act requiring reason, the deed has legal consequences neither for the master nor for his slave. Let us begin by demonstrating that when the master authorizes the activity of his bondman, the acts take legal effect. This becomes clear from the bondman's capacity to act as his master's agent in three different settings: within the household, between his master and another householder, and with regard to his master's cultic duties.

The first case concerns the bondman's service as his master's agent within the realm of a household. Here, the bondman makes decisions that dictate his master's further activity in the same manner as would a free person in the capacity of an agent. The pericope concerns the festival of Passover, on which the members of each Israelite household must eat a lamb or a kid in commemoration of Israel's bondage in Egypt (Exodus 12). The householder here directs his bondman to slaughter an animal. At issue is whether the bondman should slaughter a lamb or a kid.

A. He who says to his bondman,"Go and slaughter a Passover-offering for me" [and neglects to tell the bondman whether to slaughter a kid or a lamb] —

B. if [the bondman] slaughters a kid, [the householder] should eat [it],

C. [if the bondman] slaughters a lamb, [the householder] should eat [it],

D. [if the bondman] slaughters a kid and a lamb, [the householder] should eat from the first [animal slaughtered].

E. [Concerning a case in which the master told the bondman which animal to slaughter, but the bondman] forgot what his master said to him, what should he do?

F. [The bondman] should slaughter both a lamb and a kid and say, "If my master told me to slaughter a kid, the kid is for him and the lamb is for me,

G. "but if my master told me to slaughter a lamb, the lamb is for him and the kid is for me."

M. Pes. 8:2

Sages imagine two situations here, one in which the householder tells his bondman which animal to slaughter, and one in which he does not. If the master specifies (E-G), the bondman must take great care to slaughter the correct animal. Should the bondman forget his master's instructions, he must slaughter both a lamb and a kid in order to be sure to carry out his master's wishes, even if this means killing an extra animal at his master's expense. If the master does not specify (A-D), however, then the bondman himself must decide which animal to slaughter. The household must eat the animal chosen by the slave, and the householder cannot change his mind and slaughter another. So in both cases, sages picture the bondman performing actions that have certain consequences for the householder himself. Yet these actions are effective only because the householder has authorized the bondman to act for him. The bondman's power in this matter is equal to that of a free person serving as an agent.

Having seen that the bondman may act for the householder in matters of concern only to the household, let us now examine the bondman's capacity to act in the context of dealings between householders. Here again the householder's authorization allows the bondman to act on his master's behalf. The case concerns a bondman who takes a cow from its owner to another householder who is borrowing it.

A. [Concerning the case of a householder] who borrowed a cow
B. and the [cow's owner] sent [the cow, without consulting the borrower,] at the hand of his son, at the hand of his bondman, or at the hand of his agent, or at the hand of the borrower's son, at the hand of the borrower's bondman, or at the hand of the borrower's agent, and [the cow] died [along the way] —
C. [the borrower] is exempt [from any liability].
D. But if the borrower said to [the owner], "Send [the cow] at the hand of my son," "... at the hand of my bondman," "...at the hand of my agent," or "...at the hand of your son," "...at the hand of your bondman," or "... at the hand of your agent."
E. Or the lender said to [the borrower], " Lo, I am sending [the cow] to you at the hand of my son," "...at the hand of my bondman," "...at the hand of my agent," or "...at the hand of your son," "...at the hand of your bondman" or "...at the hand of your agent,"
F. and the borrower said, "[OK,] send [it]."
G. and [the lender] sent [the cow] and it died [along the way] —
H. [the borrower] is liable [to pay damages].
I. And so when [the cow] is returned [the same rules apply].

M. BM 8:3

The bondman here acts as an agent for one householder or the other. This is clear from the framers' discussion of responsibility for the cow, for if the cow dies in transit, one of the householders is liable; sages do not even consider the idea that the person leading the cow might be responsible. Therefore, the bondman acts as an agent. The Mishnah's authorities of course expect the bondman to prevent the cow's death, but if he does not or cannot, then his lack of action is legally binding on the householder. Thus, we see that the bondman's acts requiring mental capacity have legal effect when authorized by a householder.

We finally turn to a case in which a householder may allow the bondman to act for him in cultic responsibilities. In this way, the slave acts as an agent between his master and God. The case at hand concerns the designation of priestly rations from a farmer's harvested produce. A householder must separate such gifts from his produce before he can eat it, and his act imparts sanctity to the designated crops. According to the Mishnah's system, these holy offerings must then be taken to Jerusalem and given to the priests. Neither Scripture nor the Mishnah specify the amount to be separated, so the householder may choose the amount to be given. If he wishes, a householder can assign this task of separation and sanctification to a bondman.

> A. [If a householder] authorized a *ben bayit* [i.e., a free person attached to his household], or his bondman or bondwoman to separate [a specified amount of] priestly rations [from his crop],
> B. that which [the individual] separates is [valid] priestly rations.
> C. [As regards a case in which the householder] voided [his authorization] —
> D. If [the householder] voided [his authorization] before [the individual actually] separated the priestly rations,
> E. that which [the individual] separated is not [valid] priestly rations.
> F. But if he retracted after [the individual] had separated the priestly rations,
> G. that which [the individual] had separated is [valid] priestly rations.

> ·M. Ter. 3:4

The point here is that, under his master's authorization, the bondman can separate the priestly rations. This produce becomes imbued with sanctity and can only be eaten by members of the priestly caste. Thus, when his master allows, the bondman may use his mental capacity to perform legally and cultically effective acts. But the bondman's acts are binding not only on the cult, they are also binding on his master. The householder must now give to the priests the produce he has designated. He no longer has any choice in the matter. So we see once again that the householder controls when his bondman's exercise of his mental capacity is effective.

We have now demonstrated that when a householder authorizes his bondman to perform an act requiring the use of reason, that act has legal consequences. However, before we can conclude that the householder has complete control over those acts of his bondman that require reason, we must also show that when the householder does not permit his bondman to act, the deed has no legal consequences. Two passages in the Mishnah illustrate how the householder's control voids those acts of his bondman that require reason and which, furthermore, the householder did not authorize before their perpetration. First, the householder may cancel a commitment his bondman made on his own concerning his future actions. The following passage focuses on a bondman who vows to become a Nazirite, a vow that can be taken only by a person who possesses mental capacity. According to Scripture, a person who makes this vow becomes consecrated to God and must abstain from drinking wine, stop shaving his beard and cutting his hair, and take utmost care to remain in a state of cultic purity (Num. 6:1-21). A bondman may take this vow, but his master may keep him from fulfilling it, and thus render the vow legally ineffective.

> A. [When] women and bondmen [vow to become Nazirites, they] are subject to [their] Nazirite-vow.

B. It is more strict for wives than bondmen [in one respect],

C. for [a householder] may compel his bondman [to break his vows],

D. but he may not compel his wife [to break her vows].

E. [The Nazirite-vow] is more strict for bondmen than wives [with regard to a second consideration],

F. for [a householder] may [permanently] revoke his wife's vows,

G. but he may not [permanently] revoke his bondman's vows.

H. [How so?] [If] he revokes his wife['s vows] — they are revoked forever.

I. [If] he revokes his bondman['s vows] — [when the bondman] is freed, [the bondman] must complete his Nazirite-vow.[7]

M. Naz. 9:1

The householder has two options by which he can force his bondman not to undertake the terms of his vows and thus invalidate the bondman's act. First, the master can simply compel the bondman to break the vow (B-D). That is, he can force the bondman to abrogate the requirements of Nazirite-status. In this way, the householder can treat the bondman's vow as inconsequential, even though the vow binds the bondman himself (A). This is significant because the Nazirite-vow consecrates the votary to God. By allowing the householder to force his bondman to profane the vow, sages reveal that the householder constitutes the highest authority over the bondman, even higher than God. In contrast, the householder may not force his wife to break her vow. As long as her vow stands, the husband cannot force his wife to ignore it.

Second, the master may revoke the bondman's vows instead of forcing him to break them (E-I). In other words, he may void the vow and thus postpone the bondman's obligation. We can see how this act stems from the householder's control by comparing the bondman with the wife. At B-D, the husband must allow his wife to fulfill her vow because the vow stands. But E-I reveals that the husband may cancel the vow, thereby ending her obligation. Since, in the framers' view, the wife is permanently attached to her husband, her vow remains void even if he dies (H). With regard to the bondman, however, the householder can only suspend the vows for the duration of the bondman's servitude. Once the householder's control ceases, the obligation to fulfill the vow returns to the

---

[7] I translate line I in accord with Albeck and Bert., who follow the consensus of nearly all previous commentators. The main dissenter from this interpretation is Maimonides. He holds that upon revocation of the bondman's vow, the slave immediately goes free and must complete the vow. Such an understanding, however, goes against the passage's point. At I, sages are making the point that the vow is "hard" on the slave. I would not consider emancipation to be "hard." Maimonides' interpretation would furthermore provide the bondman with an easy road to freedom and escape from his master's control. He could simply take a Nazirite vow and hope that his master revokes it, thereby setting him free. Such an understanding goes against the fundamental principles of the Mishnah's system of slavery.

bondman. The fact that the vow is not permanently cancelled but merely suspended shows that it is the master's control over his bondman which enables the master to revoke the vow. Thus, we see that those acts of a bondman that require reason — even those that bind him to God — are legally effective only if the master permits.

That the householder controls the effectiveness of his bondman's acts involving reason is further made plain in cases where a bondman injures a person. In sages' view, causing injury is an act requiring reason. Damages bear legal consequences only when caused by persons having an unfettered use of their reason. Thus, the bondman does not become liable to pay any damages that a free Israelite householder would be required to pay.

A. A deaf-mute, an idiot, and a minor — coming into contact with them is bad:
B. He who injures them is liable [to pay compensation].
C. But should they injure others, they are exempt [from paying compensation because they lack reason].
D. The bondman and the wife — coming into contact with them is bad:
E. He who injures them is liable [to pay compensation].
F. But should they injure others, they are exempt [from paying compensation].
G. But [under conditions spelled out at H-J] they may pay compensation at a later time.
H. [If] a wife becomes divorced,
I. [or if] a bondman becomes free,
J. they are liable to make compensation.

M. BQ 8:4

The fact that the householder suspends his bondman's culpability, but does not cancel it, reveals both the bondman's humanity and his master's power to deny it. G-J show that the bondman becomes liable for his deeds just like any other adult Israelite. Since the bondman's liability becomes evident when he gains his freedom, we know that he incurs culpability at the time of the deed. However, the master's control over his bondman removed his slave from immediate culpability (D-F). As long as the bondman remains enslaved, his master's control protects him from culpability. Thus, the householder's control over his bondman keeps the damages caused by the bondman from taking legal effect. This result confirms our contention that the householder dictates when his bondman's acts requiring reason are not effective.

In sum, the Mishnah's authorities recognize the bondman's nature as a human being by granting him the capacity of reason. Their picture of the bondman equates his power with that of the adult Israelite householder. They leave us in no doubt that the bondman is a human being. However, it is just as clear that the householder has complete control over the legal consequences of his bondman's capacity to perform acts of reason. Thus, the master controls the slave even when the slave is at his most human. The bondman's humanity therefore serves to distinguish him as a separate category within the Mishnah's system of property.

Merely Physical Acts and Bodily Conditions

The second means by which bondmen, like other human beings, exercise power is through merely physical acts and bodily conditions. Here, the deed or condition bears legal consequences whether or not the performer possesses the capacity of reason. Merely physical acts include touching, sitting, becoming pregnant, and so on. Bodily conditions happen to a person, rather than being actively performed by a person. These involuntary conditions include events such as a flux and the contracting of a disease.

To begin our investigation, let us explain how merely physical deeds operate by comparing them to deeds requiring reason. The main difference between physical acts and those that require the exercise of reason lies in how they produce legal effects. As we demonstrated above, two conditions must be fulfilled before an act requiring reason may take effect; it must be performed by a person who possesses both 1) the capacity of reason, and 2) the free ability to exercise that capacity at the moment of the deed. These two conditions of reason mean that the person who acts must either be an adult who is not subject to a householder's control or a dependent acting under a householder's authorization. Merely physical acts and bodily conditions, by contrast, produce legal consequences merely by taking place.

Both acts requiring reason and merely physical acts and bodily conditions can produce physical and legal consequences. While physical effects occur in the same manner for the two types of power, the deeds differ with regard to how their legal effects are registered. Those acts that require the exercise of reason have legal consequences only if both conditions mentioned above are fulfilled. That is to say, legal effects ensue when a person who possesses reason, and the freedom to exercise it, does something. For example, if a householder breaks his neighbor's arm, he must pay compensation. This is because the householder possesses reason. However, if a minor son breaks his neighbor's arm, no compensation is paid. This is because the minor has no capacity of reason. Merely physical acts, by contrast, produce legal effects in the same way they produce physical effects. That is, when an event occurs, legal consequences ensue regardless of the actor's mental capacity or any other condition. For instance, suppose a bondman impregnates a free woman. From the moment of intercourse, the deed has both physical and legal consequences. Physically, the woman becomes pregnant, and legally, the bondman influences the status of the offspring.

The bondman's capacity to cause legal effects through merely physical acts and bodily conditions becomes evident from a passage in which sages hold that a bondman can contract leprosy (a mistranslation of the hebrew word *sara'at*). The framers, following Scripture (Lev. 13:1-46), view leprosy as a disease that makes a person unclean. The legal consequence of leprosy is that a person who contracts the malady is forced out of the community until he is healed. Once healing occurs, the matter is not yet over. The former leper must be approved by the priesthood and then cleansed. The process of cleansing entails the leper giving a sacrifice to the Temple for his purification. The following passage shows that, if a bondman had been a leper, he must perform this rite.

> A. A man may bring, for his son, for his daughter, for his bondman, [and] for his bondwoman, a poor-man's offering[, instead of a rich man's offering, for the purpose of cleansing the person from a previous condition of leprosy].
>
> M. Neg. 14:12

The fact that the householder supplies the offering shows that the legal effects of the bondman's bodily conditions can encompass even his master. In this case, two things happen to the slave: he contracts leprosy and subsequently becomes healed. The legal consequences stem from sages' requirement that the bondman perform the cleansing ritual. Since the bondman has no possessions, his master must supply the necessary sacrifice. Thus, the bondman's merely physical acts and bodily conditions bear legal ramifications, even for the slave's master.

The bondman's ability to perform merely physical acts does not lead directly to the conclusion that the framers consider him a human being in this respect, for sages hold that animals, as well as human beings, can produce legal consequences through physical deeds. Since animals and human beings share this type of power, it is not immediately apparent whether sages grant it to the bondman because they deem him a human being or because they hold him to be analogous to an ox.

A closer look, however, reveals that in this context the framers consider the bondman a human being, for the types of deeds they categorize as physical when performed by human beings differ from those considered so for merely animate property. The framers categorize the bondman's activity like that of other human beings, and not like that of animate property. Clearly, sages grant the bondman this type of power because of his human qualities. Let me explain how they perform their classification. Both human beings and animals do things that the framers consider to be merely physical acts. Since animals lack reason, sages treat everything they do as physical deeds. They divide the actions of human beings, however, into those that require reason and those that do not. Furthermore, when deciding how to categorize specific acts, the framers classify the same act differently depending upon whether an ox or a bondman performs it. An act that they treat as merely physical for an animal, they usually view as an act requiring reason for a human being. The framers illustrate this point by contrasting oxen and donkeys with bondmen, as in the following passage. Here, the Sadducees dispute a position held by the Pharisees, the predecessors of the Mishnah's framers. At issue is the householder's culpability for damages caused by his animals and by his slaves.

A. The Sadducees say, "We cry out against you Pharisees, [for according to you,] my ox and my donkey who cause damage are culpable,

B. "but my bondman and bondwoman who cause damage are exempt [from culpability].

C. "If [for] my ox and my donkey — which I am not required [to raise] in the Commandments — I am held culpable for their damages,

D. "how much the more so should I be held culpable for the damages of my bondman and bondwomen — whom I am required [to raise] in the Commandments (see Gen. 17:12)."

E. They [i.e., the Pharisees] said to them, "No. If you argue [that I am responsible for] my ox and my donkey, who have no [capacity of] reason (דעת),

F. "would you argue [that I am responsible] for my bondman and my bondwoman, who have [the capacity of] reason?

G. "For if I cause them to be angry, they may go and light a fire in another's corn stack, and I would be liable for all of it!"

M. Yad. 4:7

The Pharisees' position with regard to the slave (E-F) is the same as the framers' ruling in M. BQ 8:4, which we examined above; neither the bondman nor his master bears responsibility for damages caused by the bondman. In other words, no legal effects ensue for the damages he causes. This is because the householder dictates when his slave's acts requiring reason yield legal effects. The bondman's act constitutes an exercise of reason unauthorized by his master. In similar circumstances, however, the householder incurs liability for his ox's or donkey's damages. These legal consequences ensue because sages hold that the animals lack reason (E) and hence their deeds fall into the category of the merely physical. Thus, we see that sages classify the power of bondmen differently from that of animals. Since they consider a bondman's act like that of a human being — that is, as one requiring reason — and not like an animal's deed — merely physical — they obviously consider the bondman a human being here.

In general terms, the fact that the bondman is a human being possessing the capacity of reason motivates sages to place the damages he causes in a different classification from those caused by an ox. But it is unclear at this stage why the bondman's reason should cause this difference. After all, if an ox tramples a field or a bondman burns it, the result is the same, namely, the crops are ruined. Why should the householder incur culpability for the damage caused by his ox but not for that caused by his slave? The answer lies in the framers' concern with the householder's control over his property. They want to ensure that, in as many situations as possible, the owner can dictate the legal outcome of deeds perpetrated by his animate property. That is to say, since sages recognize that both the bondman and other forms of living, mobile property can cause injury, they want the householder to be able to protect himself from the legal consequences. In order to accomplish this goal, the bondman's capacity of reason requires the framers to classify some of the bondman's deeds differently from those of other types of property. This difference means that the householder's control over his bondman and that over other types of property do not always function in the same manner. We can discover where reason affects the classification of physical deeds by investigating how the householder's control functions with regard to his bondman's merely physical acts. If we can determine when the householder's control over his bondman does not match his control over his animate property, then we shall know reason's affects.

We recall that the householder's power over his bondman functions according to the same guidelines as his control over other types of property. We can summarize those rules as follows: when the bondman shares certain features with other types of property, then the householder controls those features of his bondman in the same manner as he would the same features in the other types of property. For example, during the sale of a slave, the householder's power works as it would during the sale of a cow. Conversely, when the bondman possesses features not shared by other types of property, only then do the framers need to design special rules governing the householder's power over him.

To preview our findings, the householder influences neither the legal consequences that ensue from deeds of his bondman nor those stemming from his other animate property. Once an action is performed, it bears legal effects. If, by contrast, we ask whether the householder can prevent these acts from taking place, we find a clear difference. Sages grant the householder the full capacity to control the actions of his livestock and hence to prevent the animals from performing any misdeeds. By contrast, they give the master no capacity to prevent the deeds of his bondman. The bondman's capacity of reason places any deeds he may perform, whether acts of reason or merely physical deeds, beyond the capacity of his master to prevent. Before we can develop this point further, we must study the householder's control over the physical actions of the bondman and compare it to his power over his livestock's deeds.

Since both bondmen and animate property share the capacity to perform physical acts, the framers treat in the same way the householder's control over the legal effects in either case. That is, they grant the householder no control over legal effects brought on by his bondman's or animal's merely physical acts because the legal effects stem from the deed itself and do not depend on any further conditions. A brief comparison of physical deeds with those requiring reason will show why. As far as his bondman's rational acts are concerned, the householder dictates when these take effect, for he determines when his bondman's exercise of reason is valid. That is to say, the master must authorize any deed of his slave that requires reason. But in merely physical acts, reason is irrelevant. Since the deed produces effects when it is performed, there is no opportunity for the householder's will to intervene. Thus, the householder cannot alter the consequences of either his bondman's or his livestock's merely physical deeds.

The householder's lack of control over his bondman's physical deeds and bodily conditions comes to light when the framers state that the slave can become unclean. Sages depict the slave as subject to a specific type of uncleanness, that of the *zab*, which a man enters by having an unexpected flux of liquid from his penis.

> A. Everyone becomes unclean on account of a flux [and thus become a *zab*], even proselytes, even bondmen, whether free or not free, a deaf-mute, an idiot, or a minor.

M. Zab. 2:1

That the slave can become a *zab* provides evidence of his power to produce legal effects through merely physical conditions or activity. Here we find evidence for both the involuntary acquisition of a physical condition and the transference of that condition to others. Moreover, his master cannot affect the legal consequences of either. On the one hand, the bondman enters the status of a *zab* through the involuntary event of having a flux (A). Clearly, the householder cannot prevent the legal consequences of the bondman's becoming unclean. On the other hand, the slave can pass on this state of uncleanness to other people and objects. Sages describe several different ways in which he can cause others to become unclean; each one belongs to the classification of merely physical act and hence lies outside the householder's influence. For example, if the slave touches someone, he renders that person unclean (M. Zab. 5:1). So too, if the bondman sits on a bench with another person, he conveys uncleanness to the other without touching (M. Zab. 3:1). And since both touching and sitting are merely physical acts, and hence take effect immediately, the bondman's master has no power to alter the legal consequences.

Sages treat the householder's control over his animal's physical deeds in exactly the same manner, again granting the owner no influence over legal effects of such deeds. Indeed, the householder actually may be required to suffer the consequences of his livestock's actions. This is apparent in cases where an animal causes damage to someone else's property.

> A. [In the case of a] dog and a goat who jumped from the top of a roof and[, when they landed,] broke some vessels —
> B. [their owner] must pay full damages.

M. BQ 2:3

The main consequence stemming from breaking vessels is that the owner of the dog or goat must pay compensation. The householder's culpability is automatic; he can do nothing to avoid it. He lacks any influence over the legal effects that stem from the deeds of his animate property, even when those effects impinge directly on himself.

So when a merely physical act occurs, sages treat the legal effects in the same way whether it is performed by a bondman or an animal. In neither case does the owner have any influence on the legal consequences that ensue. But this similarity tells us nothing that could explain why the bondman's humanity makes him different from livestock. If, however, we turn our attention from the householder's lack of power after the act to his control before it, we find a different situation. Sages hold that the householder can prevent his animals, but not his bondman, from performing physical acts. That is to say, the owner has complete control over his livestock and therefore can stop a deed before it happens. In contrast, the master has no power to prevent his bondman from performing a physical act.

Consider a flock of sheep. The framers expect the householder to keep them in line as his property and hold him responsible when he does not. Since the owner's culpability depends on the care he takes to prevent mishaps, sages clearly consider him capable of preventing them. We can see this in the following passage.

A. [A man who] brought his flock [of sheep] into the fold...
B. [if] he did not close them in properly and they got out and caused damage [to his neighbor's crops]—
C. he is culpable.
D. [If the wall of the fold] was breached during the night, or robbers broke into it, and [the flock] got out and caused damage [to nearby crops] —
E. [the owner] is exempt [from culpability].

M. BQ 6:1

Sages discuss the householder's culpability in two different situations. First, if the owner fails to take proper care to prevent his flock from getting out of the pen and damaging nearby crops, then he bears culpability. Conversely, if the damage caused by his sheep was beyond his control, then he does not bear culpability. In this way, sages show that, in normal circumstances, they consider the owner capable of preventing any misdeed of his animals.

In contrast, the framers hold that the householder cannot prevent his bondman's merely physical acts. There is no way in which the householder can keep his bondman from receiving or conveying physical conditions to another person or an object. For instance, if the slave becomes unclean, he need only touch someone or something and they likewise become unclean. While the householder might be able to prevent the contamination of a specific person or object, he lacks the capacity to protect everything and everyone from his unclean slave. Thus we see that, in sages' eyes, the householder cannot prevent his bondman from performing physical deeds.

To understand why the householder's power over his bondmen and livestock function in the same way in one case and not in the other, let us turn to the problem of classification. The criterion by which the framers categorize deeds performed by bondman and animals reveals the logic of their system. The similarity in the influence over legal effects stems from the fact that bondmen and livestock perform the same type of deeds, that is, merely physical. The difference, by contrast, is caused by the fact that livestock meet the taxonomic criterion for the category of physical deeds in a different manner from bondmen. Animate property completely lacks reason and so its deeds always fall into the classification of merely physical. But bondmen possess reason and this changes how their deeds are categorized.

We can understand sages' classification of the bondman's deeds more readily by focusing on what the Mishnah's authorities consider the primary function of reason, namely, the capability to plan ahead. To them, any deed that can be planned by its perpetrator is a deed requiring reason, and any that the performer cannot plan is a merely physical act. Thus, the question for the bondman becomes; what act can a bondman perform that he cannot also plan? The only type to fit this description are those acts over which the bondman has no conscious control prior to doing them: merely physical acts and bodily conditions. All other types of actions can be planned and hence fall into the category of acts requiring reason.

Relationships: Kinship Ties and Caste Status

Actions are not the only cause of legal effects; relationships may also produce them. These effects are continual, however, not momentary like those caused by actions. Wherein lies the difference? When a person performs a deed — for instance, he hits someone — all ensuing legal consequences stem from that single incident. The legal effects of a bond between two people, in contrast, begin with its establishment and continue as long as it exists. If the liason should end, the effects likewise cease. Furthermore, relationships comprise a third means, in addition to acts requiring reason and merely physical deeds, through which one person can exercise power over another. For example, when a woman marries, she forms a tie to her husband. Through this link, the husband determines his wife's caste status. If the woman's husband belongs to the caste of priests, she enters the caste of priests.[8] If the husband should ever divorce her, thereby cutting the link between them, he ceases to determine her

---

[8] As I explain in Chapter Four, although she enters the caste of priests, she does not become able to perform any of the priestly duties. She does however become permitted to take part it the castes's privileges, such as eating priestly rations.

caste position. Thus, a relationship is a state of being; while a person remains in a particular state, the effects of that state persist.

The main question for our study is whether the bondman possesses the power to control other people through his ties to them. To determine the answer, we shall examine the most commonly discussed legal effect of relationships, namely, the control of a person's caste status. Every householder has an inherent caste standing and, through his ties to his family, dictates the caste of each member. Thus, if a householder belongs to the caste of "Levite," so does each member of his family. We can use sages' interest in the caste system to determine whether the bondman controls other people through such a link.

Before we begin our study, let us review the place of caste status in the Mishnah. In the society imagined by sages, all Israelites fall into one of several levels of caste. The three divisions relevant to our immediate investigation are those of priest, Levite and Israelite. Following Scripture, sages view priests as the main Temple functionaries, Levites as secondary Temple officials, and Israelites as comprising the main body of Israelite society. Unlike priests and Levites, the Israelites' only connection with the Temple cult is as worshippers. In the Mishnah, sages distinguish among these three caste levels by the food they eat. Members of the priestly caste eat priestly rations — food set aside from a farmer's crops and sanctified for the sole use of the priests. The Levites eat tithe, food separated for consumption by the Levites. Israelites, by contrast, may eat only profane food, that is, food that has not been sanctified in any way. They have no right to that set aside for the priests and Levites.[9]

A person's caste status derives from his relationship, past or present, to a householder. These relationships are formed, in general, within the household. The householder always plays the dominant role, his caste controlling that of the other members. Let me specify each in turn. The householder has a kinship tie with each female member of this household. Thus, the householder controls the caste of his daughter or wife while they remain in the household. Should the daughter marry or the householder divorce his wife, however, then the relationship between them is broken and he no longer dictates their status.

The householder's control over the caste status of his son brings in a further complication, for the householder permanently transmits his standing to his son. The son takes on his father's status and makes it inherently his own. This transferral of status takes place at conception. The relationship between the householder and his son need exist only at that particular moment for the

---

[9] This description of agricultural offerings applies to the system of the Mishnah, later rabbinic texts present a different view. See M. Yeb. 9:4-6. BT Yeb. 85b assumes that the tithe set aside for the Levites can be eaten by anyone. Maimonides elaborates the Bavli's view and, in *Mishneh Torah, Maaser* (Tithe) 1:2, bases this position on an interpretation of Num. 18:27.

transmission of caste to happen. Except for this difference, the kinship ties between a father and his son operate the same as those the householder forms with the women in his family.

Sages determine the caste standing of bondmen by the same process they use for women. The main difference is that the link is one of ownership, not kinship. Thus, the bondman's position as his master's property, not his biological ancestry, determines his caste status. Indeed, whoever owns a bondman — whether, for example, it be a householder, his wife or a widow — controls that bondman's caste. He has no inherent caste standing of his own. This becomes clear in the following passage. The situation concerns a woman who enters a marriage bringing two types of bondmen with her as part of her dowry. One group of slaves are designated as *son barzel* (צאן ברזל) and pass into the control of the husband.[10] He owns these bondmen for the duration of the marriage, but must return them to his wife when the marriage ends. During the marriage, he has full control and use of them. The other group of bondmen, known as *melog* (מלג) slaves, remain under the wife's control.[11] Although the husband may use them, he must seek his wife's permission to do anything that might affect her ultimate power over them. The problem that sages address below is that the man and woman have contracted an improper marriage. The framers attempt to determine whether the woman takes on her husband's caste position by analyzing the caste of the two groups of bondmen. The way in which sages determine the caste status of the bondmen reveals how the slaves' caste depends on the person who owns them.

A. [As regards] (1) a widow [who married] a High Priest, [a union forbidden by Lev. 21:14, which, if consummated, would not allow the wife to eat priestly rations],

B. [and] (2) a divorcee, or (3) a *halusah*, [חלוצה, i.e., a levirate widow whose brother-in-law refused to marry her after her husband died childless, and who married] an ordinary priest, [all three unions are forbidden by Lev. 21:7 or Ezek. 44:22, respectively, and if consummated do not allow the wife to eat priestly rations] —

C. [if] she brought to him [i.e., into the marriage] *melog* bondmen and *son barzel* bondmen —

D. the *melog* bondmen may not eat priestly rations [because their mistress, the wife, is not eligible to consume priestly rations],

E. But the *son barzel* bondmen may eat [priestly rations because their master, the priest, confers on them eligibility to consume holy food].

F. This is [the definition] of *melog* bondmen:

G. If they die, the loss is hers. If they produce an increase, the gain [belongs] to her.

---

[10] See Cohen, "Dowry," pp. 353, 363-366, and Schereschewsky.

[11] See Levine for a discussion of possible origins of the term *melog*. See also Cohen, "Dowry," pp. 363-367, and Schereschewsky.

H. Even though [the priestly husband] is responsible for their sustenance, lo, [in this case *melog* bondmen] may not eat [food in the status of] priestly rations [because they belong to the wife who does not attain the right to eat sanctified produce].

I. This is [the definition] of *son barzel* bondmen.

J. If they die, [the husband] bears the loss, [i.e., he must replace them]. And if they produce an increase, the gain [belongs] to him.

K. Since [the priestly husband] is responsible to replace the loss [of them], lo, [*son barzel* bondmen] may eat [food in the status of] priestly rations.

M. Yeb. 7:1

L. [With regard to permitted marriages:] [If] the daughter of an Israelite marries a priest and she brings bondmen to him, [i.e., into the marriage],

M. [it does not matter whether they are] *melog* bondmen or *son barzel* bondmen,

N. lo, they may eat [food in the status of] priestly rations. [Upon marriage to a priest, an Israelite's daughter becomes eligible to eat priestly rations. Hence, both the *son barzel* bondmen and the *melog* bondmen are permitted to eat holy food; the *son barzel* bondmen because they belong to the priest and the *melog* bondmen because they belong to the wife who receives the right to eat sanctified produce from her priestly husband.]

O. [If] a priest's daughter marries an Israelite [i.e., a non-priest] and she brings to him either *melog* bondmen or *son barzel* bondmen,

P. lo, [the bondmen] may not eat [food in the status of] priestly rations. [The *son barzel* bondmen do not eat because the husband does not have the right to eat priestly rations. The *melog* bondmen do not eat the sanctified food because their mistress, the priest's daughter, has lost her right to consume holy things by leaving her father's household and marrying an Israelite.]

M. Yeb. 7:2

The status of these two types of bondmen reveals that the householder cannot confer his caste status on his wife in an inappropriate marriage (A-E). Although the *son barzel* bondmen (E) become the householder's property for the duration of the marriage and take on his caste, the *melog* bondmen do not gain the right to eat priestly rations (D). This is because they belong to the wife. The woman's union with her husband is improper, and so she does not take on the husband's caste standing. Therefore, since the *melog* bondmen belong to her, they take on her caste status, that of an Israelite. In this way, both sets of bondmen take on the caste of their owner. This understanding of how a bondman acquires caste standing is confirmed by the last part of the passage, L-P. There we see that when the marriage between the householder and his wife is legal, the wife and all the slaves she brings to the marriage take on the husband's status. Therefore, she and both types of bondmen may eat priestly rations.

Clearly a bondman's master or mistress controls his caste status through the bond of ownership.

Having seen how the householder controls the status of others, we now want to know whether the bondman has this same power. Specifically, we wish to discover if the bondman's kinship ties to his wife or offspring determine their caste status.[12] The answer has two parts. First, the bondman's standing influences that of his offspring. This standing, however, is not the caste status which the bondman derives from his master, but the bondman's own position as a slave. In other words, the bondman passes his slavehood, not his temporary caste status, onto his offspring. Second, bondmen lack the capacity to form valid relationships with anyone other than their master. Therefore, the effect that slaves have over their offspring stems not from a relationship with them, but from a merely physical act, that of conception. Let me spell out these two points.

First, slaves influence the caste position of their offspring through their standing as slaves. For example, a bondwoman's offspring becomes a slave. This holds true no matter who the father is. This result stems from the fact that the position "slave" is outside the caste system portrayed in the Mishnah. Since the mother stands outside the system, so does her offspring. In this sense, then, the slave is an outcaste. The following passage illustrates the effect that a bondwoman has over her offspring in contrast to that which a free woman possesses.

A.   [In] every place where [a man and a woman may effect] betrothal and no transgression [befalls because of the marriage] —

B.   the offspring takes on [the caste status] of the man.

C.   And who [does] this [statement concern]?

D.   A [woman who is] a priest, a Levite or an Israelite married to a [man who is likewise a] priest, a Levite or an Israelite. [Thus the offspring is a priest, a Levite or an Israelite.] ...

E.   And [in] every [case] in which she may not [effect betrothal] with [the specific man in question], and she may not effect betrothal with [any] other [man] —

F.   the offspring takes her own [social position].

G.   And who [does] this [statement concern]?

H.   A bondwoman and a gentile woman. [Thus the offspring is a slave or a gentile.]

M. Qid. 3:12

The framers explicitly state, at E-H, that bondwomen determine the status of their children. While the husbands of free women control the caste of their

---

12   We will not investigate whether the bondman can determine the caste of another slave through a bond of ownership because the Mishnah's framers never imagine that the bondman can own another person. They provide no evidence to answer such an inquiry.

children (A-D), any man who has intercourse with a bondwoman actually loses that power. Since the bondwoman deprives the man of his ability to control his offspring's status, she clearly possesses the capacity to dictate her children's status. We can tell that the position of slave is one of an outcaste from the fact that at H, sages equate the bondwoman with the gentile woman, a person completely outside Israelite society. As we can see from E-H, it is this definition of the bondwoman's status that dictates the social position of the child, not any caste standing she gains through her master.

The second step of our investigation is to determine how the bondman influences the status of his offspring. We have posited that the bondman lacks the capacity to form a relationship with anyone other than his master and hence cannot control the standing of his offspring through relationships with them. Indeed, bondmen can affect the status of others only through merely physical acts. To demonstrate this point, we must first ascertain how a householder determines the status of his offspring and then compare the bondman's power. After discovering the general rule, we can then apply it to the specific case of the bondman. The householder affects the status of his offspring in two ways; by relationship and by the merely physical act of impregnation. According to sages, the proper transmission of status occurs through relationships. Under improper conditions, however, status is determined by physical deeds. Let us deal with each in turn. The condition for forming valid relationships is that the man marry a woman with whom he can effect betrothal and hence contract a valid marriage. Sages recognize the establishment of kinship ties only within a suitable marriage.[13] This condition applies both to the relationship between husband and wife and to the relationship between the man and his offspring. Since an Israelite male can validly betroth nearly all unmarried Israelite women, it is easier to specify those whom he may not. Following Scripture (Lev. 18:6-18), the Mishnah's framers outlaw marriages between people whose relationship they define as incestuous. For example, sages forbid a father to marry his daughter or a nephew to marry his aunt. Thus, a valid marital relationship is formed only between people who are not close blood relatives.

When a householder marries a woman with whom he cannot form a valid betrothal, the offspring of that union enters the status of a *mamzer*. That is, the child enters a caste reserved for the offspring of invalid unions and does not take on the status of either parent. The situation is this: when the householder cannot form a valid relationship with his wife, he cannot affect her caste status. Furthermore, he cannot form any valid ties with his offspring from this liaison and thus is unable to dictate their caste position. He can, however, influence the offspring's status, for a child born of an invalid union enters the status of

---

[13] More accurately, kinship ties are created between two people who may marry each other, whether or not they actually do is irrelevant to determining caste status. That is to say, the householder affects the woman's caste, and that of his offspring, even if he does not marry her.

mamzer, the category sages use for those born of parents forbidden to marry (M. Qid. 3:12).

A. [In] every [union] where she may not [effect] betrothal with him, but she may [effect] betrothal with others —
B. the offspring becomes a *mamzer*.
C. And to whom [does] this [statement refer]?
D. To [one] who had intercourse [with someone of] one of the forbidden degrees [stated] in the Torah (Lev. 18:6-18). [These are the various incestuous connections.]

M. Qid. 3:12

Thus we see that the offspring of a forbidden union — a union between persons who cannot effect betrothal — is a *mamzer*. The caste of his parents is irrelevant to the status of the child.

Now that we understand how valid kinship ties are formed, let us turn to the bondman and ascertain whether he can establish such links. We find that the bondman cannot form any kinship ties because sages place him off-limits as a marriage partner. Neither the bondman nor the bondwoman can take part in a legally recognized marriage and hence lack the capacity to form valid ties to their spouses or to their offspring. This inability becomes clearest when we examine the slaves' incapacity to form valid marital bonds with free people.

A brief reexamination of a passage studied above reveals that bondwomen cannot enter a permitted sexual union with an Israelite male. There, we read, "And [in] every [union] in which she [that is, the bondwoman] may not [effect betrothal] with [the man in question], and she may not effect betrothal with [any] other [man] — the offspring takes her own [social position]" (M. Qid. 3:12). The important point for our study here is that the framers forbid the bondwoman from entering betrothal with any man. Since she cannot become betrothed, she cannot be party to a legally recognized marriage, and, as I shall show momentarily, no slave can form kinship ties of any sort — a necessary prerequisite of a valid marriage. Thus, in the Mishnah, the bondwoman has no capacity to form a legal marriage and cannot form a valid kinship tie with her sexual partner.[14]

_____

[14] I intend this general statement to apply to both marriages between free people and slaves and to unions between slaves. Sages deny bondwomen any capacity to form a recognized marriage. There is one possible objection to this position; in M. Qid. 3:13 and in Git. 4:5 the Mishnah's framers use the verb "to marry" with regard to unions involving slaves. This does not affect my claim. First, it is common in many slave-societies to describe unions between slaves as "marriages." However, these unions exist at the convenience of the master and the host society rarely grants them any recognition. The master may separate the partners or sell one of them at any time. (See, for example, Genovese, *Slaveholders* pp. 120-121 and Patterson, *Social Death* pp. 186-190.) This is most assuredly the case for the Mishnah's system, as we shall see in the

Similarly, sages forbid the bondman from forming a valid kinship tie to a free female consort. The fact that this is a widely accepted rule becomes evident from a passage concerning divorce. Let me introduce some information necessary to understand the pericope. A divorce must be carried out according to a set procedure. If the husband deviates significantly from the designated process, the divorce fails to take effect. One important point for the framers is that the husband must relinquish all control over his former wife. If he should attempt to set conditions governing her after the separation, the divorce is null. For example, if he forbids her to marry certain men, then he has not relinquished all control over her and the divorce does not take effect. In the pericope below, the husband forbids his wife to marry persons already forbidden to her by Scriptural and rabbinic rulings. At issue is whether his statement invalidates the divorce.

A. [If a man said to his wife while he was divorcing her,] "You are permitted [to marry] any man, except for [my] father and your father, my brother and your brother, a bondman and a gentile,"
B. or any other man with whom she may not contract a valid marriage —
C. [these unnecessary remarks do not affect the divorce and so the divorce remains] valid.

M. Git. 9:2

The point relevant to our study is revealed at A; the law forbids Israelite women to marry slaves. Specifically, the husband's statement that his divorced wife may not marry anyone with whom she cannot contract a permitted marriage has no effect on the divorce's validity. This is because he has merely stated the law to which she was already subject. Since such a statement does not invalidate the divorce, we know that sages consider the bondman a forbidden union for the woman.

The principle just demonstrated for unions between slaves and free Israelites also applies to unions involving only slaves. That is to say, just as sages declare invalid marriages between bondmen and free people, so too they view as null unions between slaves. Indeed, in a family of slaves the father, the mother and their offspring are not legally related to each other. A passage concerning the institution of levirate marriage demonstrates this assertion. Levirate

following discussion. Slaves cannot form kinship ties of any sort. They can form neither marital ties nor kinship links between parents and offspring. This constitutes part of a second point, namely, the Mishnah's system nowhere indicates that slaves have any of the rights, privileges or duties of marriage. Third, the Mishnah's framers recognize that masters often use their female slaves as sexual partners. Although sages do not approve of this practice, they do not treat such practice as adultery, seduction or rape. In fact, the framers assume that after the age of three, a slave-girl is no longer a virgin. (See M. Ket. 1:2, 4 and 3:1, 2.) For these reasons, it is clear that slaves cannot enter valid marriages.

marriage, we recall, is an institution that provides for the continuance of a dead man's family. It is invoked when a married Israelite dies before any of his wives bear him offspring. The Mishnah's authorities, following Scripture (Deut. 25), consider this an undesirable situation and resolve it by requiring the dead man's brother to marry one of the widows and produce an heir to his name. At issue below is whether this law applies to the offspring of bondwomen and gentile women.

A. [A dead man] who has any kind of brother, [this brother] imposes the duty of levirate marriage on his [deceased] brother's wife [if she has borne no children],

B. and he counts as [the dead man's] brother in every respect, unless he is the son of a bondwoman or a gentile woman.

C. [A man] who has any kind of son, [this son] exempts his father's wife from the duty of levirate marriage [if his father should die]...

D. And he counts as a son in every respect, unless he is the son of a bondwoman or a gentile woman. [These rules apply to two different situations: when the woman and her offspring are slaves or gentiles and the father and his other sons are free Israelites, and when the father, the mother and all the sons were originally slaves, but have been freed (M. Yeb. 11:2).]

M. Yeb. 2:5

Our interests center on the latter situation, that is, when all family members were originally slaves but have since been freed. In such cases, sages do not consider the father to be related to his sons, or the sons as related to each other.[15] Hence, such sons do not free the widow of a childless man from levirate marriage nor are such sons subject to levirate marriage themselves. This is because no member of a family of slaves can form a kinship tie to any other. This fact stems from the incapacity of their enslaved parents to form valid kinship ties. The fact that the father is not his son's kin shows, on the one hand, that they are not directly related. On the other hand, it also shows that neither the father nor the son forms a kinship tie to the woman, otherwise they would be related to each other through her. Thus, slaves are incapable of forming recognized kinship ties with other slaves, just as they cannot form such links to free persons.

Since we now know that the bondman and bondwoman lack the capacity to form kinship ties and hence cannot affect the status of their offspring through them, we need to determine how they do make an impact. That is to say, having shown the type of power the slave lacks, we must ascertain what kind he possesses. Once again, the householder provides the clue for answering our question. The householder, we recall, affects the status of his offspring in two ways. When his union with his wife is valid, he passes on his own status to the

---

[15] This is similar to the relationships of a proselyte, as we shall see below in this chapter and in Chapter Five.

offspring through kinship ties. But when the householder cannot contract a proper marriage with a woman, his influence over his offspring's status comes through the merely physical act of impregnation. In such a case, the offspring takes on the status of *mamzer*, not the caste of the father. This latter rule also explains the effect slaves have on their offspring. In sages' view, since slaves cannot form valid marriages with anyone, they influence the status of their offspring only through the physical deed of impregnation. To demonstrate this point, we need to examine the bondman separately from the bondwoman, for they influence their offsprings' status differently.

We begin by examining the bondman. Since the bondman cannot form a valid marriage with any woman, he affects his offspring's status in exactly the same way as a free man who cannot marry his sexual partner. That is, his offspring enters the status of a *mamzer*. Sages reveal this effect in a passage concerning the son of a bondman and a free woman. At issue here is the boy's effect on the status of his free, widowed grandmother, the mother of his mother. Let me explain why this is a problem. Generally, women derive their caste position from the dominant male in their life. A daughter takes on her father's caste and a wife takes on her husband's caste. But who is the dominant male in a widow's life, the father or the dead husband? Following Lev. 22:12-13, sages hold that this question is determined by whether she has borne her husband any offspring. Leviticus states:

> If a priest's daughter is married to an outsider [i.e., a non-priest] she shall not eat of holy things [such as priestly rations]. But if a priest's daughter is a widow or divorced, and has no offspring, she may return to her father's house, as in her youth, [and] eat of her father's food [i.e., priestly rations].
>
> Lev. 22:12-13

The Mishnah's framers interpret the word "offspring" as applying to all of a woman's descendents, not just her own children. Thus, if a widow has a descendent — her own offspring or her children's offspring — that person causes her to remain a member of her deceased husband's household and therefore she retains his caste. But if she has no descendents, the widow returns to her father's house and reassumes the status she had at birth. Furthermore, although Leviticus discusses only the daughters of priests, sages apply this principle to all women regardless of their caste status. In the passage below, the Mishnah's authorities address the question of whether these general rules apply to the son of a bondman and a free woman.

L.   A *mamzer* [i.e., the offspring of a forbidden marriage] disqualifies [a daughter of a priest from eating holy food] and permits [a daughter of an Israelite] to eat priestly rations.

M.   How so?

N.   (1) [In a case in which] an Israelite's daughter [was married] to a priest, [and thus gained the right to eat priestly rations,]

O. (2) [and in a case in which] a priest's daughter [was married] to an Israelite, [and thus lost her right to eat priestly rations,]

P. and she [i.e., the woman in N or O] bore a daughter by [her husband],

Q. and the daughter went out and married a bondman or a gentile, and bore a son by him —

R. lo, this [boy, the grandson of either the Israelite daughter at N or the priest's daughter at O)] is a *mamzer*. [This is because the boy's father and mother could not form a valid kinship bond.]

S. (1) If his grandmother was an Israelite's daughter [married] to a priest (N),

T. [and if her husband and her daughter die] she may eat priestly rations [because her grandson, the *mamzer*, causes her to remain a member of her husband's household (Lev. 22:12-13)]. [Thus, the *mamzer* is viewed as the grandmother's descendent.]

U. (2) If, [however, his grandmother] was a priest's daughter [married to an Israelite (O) and her husband and her daughter die],

V. she may not [return to her father's house where she would once again] (Lev. 22:14) eat priestly rations. [The *mamzer*-grandson likewise causes her to remain in her husband's household because sages view him as her descendent.]

M. Yeb. 7:5b

In this complex passage, sages address two separate questions: what is the caste of the son at Q, and to whom is he related? In the cases we have examined up to this point, these two issues are intertwined. That is, a child derives his caste status from his closest relatives, his parents. He forms kinship ties with both his mother and his father and, like his mother, takes on his father's caste standing through these links. The case at hand, however, does not conform to this general picture because the boy's father is a slave, not a free Israelite (Q). The slave cannot form kinship ties to the woman or to the offspring. Thus, at S-V, the son is related to his mother and therefore her family — that is, his grandmother — but this bond does not determine his caste. At R, by contrast, the boy's caste status derives from his father, even though there is no kinship link between them. How does this process work? The son's caste — that of *mamzer* — provides the clue for answering this question. A person enters the status of *mamzer*, we recall, when his father and mother cannot establish a valid marital union. In this case, the father forms no relationship to his offspring. The father's control over his offspring's status stems from the physical deed of intercourse. Just as if his father was a free Israelite, a bondman's offspring enters the position of *mamzer* at the moment of conception. No further relationship or contact between the slave-father and the mother or between the father and the offspring is necessary to pass on this status. Thus, a bondman dictates the caste of his offspring through the merely physical act of impregnation, not through any ongoing relationship with the child.

Having shown how the bondman determines his offspring's status through a merely physical deed, we must now demonstrate the same for the bondwoman, for the incapacity of slaves to form valid marriages affects the bondwoman in a manner different from that of the bondman. As we saw above, the bondwoman's standing determines that of her children, while the free father has no effect whatsoever. But we have yet to show that her control stems from a merely physical act — such as conception — and not from a kinship tie between her and her offspring. The framers reveal this fact in a discussion about levirate marriage. Levirate marriage, we recall, occurs in situations where a married man has died before his wife has borne him an heir. To remedy this lack, sages require the dead man's brother to marry the widow and produce offspring in the dead man's name. If the living brother refuses to perform this duty, then he undergoes the rite of *halisah* (חליצה), which frees the wife from her duty to marry him. In the passage below, the question arises of whether these laws apply to the sons of a bondwoman or of a female proselyte. If they do, then we know that sages view the sons as kin and hence their mother is likewise related to them. If the laws do not apply, then the sons are not related to each other and their mother likewise forms no kinship ties with them.

A.   [If] the sons of a female proselyte convert with her,
B.   they are not [subject to the law of] *halisah* or [to the law of] levirate marriage [because the framers do not consider them to be brothers].
C.   Even if the first [son] was not conceived in holiness [i.e., was conceived before his mother converted] but was born in holiness [i.e., after his mother converted],
D.   and the second [son] was [both] conceived and born in holiness, [they are still not considered to be brothers and hence do not make each other subject to *halisah* or to levirate marriage].
E.   [The same is true for] the sons of a [freed] bondwoman who have been freed with her.

M. Yeb. 11:2

The important point for our study here is that the sons of a bondwoman are not kin. This means that the freed bondwoman is not related to her offspring and hence dictates their status only through the merely physical act of conception. To understand how this process works, we must consider the implications of the case at C-D. These implications apply to bondwomen as well as gentile women. The point made at C-D is that the mother's status at the point of conception determines whether her offspring is related to her. If the child is conceived when the mother stands outside Israelite society, then the offspring, when born, also stand outside society (C). The sons are not related to each other because they are not their mother's kin. But D implies that children conceived when the mother belonged to the people Israel would, in sages' view, be related to each other because they would be related to their mother. Thus, a bondwoman transmits her status — that of a slave — to her offspring at conception. There is no ongoing relationship between her and her children that has any effect.

In sum, it is clear that the bondman lacks the ability to form a relationship with anyone except his master, and hence he cannot exercise power through relationships with other people. All power that slaves possess over the status of their offspring derives, as we just demonstrated, from the physical acts of impregnation and conception. Does this lack of power through relationships mean that in this situation the framers do not regard the bondman as a human being? Most assuredly not, for the mere fact that caste status is a concern relevant to the bondman indicates that sages here view him as a human being. The slave forms a property tie with his master and this link with the master determines his caste status.

Instead, we can explain the bondman's inability to form valid relationships by appealing to sages' concern for giving the householder the greatest possible control over the slave. Any relationship a bondman could form other than the one between him and his master would interfere with the master's control over both the slave himself and the other people. Specifically, if the bondman could form a valid kinship tie to his sexual partner (a bondwoman) or to his offspring (also slaves), he would obstruct the master's control over those people. Since sages do not tolerate such interference, they deny the bondman the right to form valid relationships with these people. Thus, the bondman's incapacity to form kinship ties stems from his master's control over him, not from a subhuman standing.[16]

In contrast, the householder has no control over the legal outcome of his slaves' physical act of impregnation or conception. Their effect on the standing of their offspring is irreversible. The master's lack of control in this situation is not surprising, for he cannot control the legal consequences of any of his bondman's merely physical deeds. The reason for this lack of control, we recall, stems from the bondman's inability to control his physical activity. Since the slave himself cannot control his actions, sages do not allow his master to control them. The same explanation applies in this case. Since it is uncertain whether a woman will conceive after having intercourse, of course neither the bondman nor the bondwoman can control it. Obviously, if the couple who had intercourse cannot dictate whether conception will occur, sages cannot posit that their master can either. Once again, we see that slaves' merely physical actions are beyond their master's control.

Conclusion

In the system of the Mishnah, the bondman conforms to a simple definition; he is a human being who stands subject to the full control of a

---

[16] For a more complete discussion of the change undergone by a slave upon manumission and a comparison between the freedman and the proselyte, see Chapter Five. There I show how the system of the Mishnah treats freedom and conversion as the rebirth of the individual.

householder. This definition constitutes a powerful indicator, for it identifies the bondman's exact location in the complex organization of the Mishnah's cosmos. Specifically, it places him into both the system of property and the system of humanity. In each system, the definition identifies the bondman as a member of the system and also as a distinct category within it. On the one hand, the system of property comprises categories belonging to the genus defined as all items subject to a householder's full control. Since the framers place the bondman completely under householder's power, the bondman belongs within this genus. Within the genus itself, the species "bondman" can be clearly distinguished from the other species by his membership in the human race. On the other hand, the system of humanity comprises the collection of all members of the genus "human being," and the bondman's humanity clearly makes him a member of this genus. The bondman can be distinguished from other categories of human beings by his subjugation to a householder's full control. No other category of human being stands under the full range of the householder's power. For both systems, then, the definition of the bondman provides the grounds for inclusion and for distinguishing him as a separate category within each one. To understand in greater detail how this works, let us examine the bondman within each system.

At the most fundamental level, we know the category of bondman fits into the system of property because it conforms to the system's governing principles. We have identified four principles that help describe the bondman's treatment in this system. First, sages view the bondman, like all other categories of property, as a collection of features. Second, coupled to each feature are rules that govern how householders exercise power over that feature. As for all types of property, the framers spell out how the householder controls the bondman's different features, not how he controls the bondman as a whole. Third, when the bondman shares a feature with other categories of property — such as being subject to sale — the householder controls that feature in the same way he controls it in other categories. Fourth, when the bondman possesses a feature that is distinctly his, by contrast, sages delineate the workings of the householder's control for that feature in particular. The bondman's conformity to these four principles shows that he belongs to the system of property.

The fourth principle is particularly important to our study, for it indicates the way in which the category of the bondman is distinguished from the other categories of property. That is, when the bondman differs from other objects of property, his master's control over him also differs. This is particularly true for the three types of human power exercised by the bondman: the power of acts requiring reason, the power of relationships, and the power of merely physical acts and bodily conditions. Within the system of property, the definition of each type of power and the manner in which it is exercised is distinct to the bondman. Two of these distinctively human features fall under a householder's control. First, the householder controls the bondman's acts requiring reason by cancelling their legal effects. When a bondman's act does not cause legal effects, therefore, it is as if he had never acted. Second, the master likewise controls the slave's power to enter and maintain relationships by cancelling all links the slave may have to other people and by preventing him from forming any new ones. The only relationship the bondman possesses therefore is the one to his master. The third form of power that the bondman can exercise — that of merely physical acts and bodily conditions — should fall under a householder's control. But it does not, for this type of power cannot be subjected to any form of control. Not even the bondman himself can control his own power of merely physical acts and bodily conditions. Since the bondman cannot control it, neither can his master. The master's inability to control this form of power stems from its particular nature; the master's inability indicates nothing about the bondman's status as a category of property. In sum, the bondman's subjection to his master's full control includes him in the system of property, while his human forms of power distinguish him as a separate category within it.

In the system of humanity, the situation is reversed. Sages place the bondman within the system of humanity because of his humanity and distinguish him as a separate category by his subjugation to the full control of his master. The bondman's possession of the three forms of human power indicates that he belongs to the system of humanity. His master's control over his exercise of these powers — specifically, those of acts requiring reason and of relationships — differentiates him from other categories of human beings. To understand how this full control differs from the householder's control over other categories of people, we must briefly review how a householder's power affects those other categories. Two categories of Israelites are not subject to any control by a householder. Householders, we recall, are independent categories of human beings; no class of people exercises control over them. Similarly, the minor son — who lacks the power of acts requiring reason — stands free from the householder's control over his powers exercised through merely physical acts and bodily conditions and through relationships. Thus, these two categories of people differ from the bondman in that no householder controls their exercise of power.

A comparison between the bondman and the categories of women provides a more telling picture, for some classes of women, like the bondman, stand subject to a householder's control. By comparing them, we shall see how the full householder's control over a bondman differs from the lesser control exercised over the women. This comparison will leave no doubt that the bondman is mere property — human chattel, if you will — while, in terms of their freedom to exercise power, women rank far above him. In fact, of the six categories of women, only three have a householder over them. The other three classes constitute independent women whose ability to exercise their personal power is as unfettered as that of a householder. This difference stems from the way the Mishnah's framers classify women. The Mishnah contains six categories of women which, as we recall, are separated into three pairs. The members of each pair share the same form of sexuality. The sexuality of minor daughters and adult daughters is that of virginity. For wives and divorcees, sexual activity comprises the operative form of sexuality. For widows and levirate widows, the important form of sexuality is productivity, that is, whether or not they bore their dead husband an heir. Furthermore, in each pair of categories, the sexuality of one is subject to a householder's control, while that of the other stands free from such control. Thus, the minor daughter's virginity is controlled by her father, while that of the adult daughter is not. The wife's sexual activity is controlled by her husband, while the divorcee's is not. Finally, the parentage of the levirate widow's future offspring — that is, her future productivity — stands subject to her brother-in-law, while that of the ordinary widow does not.

The three categories of women whose sexuality is controlled by a householder have their capacity to exercise power through relationships controlled by him. In particular, this means that the householder controls the woman's capacity to enter a new relationship, namely, a marital or conjugal relationship. The householder dictates whom the woman may marry and with whom she may have sexual relations. The father of the minor daughter has full responsibility for and final say in choosing the man his daughter marries. A wife's husband automatically denies her the right to cohabit with any other man. The brother-in-law of a levirate widow has the right of first refusal to take the woman as his wife. To control a woman's sexuality, therefore, means to control her capacity to form new relationships.

When we compare a householder's control over power of relationships held by a minor daughter, a wife or a levirate widow with his control over his bondman's power to maintain and enter relationships, we notice two important differences. First, the householder merely prevents these women from forming new relationships. By contrast, he not only prevents the bondman from forming new relationships, but also cancels old ones. Thus, the bondman is tied only to his master, whereas the women are part of a whole network of kinship ties. The householder merely hinders the women's expansion of their network. Second, the householder's control over, say, his daughter's power to form new relationships, takes the form of prevention. Sages hold that he can prevent her from forming a link to a man, but if he fails to do so, a relationship is formed. For example, if a minor daughter has sexual intercourse with a man and becomes pregnant, a relationship forms between them; the father can do nothing to alter that fact. This is not a problem with the bondman, by contrast, for the bondman simply cannot form relationships to anyone other than his master. His master's control cancels all attempts to establish new relationships. Indeed, the bondman is not even permitted to marry. Thus, although the householder controls the power of relationship for three categories of women and for the bondman, he does not do so in the same manner. The control he exercises over the bondman applies to all relationships — past, present and future — and is insurmountable, while the power he exerts over the categories of women applies only to future relationships and even then it can be overcome.

Although the power of relationships directly corresponds to sexuality, we can also ask about the householder's control over the other two forms of power exercised by these categories of women — the powers of merely physical acts and bodily conditions and of acts requiring reason. First, householders exercise no control over the power of merely physical acts and bodily conditions possessed by minor daughters, wives and levirate widows. Since, like the bondmen and other human beings, these women cannot control their own exercise of this power, neither can a householder. Second, a different situation arises for acts that require reason. The three categories of women differ with regard to their possession of this power and with regard to whether a householder controls their exercise of it. First, minor daughters possess no capacity of reason and thus cannot perform acts requiring reason. Consequently, the question of whether their father can control such acts is irrelevant. Second, the levirate widow possesses reason and hence can perform acts requiring it. Her brother-in-law cannot control her exercise of this type of power. Until he actually takes her as his wife — thereby altering her classification — she is free to act as she pleases. For example, she can sell her inherited land as if she was a householder and all vows she takes are permanently binding and irreversible.[17] Third, some acts requiring reason performed by the wife are subject to her husband's control. For example, a husband may annul many vows which his wife takes. He cannot annul every vow, however, only ones that impinge upon him.[18] If a wife vows to refrain from intercourse, for example, her husband can cancel the vow. It is important to note that although this control does not apply to all acts of reason, when it does apply, this control over a wife's acts of reason functions like the householder's control over his bondman's acts of reason. That is to say, the householder's power cancels the legal effects of an act, rather than preventing the act itself. The upshot of this discussion is that the wife constitutes the only category of women for whom the householder can control acts requiring reason. She is not like the bondman, however, for the householder exercises control over only some of her acts, although the same householder can control all of his bondman's acts requiring reason.

If we now ask the question, "In terms of their exercise of personal power, is the bondman equivalent to a woman?" the answer is clearly no. The bondman is a chattel, while women appear more like a householder. Even though three categories of women are subject to a householder's control over some form of

---

17 See the insightful discussion of this matter in Wegner, *Women*, in the sections entitled "Wife's Vows Inimical to Conjugal Relations," and "The Wife as a Owner of Property."

18 This point has been clearly demonstrated by Wegner, *Women*, in the section entitled "Wife's Vows Inimical to Conjugal Relations."

their power, that control is neither as extensive nor as effective as that over the bondman. This fact holds true for both forms of power subject to external control: that exercised through relationships and that exercised through acts requiring reason. The householder's control over his bondman's relationships is strong enough to cancel all the slave's relationships. For minor daughters, wives, and levirate widows, the householder merely controls their capacity to form new relationships. Similarly, his power over his bondman's acts requiring reason is all pervasive. He can cancel the legal effects of all his bondman's rational acts. The wife — the only category of woman whose acts requiring reason are subject to a householder's control — can perform many acts outside her husband's control. He can cancel the effects only of those that affect his privileges. Thus, the bondman's status as property — his subjugation to his master's full control — marks him as a separate category within the system of humanity. The similarities between him and the dependent categories of women are of minor importance.

The final point leads us beyond the bondman to his immediate social context, that is, to the household. Throughout our comparison of the bondman to categories of both human beings and property, we have uncovered the basis by which sages organize the household, namely, the relationship between each category and the householder. This means that those categories whose members have a relationship to a householder — bondmen, minor daughters, wives, levirate widows, minor sons and the various forms of property — belong to the household. Those categories lacking such a relationship — adult daughters, divorcees, and widows — stand outside the household. Our understanding of these relationships now permits us to delineate the hierarchy of the categories within the household. For each category's capacity to exercise the three forms of personal power — a matter directly affected by the type of relationship between the householder and the category in question — reveals its rank within the household. The householder constitutes the primary category to which each of the categories relates. He stands at the top of the household, constituting the supreme authority whose power remains unchecked by its other members. Below him we find the minor son. His personal power is uncontrolled by his father, but since he lacks the power exercised through acts requiring reason, he remains within the household. Next stands the levirate widow. She is tied to the householder by his power over her capacity to form a new marital bond. Other than that, however, she remains free from his control. Below her we find the wife. Her husband controls her power to form relationships and can cancel many of her acts requiring reason. But as we saw, she retains some capacity to act independent of her husband. Of the categories of women, the minor daughter has the least amount of power she can freely exercise. Her father controls her capacity to form new relationships and she has yet to develop the power exercised through acts requiring reason. The bondman constitutes the lowest human category. He has no capacity to exercise power outside of a household's control; his master cancels all relationships except that to the master himself, and he can cancel the legal effects of all the bondman's acts requiring reason. Below the bondman lie the categories of property. Some categories, such as those of livestock, can exercise the power of merely physical acts, which is of course controlled by their owner. Nonanimate property has no power at all. Such is the hierarchy of the household according to the criterion of the exercise of power.

This brings us to the next stage of our investigation, the bondman in the larger realm of Israelite society. Here we wish to discover how the Mishnah's framers portray the category of bondman — which they define completely in terms of the control held by an individual householder — in the world beyond a householder's control.

Chapter Four
The Bondman and Israelite Society

Just as a householder's private power operates within his household, so, in the Mishnah's system, public power is centered in community institutions such as the Temple, the courts, and the market place. These institutions stand separate from each other, each one forming a self-contained entity, possessing its own purposes and goals, as well as its distinct organization and rules of operation. Moreover, these institutions serve as loci for different types of activity within Israelite society. The marketplace constitutes the locus for economic activity, the courts provide the arena for legal affairs, and the Temple comprises the center for cultic matters.

The Mishnah's portrayal of Israelite society as a collection of separate institutions has important ramifications on the determination of social status. Specifically, each institution hierarchizes, on its own and for its own purposes, the members of Israelite society. The Mishnah's framers lack the concept of a social scale that applies to all aspects of Israelite society. Each institution, such as the Temple cult, requires its own social scale. In the cult, priests rank as cultic officials who attend the Temple full time, Israelite males as full worshippers who attend on designated occasions, and women as second-class worshippers who go there only at a few specific times. More important, social scales vary from one institution to another. Since each institution comprises the locus for a different type of activity, the criteria for allowing people to participate differ. In contrast to the cult, for example, the courts make no distinction between priest and Israelite; members of both castes are subject to the same laws of litigation. Instead, the main distinction is between householders and secondary social categories such as women. Similarly, the framers design a scale for the market place — more exactly, two scales — to regulate participation in its activity. For real estate transactions, the parties must belong to a category of independent persons, such as householders, adult daughters, divorcees, or widows, and not to a category of dependent persons, such as wives or minor daughters. For buying movable goods, the main criterion is the possession of money. So, in the Mishnah's system, social status stems from community institutions, not from society in general, and therefore it varies from one institution to the next.

Our interests lie in determining how these community institutions treat the bondman. Within the system of the Mishnah, this question is complex, for it concerns the effects of one person's action, the householder's, on each institution's recognition of another person, the slave. By bringing a bondman into his domain, the householder gives the slave a new identity; the slave now constitutes the householder's personal property. As we observed above, this act cancels out the bondman's previous identity.[1] The Mishnah's system provides no clue to indicate the ethnic background of the bondman. We can therefore state the issue in the following manner: if an Israelite becomes enslaved, he loses his birthright and his full membership in Israelite society; if a foreigner becomes enslaved, he loses his birthright and membership in his own community. Each becomes a person without a past. The question now facing us is how, in the Mishnah's system, community institutions register the bondman's new identity. Let me spell this out. In the framers' portrayal, when an Israelite householder purchases a human being, he, on his own accord, acquires the slave's person as his property. The purchase constitutes the act of a private individual; no outside authority sanctions his action. Within the owner's private realm this lack of public sanction does not matter; since the householder brings the slave into his own domain, where he is the sole authority, no second authority is affected. But in the Mishnah's system, the bondman does not live solely within the household, he also exists in the context of Israelite society. In that society, institutions such as the government, the courts, and the Temple exert power far beyond that of a householder. We want to determine how these institutions acknowledge the identity given to the bondman by his master. That is, we must ascertain whether they grant the bondman a public status in accordance with his position in his master's household.

The importance of analyzing a slave's status in one area of society separate from that in others is demonstrated by the well-known but extreme example of Roman imperial slaves. Most Roman emperors used slaves as high government officials who, in turn, used their positions to amass great wealth. So on both political and economic scales, they were superior to all but a tiny handful of Romans. As slaves, however, their position in the social order remained lowly; they lacked both access to the courts and Roman citizenship. A study of the overall social position of these slaves can succeed only by examining the slaves' position in each area separate from that in other areas and then bringing together the results for final analysis. To analyze, for instance, the slaves' political power without distinguishing it from their exclusion from the legal system would result in certain confusion. Similarly, to determine the Mishnah's overall placement of the bondman, we must delineate the bondman's standing in each institution separate from his position in the others. When this has been

---

[1] See the explication of this question in Chapter Two. There I show that the Mishnah ignores Scripture's categories of slavery and designs its own categories (bondman and freedman), which are ethnically unmarked. Whatever the ethnic background of the bondman, it is forgotten totally once the person becomes enslaved.

accomplished, we can then compare the different rankings and attempt to discern the principles that determine the bondman's overall place in Israelite society.

Only one institution, the Temple and its cult, provides us with sufficient data to analyze confidently its treatment of the bondman. In fact, the Temple cult constitutes by far the most frequent context for the bondman when the Mishnah's authorities depict him outside his master's household. By Temple cult, I mean to indicate the whole scheme of worship outlined in the Pentateuch. Although this scheme focuses on the Temple, it is practiced in the household as well as in the Temple proper. The Temple and its cult therefore includes, among other observances, sacrifices, rites of purification, annual festivals such as Passover and the Feast of Booths, and Sabbath observance. For example, sages discuss what Temple festivals slaves attend, the types of cultic impurity to which they are subject, and their role in certain types of sacrifice. In all, forty two[2] of the fifty five passages[3] that portray the bondman outside the household depict him in some relationship to the Temple (76%). The bondman receives little attention with regard to any other important institution of Israelite society; he appears in the context of the courts only five times, and sages do not even depict him buying, selling, or otherwise figuring in market place activities.[4] Thus only the Temple and its cult provides sufficient material for studying the bondman outside his master's household.

A closer look at the Temple cult, however, reveals that it requires people to perform many different tasks, and each task applies different criteria to select its participants. For example, to offer sacrifices, a person must belong to the priestly caste; to touch food susceptible to uncleanness, one must be cultically clean. Obviously, to evaluate people's suitability to perform different cultic activities, different scales must be used. In this way, the Temple is analogous to a business; different jobs within the business require people to possess different qualifications. Since there are many discrete tasks in the Temple, we must examine the bondman's position as regards each one. Only after we ascertain his place on each scale and the characteristics that dictate that position can we then attempt to piece together a general picture of how he fits into the Temple cult as a whole.

---

[2] The forty two passages that depict the bondman acting within the realm of the Temple and its cult are: M. Ter. 3:4, 7:3, 8:1; Bikk. 1:5b; Pes. 7:2, 8:1a, 8:1b, 8:2, 8:7; Sheq. 1:3, 1:5, 1:6; Suk. 2:1, 2:8, 3:10; Hag. 1:1; Yeb. 7:1, 7:2, 7:3, 7:5, 8:1, 8:2, 11:5; Ket. 2:9, 3:1, 3:2; Naz. 9:1; Sot. 1:6; Qid. 3:12, 3:13; Zeb. 3:1, 5:5, 5:6, 5:7; Men. 9:8; Ker. 1:3, 2:2, 2:3, 2:4, 2:5; Neg. 14:12; and Zab. 2:1.

[3] In addition to the passages in the previous note, see M. Erub. 5:5; RH 1:8; MQ 2:4; Yeb. 16:7; Sot. 6:2; Git. 4:4; BQ 8:4; BM 7:6, 8:3; Shebu. 4:12; Arak. 1:1; Oh. 18:7; and Yad. 4:7. These thirteen passages depict the bondman acting outside the household, but not within the realm of the Temple and its cult.

[4] The five passages that focus on the bondman in the courts are: M. Yeb. 16:7, Ket. 2:9, Sot. 6:2, Shebu. 4:12, and Oh. 18:7.

The bondman appears in discussions concerning two kinds of activity that center on the Temple cult. These are the issue of assigned roles in Temple worship and the question of entering the Temple precincts. Our interest focuses on the bondman's place on the social scales that govern participation in these activities. These scales are, respectively, those of caste status and cultic purity. As we have seen, caste status addresses the capacity of people of different castes to marry one another and determines the standing of any offspring they produce. This standing in turn determines the cultic role to which a person is assigned. The system of cultic purity measures whether a person is in a state of cleanness and may therefore enter into the Temple. Our interest in these different social scales is to discover where the bondman fits on each of them. We need to discover at what level, if at all, he participates in the caste system and in cultic purity. Once we answer these questions, we can attempt to discern what they tell us about the framers' overall picture of the bondman.

Cultic Worship and the Caste System

The first stage in our study of the bondman's social standing focuses on his place in the Temple cult. To assign Israelites different tasks in cultic worship, sages use a caste system. This system organizes Israelite society into a hierarchy of social groups, ranking them according to the importance of the cultic duties performed by their members. Our interest lies in determining the bondman's place on this scale of caste status, and thus in ascertaining what role in worship the Mishnah's authorities grant him.[5] The point of such a study is not merely to ascertain the slave's status, but also to discover the rationale that sages use to assign it. In particular, we wish to discern how the bondman's enslavement — that is, his position as the property of an Israelite householder — influences his rank in the caste system. Since, within the household, the slave's definitive characteristic is his master's power over him, our investigation of the bondman's standing outside the household must begin with this question.

To accomplish this task, we shall proceed through three stages of investigation. First, we must delineate the categories that make up the caste system and ascertain in which category, if any, the bondman finds a place.

---

[5] There is one indicator of status that places the slave clearly within the bounds of Israelite society, namely, the slave is circumcised. Unfortunately, the Mishnah's framers never refer explicitly or implicitly to this fact, leaving the reader to infer it from Scripture (see Gen. 17:10-14). Because of this lack, I choose not to use circumcision as an indicator of status for the Mishnah's bondman. I do not wish to build an argument on a point that I cannot prove.

The Tosefta (AZ 3:11) and later rabbinic texts (for example, BT Yeb. 45b-46a) assume that slaves must be immersed as well as circumcised before they fully enter the household. The Mishnah makes no mention of immersion of slaves. For further information about the role of immersion in later rabbinic thought, see Bamberger, pp. 127-128.

Second, we must delve beneath the surface of this scale and discover how it organizes Israelite society. That is, we need to discover the criteria sages use to rank the different castes and the corresponding human characteristics they use to place people in them. With such knowledge, we can deduce from the bondman's place on this scale the degree to which he possesses these features. Our study's final stage involves discovering why the Mishnah's framers grant the bondman the social position they do. In other words, we want to delineate the factors dictating the bondman's position in the caste system. Once we discover that, we will know the effect of the bondman's enslavement on his social standing.

We begin our study by ascertaining where sages place the bondman vis-à-vis the caste system. To accomplish this task, let us start by examining the system in its own terms and attempting to see how it views the bondman. By examining how the Mishnah ranks the different castes, we can accomplish both aspects of our investigation at once. That is, we can ascertain how the caste system serves to organize Israelite society and we can discover where it positions the slave. The following passage neatly shows us the castes in their respective rank:[6]

A. Ten castes came up [to Jerusalem] from Babylonia:[7]
B. (1) the priests,
    (2) the Levites,
    (3) the Israelites,
C. (4) the impaired priests [who have transgressed the rules of Lev. 21:1, 7, 13-15 and married women who are divorcees, or, in the case of a High Priest, a non-virgin],
D. (5) the proselytes [foreigners who have chosen to worship Yahweh] and,
    (6) the freedmen,
E. (7) the *mamzers* [who are the offspring of incestuous marriages, (Lev. 20:17-21)],

---

[6] M. Hor. 3:8 presents a ranked list of social groups containing many of these castes. These groups are arranged in a different order from M. Qid. 4:1. There is no incompatibility between the two lists, however, for the criterion here in Qiddushin is role in worship, and the one in Horayot centers on the legal system.

[7] Albeck (following the Yerushalmi to this passage) suggests that this Mishnah pericope is based on the categories of Neh. 7:5-65, which lists the different classes of people who returned to Israel from the Babylonian exile. (See Albeck, *Mishnah*, vol. 3, p. 325 and Yer. Qid. 4:1, for English translation see Neusner, *Yerushalmi*, vol. 26, pp. 214-225.) However, the lists of people in the two passages only partially correspond. Both lists contain categories not found in the other and leave out categories that are found in the other. Furthermore, the passage in Nehemiah focuses on listing the subfamilies of each class. It does not arrange either the groups or the subfamilies into any sort of hierarchical order. Since the point of the passage in M. Qiddushin is to present a hierarchical caste system, it cannot be anything more than a faint echo of Nehemiah.

F. (8) the *netins* [foreigners who once were servants to the Israelites],

G. (9) the *shetuqs* [people who know who their mother is, but not their father (M. Qid. 4:2)] and

(10) the foundlings [who know neither their mother nor their father (M. Qid. 4:2)].

M. Qid. 4:1

Obviously, the category of "bondman" has no place in the caste system. In all of the ten castes, there is neither a caste of bondmen nor do bondmen as a category make up part of a caste with other people; there is no caste of, say, bondmen and freedmen.[8] This exclusion is significant, for it reveals that the category of bondmen lacks the features belonging to categories of the caste system. To ascertain just what these features are, let us look at what the caste system measures, and how it accomplishes that measurement.

The framers use the caste system to measure a person's capacity to participate in Temple worship.[9] It divides Israelite society into the castes whose members are allowed to participate in worship and those whose members are not. To use sages' terms, they distinguish those who may approach Yahweh in the Temple from those who are forbidden. The first six categories of people in the passage above comprise those who take part in Temple worship — priests, Levites, Israelites, impaired priests, proselytes, and freedmen — and the last four contain people denied the capacity to approach the Lord — *mamzers*, *netins*, *shetuqs* and foundlings.[10]

---

[8] To state that the category "bondman" is not a category of the caste system is not to say that bondmen as individuals have no relation to the caste system. Indeed, as we shall see below, bondmen, like women, take on a secondary caste status that is linked to the dominant male in their life. For bondmen, this male is of course the master, while for women, this male could be a father, husband or brother-in-law. The point is that there is no caste of "bondmen" to which all slaves belong; individual slaves belong to different castes.

[9] The context in which this passage appears in the Mishnah focuses on the issue of permitted marriages (see the discussion of these matters in Chapter Three, in the section "Relationships: Kinship Ties and Caste Status"). This does not alter the caste system's primary function, which is to assign roles in cultic worship.

[10] This claim is based on the use of the term "Congregation (קהל) of Israel" in the Mishnah's system. This term refers to the majority of the people of Israel, who are required to participate in cultic worship. Those outside the congregation are not allowed to worship at the Temple, even though they belong to the larger entity of the people of Israel. The framers' understanding of who is outside the congregation stems from Deut. 23:2-3 where Scripture states that *mamzers*, among others, are not permitted to enter the congregation. At M. Qid. 4:3, the Mishnah's framers show that they extend this ban from *mamzers* to the castes below them as well, namely, to *netins*, *shetuqs* and foundlings. In the Mishnah's system, to stand outside the congregation means that one is banned from participation in cultic worship at the Temple. For example, M. Pes. 5:5, referring

This task is part of the caste system's larger purpose of designating different cultic duties to the participants. Following Scripture, sages assign a specific role in worship to each caste. This is clear with regard to the three main castes of Israelite society. The priests are the Temple officials; they perform the sacrifices and are in charge of the Temple. Members of the Levitical caste, by contrast, constitute assistants to the priests; they help the priests in various ways behind the scenes of worship and accompany the rites with music. Members of the Israelite caste comprise the worshippers. The framers require them to attend the various Temple rites, to provide the sacrifices offered on the altar, and to give donations for the upkeep of the Temple. Clearly, each caste is linked to a specific role in Temple worship. This logic applies to the other castes who have a role in worship. The proselytes and freedmen, whom we shall study further in the next chapter, in general take on the same duties as members of the caste of Israelites. While it is is not clear what role in worship the impaired priests possess, that they have a role is apparent from the fact that sages place them in the group of castes who take part in the cult.[11] In this way then, the framers use the caste system to assign different roles in worship to members of Israelite society.

To understand the bondman's position vis-à-vis the caste system and the roles it assigns, we need to examine the basis on which the Mishnah's framers determine caste membership. This will reveal the true character of the category bondman, a problem with which we have struggled throughout this book. Earlier we saw that the Mishnah was silent on the ethnic background of the bondman. We claimed that was because the past kinship ties of the bondman had been wiped out. On this basis, we argued that we had to treat the category as if it had been designed for both Israelites and non-Israelites. Now we shall see that the category of bondman has indeed been designed to accept bondmen of both Israelite and gentile origins. In fact, the category of the bondman occupies the only location within the caste system that could enable it to take members of both ethnic groups and to treat them in the same way.[12]

---

to Ex. 12:6, assumes that only members of the congregation take part in the Festival of Passover.

[11] In the Mishnah, as well as in Scripture, the impaired priest's capacity to participate in cultic worship is unclear. This is because the Mishnah mentions impaired priests in only four passages: M. Yeb. 9:1, 9:2; and Qid. 4:1, 4:6. Sages certainly exclude him from any duties specific to priests, but they do not deny him the right to take part in worship. He apparently remains a member of the "congregation" of Israel and hence remains an active participant in the cult. See Albeck, *Mishnah*, p. 325 and Qehati on M. Qid. 4:1 and 6. The extent of this participation is unclear even in later texts; for instance the Yerushalmi (Yer. Qid. 4:1), following Ezra 2:61-63, holds that the impaired priest cannot eat the agricultural offerings due to priests.

[12] For a fuller version of the following discussion, see Flesher, "Hierarchy."

The criteria by which sages assign roles are complex, for the caste system reflects two different views of Israelite society. Each view determines membership in a caste, and indeed membership in Israelite society as a whole, according to different criteria. On the one hand, the caste system reflects the portrayal of the people Israel as an extended family. This depiction, we recall, derives from the Biblical myth that all Israelites have descended from the patriarch Jacob. As such, they are the inheritors of the promises that God made with Jacob and of the Covenant that God made with Moses on behalf of the people Israel. On the other hand, the caste system embodies the view that Israelite society constitutes a collection of households. Everyone who belongs to an Israelite household belongs to Israelite society. The issue of their membership in the extended family of Israel is peripheral. These two views of Israelite society are closely related; they constitute different ways of ranking the same categories of people in the same positions — except, as we shall see, for the category of bondman.

The myth of Israelite society as an extended family provides the foundation for the caste system. Since all members of a family are related to each other, this image of Israelite society centers on the notion of kinship ties; all those who have Israelite ancestry and marital bonds belong to the family Israel. The Mishnah's authorities, however, have hierarchized the members of this family. Some subfamilies have a higher rank than others. In the Mishnah's system, the framers use the scale of the caste system to formalize this inequality. In this view of society, a person's ancestry and marital bonds combine to place them into one of the ten castes listed above. In general, a person's initial caste standing derives from his or her parents, but the transmission of parental status to offspring depends on the validity of the parental union. In a marriage between two members of the same caste — the most straightforward case — the offspring take their parents' caste. So too the child of two Levites, for example, belongs to the caste of Levites. But in marriages between members of different castes the validity of the marriage takes on a greater importance in determining the offspring's caste. In general, if a man and a woman are from compatible castes, the offspring takes the father's caste. Thus, if an Israelite man marries a levite woman, their children are Israelites. Similarly, if a priest marries an Israelite girl, their children are priests. But if the castes are incompatible, or if for other reasons the union is invalid, then sages determine the child's status according to different rules, which we examined in Chapter Three.[13] Yet these rules too accord with the parents' standing. In all cases, then, a person's ancestry interacting with the validity of his parents' union determines his or her caste position.

---

[13] With regard to the question of how the status of the parents affect the status of their offspring, see the discussion concerning the various parts of M. Qid. 3:12 in the previous chapter.

According to the portrayal of Israelite society as a collection of households, membership in a household determines a person's caste status. The Mishnah's authorities envision that all members of a typical Israelite household — one in which the householder has formed an approved marriage — belong to the same caste. The wife takes her husband's caste and their offspring do likewise. In this way, the caste of the householder determines the caste of the other members of the household. Furthermore, the household serves to divide each caste into two levels, which we shall call primary and secondary. The primary level consists of assigned roles in the Temple cult. Only the householder receives an assigned role in Temple worship.[14] This role consists of a set of required tasks and privileges. The other members of the household — women and minor sons — belong to the secondary level of the caste system. They do not receive any assigned duties linked to the caste, but they do partake of its privileges. In this way, then, the household differentiates members of each caste.

Each of these two portrayals of Israelite society treats the bondman in its own way. On the one hand, the bondman belongs to an Israelite household. The master joins him to his household through the property link between them. Through it, the bondman becomes an Israelite and takes on a secondary status in his master's caste. On the other hand, the bondman has no part in the network of kinship ties that indicates membership in the extended family of Israel. The tie to his master cancels all kinship ties the bondman may possess — whether to members of Israelite society or some other culture. In so doing, it denies him a place in the extended family of Israel. His property relationship to his master, therefore, causes one image of Israelite society to exclude him from the caste system, while at the same time, causing the other to include him.

From this interstitial position, the category of bondman derives the power to accomplish a task otherwise treated as impossible by the Mishnah's framers; it removes the differences between Israelites and gentiles and makes them the same. Specifically, the bondman comprises a category that accepts people of every ethnic background and places them into a single category that obscures all traces of their ethnic origins. The householder's control over bondmen produces the same effect on everyone, whether they derive from the family of Israel or from foreign origins. That control abrogates the former kinship ties of the slave and substitutes a property tie to link him to Israelite society and its caste system. This tie places the bondman within Israelite society — that is, Israelite society defined as a collection of households — but outside the kinship network of the family Israel. On the one hand, the householder's power cancels the ancestral and marital ties of an enslaved Israelite, thereby removing him from the extended family of Israel. The householder's control does not place him outside

---

[14] In theory, adult sons who have yet to leave the household also have assigned roles in the Temple cult. The Mishnah's authorities, however, do not discuss this particular situation.

Israelite society, however, but only outside the family Israel; his status as property now links him to the Israelite community and determines his caste status. On the other hand, a slave originating outside Israelite society has radically different social ties, but his enslavement puts him in the same place occupied by enslaved Israelites. Prior to enslavement, the gentile's kinship ties bind him to a foreign society and he has no links whatsoever to Israelite society. But once enslaved, the householder's control places him in the same interstitial position; the householder's power cuts his kinship ties, places him within Israelite society defined as a collection of households, but does not bring him into the family of Israel. In this way, sages have positioned the category of bondman vis-à-vis the caste system in the one place it has the power to accept both Israelites and gentiles and homogenize them into identical people.

To place the bondman's status into comparison with that of other categories, we can chart how the two perspectives of the caste system rank the categories of Israelite society. In this way, we can graphically pinpoint the bondman's position.

Social Category	Extended Family of Israel: Kinship Ties	Households: Level in Caste System
Householder	Full member	Primary
Minor son	Full member	Secondary
Women	Full member	Secondary
Bondman	Non-member	Secondary
Foreigner	Non-member	Non-member

Figure 5

As we can see from the chart, the bondman straddles the boundary of Israelite society. He stands at the only point where the view of the caste system as a network of kinship ties is not coextensive with the portrayal of the caste system as made up of members of households. While the slave stands totally outside the extended family of Israel, his enslavement gives him a secondary status in his master's caste. He participates in cultic worship — which is governed by the caste system — like other categories that have secondary caste status, namely, women and minor sons.

Despite the importance of the bondman's interstitial position in the caste system, we must be careful not to overstate it. For this anomalous placement actually results in the bondman's standing in a perfectly routine relationship to the caste system; he belongs to the secondary level of his master's caste, just like every other member of his master's household.[15] The complex means of determining the bondman's caste status thus functions to provide him with a normal caste status within Israelite society. The next stage of our investigation is to determine whether the bondman's secondary caste membership determines his actual capacity to participate in the Temple cult, or whether in that too he takes an interstitial position.

The Bondman's Participation in Cultic Worship

The caste system's portrayal of the bondman has provided a theory about his place in the Temple cult. This theory must now be tested. At issue is whether the Mishnah's framers describe the bondman's participation in Temple observances in line with their description of his caste status. Specifically, we must discover whether the bondman's ability to take part in Temple worship conforms with his position on the secondary level of his master's caste. Two important points demonstrate that it does. First, sages never require the bondman to perform a cultic duty. In every case in which they discuss his participation in a specific cultic observance, they portray him as a category that is not required to take part. This conforms to the fact that the caste system does not assign him any cultic duties. Second, the framers permit the bondman to take part in cultic practices when he or his master wishes. This is because his secondary caste status — like that of women and minor sons — links him to the Temple cult and thus enables him occasionally to participate.

The law concerning attendance at the pilgrim festivals provides the first demonstration that the bondman is not required to participate in cultic observances. Instead, he belongs to the group of people that sages exempt from attendance. To grasp the framers' point, we must briefly rehearse Scripture's view of pilgrim festivals. Deut. 16:16 specifies that all Israelite males must travel to Jerusalem three times a year to attend the pilgrim festivals: the Festival of Booths, the Festival of Passover and the Festival of Weeks. In the following passage, the Mishnah's authorities specify more exactly who is included in the designation of "all Israelite males." They accomplish this goal through negation, by detailing the types of people who are exempt from attending these three festivals. Our interest, of course, lies in discovering whether the bondman is required to attend.

---

[15] In Chapter Two, I showed that the Mishnah's framers use different criteria to distinguish the categories of bondmen, women and minor sons. Sages differentiate bondmen by their subjection to a householder's control, women by their gender, and minor sons by their lack of reason. The different criteria, by definition, give the categories different abilities and characteristics. However, the secondary caste status that these three categories share defines an area in which the different taxonomic criteria underlying each category provide them with the same features. These features, as we shall see in the following section, permit them to participate in the Temple cult to the same degree.

A. All [Israelites] are required to appear [at the Temple for each of the three pilgrim feasts (Ex. 23:17 & Deut. 16:16)],

B. except for (1) a deaf-mute, (2) an idiot, (3) a minor [because they lack the capacity to reason],

C. (4) a person lacking obvious sexual characteristics, (5) a person who has the sexual features of both sexes, (6) women [because they are not purely male],

D. and (7) bondmen who have not been freed.

M. Hag. 1:1a

Sages specifically exempt the bondman from attending the pilgrim festivals (D). By itself, this fact shows that the first part of our hypothesis tests true. But a second point strengthens it further, namely, that the bondman's exemption stems specifically from his enslavement. Sages have arranged the categories of people in B-D according to the taxonomic criteria that distinguish them from the householder. These criteria are the standard list of three opposites of the householder's characteristics: lack of reason, improper gender, and enslavement. The criterion for the minor and the other categories in B is the lack of power to reason. The categories at C are those who are not solely of the male sex. By placing the women here, the framers make it plain that women's exemption from attending the festivals stems from their sexual characteristics. And finally the bondman appears alone at D. Since he is like the householder in both the capacities of reason and sex, this can stem only from his enslavement. Furthermore, by specifying slaves "who have not been freed," the framers emphasize enslavement as the criterion for differentiating the bondman from the householder. Thus, sages exempt the bondman from the requirement to attend these festivals solely because he is a slave.[16]

Although the Mishnah's authorities exempt the minor son from the duty to appear at the Temple for the three festivals, they encourage him to take part in the journey to Jerusalem, as we can see from the following remarks.

A. Who is a minor?

B. "Anyone who is not able to ride on his father's shoulders [because he is too young] and go up from Jerusalem to the Temple Mount." The words of the House of Shammai.

C. And the House of Hillel say, "Anyone who is not able to hold his father's hand [because he is too young] and go up [i.e., walk] from Jerusalem to the Temple Mount.

D. "As it is written [in Ex. 23:14], 'Three times (רגלים) [in a year you shall celebrate a feast to Me.]'" [The word for "times" used here can also be interpreted as "feet." The House of Hillel understand this as meaning that a minor is someone who cannot walk upon his own feet to the Temple.]

M. Hag. 1:1b

---

[16] This argument explicates the rational behind the joining of the three categories of bondman, woman and minor son. See previous footnote.

Both the Houses of Hillel and Shammai hold that the minor son should go up to the Temple as soon as he is physically capable. They differ only with regard to when in the boy's life this occurs. Thus, although the minor's legal position is equivalent to the other dependents', the framers nevertheless encourage him to participate before he assumes his legal obligations. This is because the minor son is the only one of the three categories possessing secondary caste status that is expected to assume eventually primary caste status with its rights and duties. By having the son participate in these observances before he becomes permanently obligated, the framers provide him with an opportunity to learn them.[17]

The Festival of Booths provides another context showing that sages do not require the bondman to participate in cultic observances. Here, the framers exempt him from performing the distinctive observance of the Festival of Booths, namely, the duty of dwelling in a booth. This duty derives from Leviticus 23:

> You shall dwell in booths seven days...all that are native in Israel shall dwell in booths.
>
> Lev. 23:36, 42

Our interests lie in determining whether the framers require bondmen to fulfill the commandment of dwelling in a booth. To restate this question in Leviticus's terms; we wish to know whether they define "native" so as to include bondmen. Sages' answer becomes clear in the following passage.

A. He who sleeps under a bed in the booth [during the Festival of Booths] does not fulfill his obligation [to sleep in the booth]. [This is because the bed is between him and the booth's roof. Therefore the bed shelters him, not the booth.]...

B. Said Rabbi Simeon, "It once happened that Tabi, the bondman of Rabban Gamaliel, slept under the bed [in a booth].

C. "And Rabban Gamaliel said to the elders, "Observe Tabi my slave, for he is a disciple of a sage! And he knows that slaves are exempt from [the requirement of dwelling in] the booth. Therefore he sleeps under the bed." [Since the bed comes between Tabi and the booth's roof, Tabi is not in a position to fulfill the commandment. Gamaliel's point is that this does not matter because Tabi, as a bondman, is not required to fulfill it.]

D. In this manner we learn that he who sleeps under the bed [in a booth] has not fulfilled his obligation [of dwelling in a booth].

M. Suk. 2:1

---

[17] The emphasis on the father's participation in this process (M. Hag. 1:1 B & C) is not accidental; it is part of the duty laid upon the father to teach his son how to perform the different acts of worship. See, for example, Proverbs 22:6.

Sages' understanding of Leviticus 23 is plain: the term "native" does not encompass the bondman.[18] Indeed, Gamaliel's public approval of Tabi (B-D) reveals that bondmen lack any requirement to dwell in the booth. Since it is acceptable for Tabi to sleep under the bed, he does not need to sleep in the booth. The framers positive use of this story shows that they follow Gamaliel's view. Clearly, then, sages do not require the bondman to participate in cultic observances.

Again, minor sons and Israelite women possess the same status as the bondman in this matter; the framers do not require them to dwell in the booth during the Festival of Booths. This becomes clear from the following passage.

A. Women, bondmen, and minors are exempt from [the requirement of dwelling in] the booth [during the Festival of Booths].

B. A minor that no longer needs his mother, is required [to dwell] in the booth.

C. It once happened that the daughter-in-law of Shammai the Elder bore [a son during the festival] and he broke off some of the roof plaster and made a booth over the bed for the child.

M. Suk. 2:8

Sages' ruling at A is straightforward; women and minors, like slaves, lack the requirement of living in the booth. Thus women's position is clear, but the presence of B and C indicate further requirements for the minor son. A tension exists for the minor son between the duties incumbent upon him from his inherent caste status and the lack of reason that deprives him of the intention required to translate performance of these duties into their fulfillment. At A, sages use the standard list for describing nonhouseholders — women, minor sons and slaves. This use clearly indicates that they mean a child under the age of thirteen who has no capacity of reason (see M. Abot 5:21), as they do in every other occurrence of this list.[19] But this position is contradicted at B and C. There, they attempt to redefine the category of the minor by ignoring his lack of reason. Instead, they emphasize the duty inherent in his caste membership. Shammai's action at C, which follows the position at B in an extreme manner, reveals the crux of the matter. Although his deed technically places the baby into a booth, the baby can in no way be seen as performing the commandment. It is just happening. Thus, what we see in this passage is that sages encourage the minor to take part in the duties belonging to his caste, but he does not fulfill them in the same sense as adults.[20]   Therefore, none of the secondary caste

---

[18] This should not surprise us, since we just saw that bondmen stand outside the extended family of Israel.

[19] For other occurrences of this list, see M. Ber. 3:3, 7:2; M. Suk. 3:10; M. BM 7:6; M. Men. 9:8; and so on.

[20] The ruling at M. Suk. 2:8 B can be understood as a statement of the father's requirement to educate his son in the proper performance of worship. But the

members — bondmen, women or minor sons — are required to perform cultic duties linked to their caste status.

Even though the framers do not require bondmen and other secondary classes to participate in caste-based cultic practices, they permit the categories to do so. This point stands out clearly in the bondman's participation in the most holy of the Temple practices open to laymen — the slaughtering of sacrificial animals. To understand this point, let me describe how animals are slaughtered. Slaughtering consists of two separate acts: the killing of the animal (with its subsequent dressing), and the collecting of its blood. Priests must always collect the blood, and they usually perform the slaughter. But certain sacrifices permit — even require — a non-priest to slaughter his own offering. This last fact provides the interpretive crux for the following passage. At issue is the validity of a sacrifice performed by a priest who is temporarily ineligible to collect the blood. Does his ineligibility to collect the blood imply that he is ineligible to slaughter the animal as well? Sages' answer to this question reveals that they include bondmen as people who are eligible to slaughter.

A. All [priests] who are ineligible [to receive the blood of a sacrificial animal (see M. Zeb. 2:1) but] who slaughter [a sacrificial animal] —

B. their slaughtering is valid,

C. for slaughtering [of sacrificial animals] by

(1) non-priests,

(2) women,

(3) bondmen [who may slaughter when their master commands them to do so (see, for example, M. Pes. 8:7)],

(4) and those who are unclean [even though their uncleanness makes them ineligible to be in the Temple and their presence entails a heavy fine]is valid,[21]

---

story at C does not conform to such an interpretation, for a newborn babe is simply incapable of being trained.

[21] The appearance of the unclean person in the list at C presents a dilemma to the interpreter. How can an unclean person validly slaughter a sacrifice when he cannot validly enter the Temple compound? The solution is that this is an example of sages' interest in unusual circumstances. The unclean person is someone who forgot he was unclean, entered the holy precincts, slaughtered, and only then remembered he was unclean. While he must now pay the penalty for violating the area's sanctity, the animal he slaughtered remains valid.

Bertinoro's comment misses the point. He suggests that the unclean person is standing outside the Temple Court and slaughters with a (very) long knife. His view cannot be correct for two reasons. First, the stairs and walls around the Temple court would make it impossible for someone to stand outside while slaughtering inside (see M. Middot). Second, that aside, Bertinoro still does not solve the problem. The Mishnah's framers, following Scripture, hold that an unclean person is not allowed to stand outside the Court, that is, in the Court of Women. So in the Mishnah's world, the unclean person would not be allowed as close as Bertinoro's comment requires. See M. Kel. 1:6-9 and Lev. 13-14.

D.   even the slaughtering [of animals in the status of] Most Holy
     Things [the most holy classification of sacrificial animals that
     may only be slaughtered in the Court of the Priests (See M. Zeb.
     5:1 and M. Kel. 1:8)].

M. Zeb. 3:1

At C, sages reveal that bondmen may validly slaughter sacrificial animals. Their
casual use of this fact as support for the argument at A shows that the
bondman's right constitutes a noncontroversial fact; to the Mishnah's
authorities, the bondman's slaughtering of sacrificial animals is a commonplace.
Similarly, the framers view the woman's capacity to slaughter as standard
procedure. Unlike the previous two passages, this passage contains no mention
of the minor son. This is because slaughtering is valid only when performed by
a person possessing the power of reason. Since minors lack this ability, they
cannot slaughter under any circumstances. While both slaves and women may
participate in sacrificial slaughter, therefore, minor sons cannot.

The capacity of bondmen and women to slaughter animals in the status of
Most Holy Things (D) takes on even greater significance when we realize where
the slaughtering takes place — in the Court of the Priests. This area is restricted
to Priests and may only be entered by an Israelite to perform specific tasks of his
sacrifice, such as slaughtering. Even then an Israelite — adult male, woman or
bondman — may enter only if they are in a state of cultic purity. We can draw
two important conclusions from this. First, sages permit the bondman and the
Israelite woman to take part in the highest and most holy cultic observances.
Second, the bondman, as well as the woman, can achieve a state of cultic purity
equal to that of the Israelite householder. We shall examine, in greater detail, the
purity issue later in this chapter. Both points, however, make it plain that our
hypothesis concerning the place of bondmen, and of women, is so far correct.

The Mishnah contains further examples showing that the bondman may take
part in cultic practices. We now turn to a passage that shows the bondman
supporting the Temple by paying the Temple tax. The annual half-sheqel tax is
only levied on free adult male Israelites (Ex. 30:13ff), but sages rule that slaves
may pay the tax if they so desire. We discover this fact in the following
passage, where sages address the question of what happens when a person cannot
pay the tax on time. The answer is that when the date for payment approaches,
the people who expect to be late pledge that they will pay the tax. Our interest
focuses on whether or not the bondman takes a pledge or pays the tax.

A.   From whom do [the money-changers] exact a pledge [that they
     will pay the yet unpaid Temple-tax]?
B.   [They exact a pledge] from Levites, Israelites, proselytes and
     freedmen.
C.   But [they do not exact a pledge] from women, bondmen, and
     minors [because they are not required to pay the Temple-tax.]....

D. Even though [sages] have said, "They do not exact a pledge from women, bondmen and minors," If these people paid the [Temple-tax], [the money-changers] accept it from them.

E. [If] a gentile or a Samaritan paid the [Temple-tax], [the money-changers] do not accept it from them....

F. And these [types of people] are liable [to pay] the surcharge [to pay the money-changers for the cost of converting the standard currency into Temple coinage]:

G. Levites, Israelites, proselytes and freedmen,

H. but not priests, women, bondmen or minors. [This is because they do not have to pay it in the first place.]

M. Sheq. 1:3, 5, 6

The framers distinguish three classes of people — the bondman among them — by their standing with regard to the Temple tax. At B, sages list the categories of people, the male members of four different castes, who possess the duty to pay. At C-D, we find the bondman, along with the woman and the minor. Sages categorize these three groups as those who are not required to pay the half-sheqel, but may if they wish. Finally, at E, stand the two groups who may not pay the tax under any circumstances, namely, gentiles and Samaritans. By placing the slave in the second group, the framers show that they allow him to take part in this duty, even though it is not incumbent upon him. The woman's and the minor's location there likewise reveals that they may participate but are not required to do so.

Upon examination, F-H reveal an important point. Here, the voluntary payment by the three secondary caste members lacks the same status as the tax paid by those from whom it is demanded. That is to say, their participation does not have the same standing as participation by someone who is required to pay the tax. Thus, although the money-changers accept the half-sheqel from dependents, the dependents do not pay the surcharge, which is necessary to compensate for the exchange into Temple currency. The slave's contribution, like that of the woman, is thus less than the half-sheqel because the fee must come out of his payment. Their payment therefore has the status of a voluntary contribution rather than the full half-sheqel tax. In sum, the slave's participation in this cultic practice is not as effective as that of a householder.

This points to the critical distinction between the householder and the secondary categories of Israelite society. The difference stems from the householder's assigned role in the Temple cult. His requirement to perform certain tasks grants his actions a higher status than, for instance, the bondman's performance of the same tasks. The householder's duties constitute part of the Temple cult's organization of its world. It counts on the householder to perform those duties. The actions of bondmen and others who lack the obligation are random; since they cannot be relied upon to happen, the Temple does not depend upon them. The bondman's and the woman's lack of duty — that is, of an assigned role in the cult — thus makes their actions qualitatively different from those of an Israelite householder.

The same principle governs the eating of the Passover meal by the slave, the minor, and the woman. The Mishnah's framers make it clear that their participation depends completely upon the householder. They may eat the meal, but the cult does not require it and can do without it. In Chapter One, we discussed how, in Scripture, the foreign slave joins his master and family in eating the Passover meal. When we examine the framers' conception of this meal, we discover that they extend the definition of "family" to include groups of people, not necessarily related to each other, who may band together to share a sacrifice. They retain two requirements: one, the group must be headed by a householder; two, it must consist of people capable of consuming the sacrificed animal. The passage below clarifies the bondman's position, as well as that of women and minors, with regard to these two requirements.

A. Even if there is an group of a hundred [Israelites], [if] they cannot eat [among them] an olive's-bulk [of the meat] —

B. they do not slaughter the [Passover-offering] for them. [This is because they are unable to eat the requisite amount to fulfill the obligation to eat the Passover offering.]

C. And they do not form a group [for the purpose of eating the Passover offering] from [only] women, slaves, or minors. [These types of people are not subject to the command to eat of the Passover-offering and hence, by themselves, cannot constitute the valid group necessary for the slaughtering of a sacrificial animal.]

M. Pes. 8:7[22]

This passage illustrates the two rules explained above. A-B specifies that if those classes of people who are required to eat it — namely, Israelites — cannot, then an animal should not be slaughtered for them. In contrast, at C, we find groups of persons who are not required to eat the sacrifice but who can. These are groups consisting solely of bondmen, minors and Israelite women. Sages deny them the right to have an animal slaughtered for them because they lack a householder. Thus, while members of the dependent categories may perform the

---

[22] My translation presents the "plain meaning" (*peshat*) of the Hebrew text. The framers of the Babylonian Talmud, at Pes. 91a-b, argue that the point of the Mishnah passage is not to delineate the different classes of people that do not require the Passover offering, but to state that the groups may not celebrate the Passover *together* when no householder is present. (This latter interpretation is followed by later commentators such as Maimonides. See his commentary to the Mishnah on this passage.) The Talmud's interpretation of M. Pes. 8:7, however, is based on a midrashic exegesis. Its discussion even begins by implicitly admitting that the reading as I have it at M. Pes. 8:7C is the plain meaning (see the end of BT Pes. 91a). Then, at BT Pes. 91b, the Talmud's editors begin a debate on which midrashic exegesis provides the correct interpretation of the Mishnah passage. (Wegner, *Women*, reads the Mishnah passage as I do.)

same act as householders — namely, eat a Passover offering — they do so according to different rules. The absence of duty for bondmen, minors and women alters the quality of their participation in cultic practices.

To generalize from our results: bondmen, like women and minor sons, take part in cultic worship according to the theory of the caste system that we spelled out in the previous section. The Mishnah's authorities do not require slaves and women to take part but in general permit them to do so. (The same holds true for the minor son, but for him, there is second issue: sages encourage him to participate when he can, in keeping with his own inherent caste position.) Furthermore, when members of these secondary categories do participate in cultic observances, their actions possess a lower status than those of householders. This is because the householder possesses an assigned role in the Temple cult, while the secondary caste members lack such a role. Both points reveal, therefore, that the bondman, like other secondary caste members, participates in cultic activities in conformity with his place in the caste system.

The bondman's ability to take part in cultic practices makes it clear that he belongs within Israelite society. To further substantiate his place in Israelite society, let us briefly compare him with the gentile. In the three cases where sages permit the slave to take part in the Temple cult, they concurrently deny the foreigner any such right. This fact provides a negative indication of the bondman's place within the Israelite community. First, with regard to paying the Temple tax, we have already seen that a gentile's money is not accepted.[23] Second, we know from Scripture that non-Israelites may not eat the Passover sacrifice. They may do so only if they convert. Third, it is impossible for foreigners to slaughter a sacrificial animal because they are forbidden, upon penalty of death, to enter the area of the Temple set aside for slaughtering (M. Kel. 1:8). With regard to participation in the Temple cult, therefore, the Mishnah's authorities clearly distinguish between the bondman and the foreigner; the bondman belongs within Israelite society while the foreigner definitely stands outside.

Slavery and Agency

One apparent inconsistency remains unexplained. We have shown that the bondman's acts of participation have a secondary status; they lack the full efficacy that a householder's action possesses. In contrast, we have also seen that the slave may slaughter sacrificial animals as part of a sacrificial rite. Surely his act here — a central act of cultic worship — does not have secondary

---

[23] The Temple does not reject all gifts given by gentiles, only those in which the amount given is clearly specified, or that might provide some benefit for the foreigner. Thus free-will and voluntary offerings are accepted while those sacrifices offered in accordance with purification regulations are not (see M. Sheq. 1:5).

status! Indeed, it does not, for in sacrifice the bondman does not act on his own behalf, but for his master. By commanding his slave to sacrifice, a householder makes the slave an agent who thereby acquires the householder's duty to fulfill the sacrifice. Let us explicate the concept of the slave as his master's agent by examining his actions in sacrificial rites.

The Festival of Passover displays the bondman's role as an agent in the slaughter of the Passover sacrifice. According to the Mishnah, the slaughter of the lamb for the Passover meal is a sacrifice performed by the householder in the Temple at Jerusalem. After he kills the beast, and a priest takes the slain animal's blood, the householder and his family eat the animal. In the following passage we discover that a householder may assign his bondman to perform the sacrifice in his place. This is significant, for it shows that the bondman — who does not require the Passover meal on his own behalf — can function as his master's agent and fulfill his master's obligation to slaughter the sacrificial animal.

> A. He who says to his bondman, "Go and slaughter a Passover-offering for me" [and neglects to tell the bondman whether to slaughter a kid or a lamb] —
> B. if [the bondman] slaughters a kid, [the householder] should eat [it],
> C. [if the bondman] slaughters a lamb, [the householder] should eat [it],
> D. [if the bondman] slaughters a kid and a lamb, [the householder] should eat from the first [animal slaughtered].
>
> M. Pes. 8:2

The power of the bondman as an agent equals that of the householder himself. The bondman has the right to make all the decisions with regard to which type of animal is slaughtered. These decisions are binding on the householder. Thus the householder grants his slave, in assigning him as agent, the duty to make the sacrifice and that duty makes the sacrifice fully effective. It is effective not for the slave, but for his master. For upon the slave's performance, his master's obligation is fulfilled. Thus, we see that the bondman, as his master's agent, participates in the cult with full capacities. It is only when his master assigns him his own obligation for a cultic action that the bondman's actions are fully effective.

The bondman's capacity as an agent also appears in a passage concerning the designation of priestly rations from a farmer's harvested produce. A householder must separate such gifts from his produce — thereby imparting sanctity to the designated crops — before he can eat it. These holy offerings must then be taken to Jerusalem and given to the priests. Neither Scripture nor the Mishnah specify the amount to be separated, so the householder may choose the amount to be given. If he wishes, a householder can assign this task of separation and sanctification to a slave.

A. [If a householder] authorized a *ben bayit* [i.e., a free person attached to his household], or his bondman or bondwoman to separate [a specified amount of] priestly rations [from his crop],

B. that which [the individual] separates is [valid] priestly rations.

C. [As regards a case in which the householder] voided [his authorization] —

D. If [the householder] voided [his authorization] before [the individual actually] separated the priestly rations,

E. that which [the individual] separated is not [valid] priestly rations.

F. But if he retracted after [the individual] had separated the priestly rations,

G. that which [the individual] had separated is [valid] priestly rations.

M. Ter. 3:4

Under his master's authorization, the bondman may validly designate priestly rations from his master's produce. The slave decides how much produce should be given and from which produce it may be taken. His power only lasts, however, for the time in which his master grants him the duty to perform the separation (A-B, F-G). When the master removes the duty, then the right to make the designation of priestly rations also vanishes (C-E). Thus, the householder may assign to the bondman his own obligation to designate priestly rations. By doing so, the slave fulfills the householder's obligation for him.

The bondman's link to an Israelite householder, therefore, results in two types of cultic participation. First, simply by virtue of his secondary status in his master's caste the bondman can participate in certain cultic observances. The status of his participation, however, is qualitatively inferior to that of a householder, who has been assigned cultic duties. Second, when a householder appoints his bondman as an agent to fulfill a cultic obligation, the bondman then participates in the cult at the same level of efficacy as a full caste member. The slave takes on, through the agency, his master's cultic obligation. It is this obligation that gives his actions full effectiveness. This second point is important, for the householder who functions as an agent also possesses the capacity to do the action for himself, but the bondman can perform the action only when he functions as an agent for his master.

The bondman's capacity to function as an agent in matters of the Temple cult is significant, for he constitutes the only one of the three categories possessing secondary caste status that can do so. The minor son cannot be an agent at all because he lacks the necessary capacity of reason. The woman can act as an agent, but only in private matters that directly concern women. For example, one woman can function as an agent for a second woman in receiving a writ of divorce from the second woman's husband. But the capacity of women to act as agents is strictly limited to the private realm; the Mishnah's framers never depict a woman as an agent in matters of the public arena, let alone matters of the cultic worship.[24]

The bondman can function as his master's agent in the Temple cult because the Mishnah's system does not require him to meet one of the rules of agency that apply to free Israelites. This rule is: to perform a certain task as an agent for another person, an Israelite must be able to do that particular deed himself when not acting as an agent.[25] In the Temple cult, that further means that the person must be required to do that act as part of his Temple duties. The slave does not meet this requirement. As we shall see in Chapter Six, this is because the bondman acts through the will of his master, not through his own. He is the only secondary category that is not bound by this restriction. The minor son lacks all capacity to be an agent because his incapacity to reason means that he cannot do any legally binding task for himself. The woman can function as an agent in marital and household matters, but since she lacks any caste-based cultic duties, she cannot serve as an agent in that arena. In this way, the difference between slavery and freedom is apparent even in the matter of agency.

Agency thus emphasizes the importance of a category's taxonomic criterion in determining the attributes and abilities of its members. While women, bondmen and minor sons all have a secondary caste status — that is, they are not required to participate in cultic worship, but may if they desire, even though their acts of worship are not as effective as those of a householder — that status derives from different taxonomic criteria. Therefore, although they share the status, the three categories differ in other respects. First, because the minor son will eventually attain the capacity to reason and thereby become liable to fulfill caste-based duties, the framers hold that his father should encourage him to participate even though his actions have no legal effect. In this way, the son will learn how to perform those acts when he comes of age. Second, the bondman's capacity to function as his master's agent stems from the taxonomic criterion of the householder's control. Since the householder owns the bondman, he can require him to perform as an agent.[26] Third, the woman is neither

---

[24] Wegner, *Women*, argues that M. Ket. 9:4 and Shebu. 7:8 imply that women can serve as agents. Since neither passage mentions agency nor do they appear in a context concerned with agency, I do not concur. Even if Wegner is correct, however, neither passage would affect my claim that women cannot act as agents in the fulfillment of caste-based cultic duties. This is because M. Ket. 9:4 focuses on the context of the market place, while M. Shebu. 7:8 concerns the wife as the manager of the household.

[25] See the discussion of the rules regarding agency in Eilberg-Schwartz, pp. 108-114, 163-172.

[26] The bondman has an advantage over the free, adult, male Israelite who serves as an agent, for the bondman can be agent in situations where the free man cannot. This is primarily in cultic duties that must be performed during a limited period of time. For example, it would be impossible within the allotted time period for one householder, acting as an agent, to slaughter a Passover sacrifice

encouraged to participate nor permitted to function as an agent. This is because the taxonomic criterion defining the category of women — gender — does not provide her with the attributes possessed by the other two categories. On the one hand, since she will never become liable to perform caste-based commandments, she does not need to be trained in them, while, on the other hand, since she is not owned and therefore not subject to a householder's full control, she cannot function as an agent in the Temple cult.[27] The upshot of this is that the taxonomic criteria that define each category provide the primary definition of each category, overriding all other considerations. Even when the taxonomic criteria of other categories come into play, the criterion for that particular category remains dominant. For instance, the Mishnah's framers grant the bondwoman the capacity to act as an agent for her owner in matters of cultic worship (M. Ter. 3:4). This is because the framers define her primarily as a slave and only secondarily as a woman.[28] Thus, the taxonomic criteria provide the central definition of each category.

The upshot of our investigation, therefore, is that the Mishnah's framers assign the bondman a secondary caste status in the Temple cult and grant him the further capacity of agency. On the one hand, the Temple recognizes the householder's private act of enslavement and grants the slave a regular status in its organization of Israelite society. Although the bondman's secondary position does not require him to take part in cultic observances, it permits his participation when he or his master desires it. He is simply a secondary caste member, just like women and minor sons. At every point where slaves, women and minor sons appear jointly, we find that the Temple cult treats them in the same manner; they are not required to participate, but may do so if they wish. On the other hand, it enables the bondman to serve as his master's agent in fulfilling the master's cultic duties. He constitutes the only category with secondary caste status that possesses this capacity. The bondman is thus the only category both to share in secondary caste status and to carry out, in some form, caste-based cultic duties with full efficacy.

The Bondman and Cultic Purity

One division of the Temple cult treats all Israelite social categories — bondmen as well as householders — according to the same rules. That division is the system of cultic purity. In it, the bondman behaves like all other

---

for another householder and still have time to slaughter one for himself. The bondman has no such problem because he is not subject to that duty.

[27] Women are liable to perform cultic requirements that are not caste-based, as we shall see in the following section.

[28] As we demonstrated in Chapter Three, this applies to matters over which the householder possesses control, such as relationships and acts requiring reason. It does not apply to merely physical acts and bodily conditions, over which the householder lacks control.

Israelites; he becomes cultically unclean and attains purification in conformity with the regulations governing all other members of Israelite society. The bondman's status becomes apparent when we examine his susceptibility to different kinds of impurity.

The first type of uncleanness to which bondmen are susceptible is that of *saraat* (צרעת, often mistranslated as leprosy). This is the most serious level of impurity, for an Israelite who contracts this form of impurity must be expelled from his city. As a continual source of uncleanness, the impure person always constitutes a danger to his community; he cannot enter a house without rendering impure every object in it (M. Neg. 13:11). The Mishnah's framers, following Scripture, therefore require him to dwell outside the community. Bondmen, like Israelites, can contract *saraat* and thereby become impure. This becomes clear from a passage in which sages discuss the type of offering his master must bring to purify him once he is healed of the disease. Leviticus 14:2-22 distinguishes two classes of offerings the person may bring. A wealthy person must bring three lambs, but poor people can achieve purification by bringing only one lamb and two birds. In the Mishnah passage below, sages discuss what type of offering a householder must bring on behalf of his bondman who is healed from *saraat* . Must he bring a rich man's offering — presumably in accord with his own financial status — or can he bring a poor man's offering — in line with his slave's financial situation?

> A.   A man may bring on behalf of his son [who was a leper], on behalf of his daughter [who was a leper], on behalf of his bondman [who was a leper] and on behalf of his bondwoman [who was a leper] a poor man's offering. [This will enable them to complete their process of purification.]
>
> Neg. 14:12

Sages resolve the matter in line with the slave's financial standing and not that of his master; that is, his master can bring a poor man's offering for him. But the important point for our study is that the bondman and bondwoman can contract *saraat* and, like other Israelites, become unclean from it. When the slaves are healed from the disease, they go through the same process of purification as Israelite men and women. Indeed, sages explicitly treat the bondman on the same basis as an Israelite householder, for they discuss the matter of the proper offering for him as part of a discussion of the proper offering for the master's own children. Thus, the bondman's susceptibility to impurity through *saraat* shows that, with regard to purity, his status is the same as full Israelites.

The second kind of uncleanness that affects slaves, as well as Israelite men and women, is produced by an abnormal flux of liquid from their sexual organs. By "abnormal' I mean to indicate fluid such as puss or blood; predictable appearances of liquid, such as emissions of semen for men and menstruation for women, do not fall into this category of impurity. When bondmen have a flux, sages treat them in the same manner as other Israelites. That is, they can transmit their impurity to others just as Israelites do, and thus they must go through the same process of purification as Israelites. This fact becomes clear from the following passage.

> A. Everyone becomes unclean on account of a flux, even proselytes, even bondmen, whether free or not free, a deaf-mute, an idiot, or a minor...
>
> M. Zab. 2:1

By stating in this manner that the bondman is susceptible to the uncleanness of a flux, sages equate the bondman's susceptibility to impurity with that of other Israelites. By explicitly comparing his susceptibility to uncleanness with that of Israelite minors and implicitly to that of adult Israelites, the framers reveal that the bondman has the same rank in the purity system as Israelites.

Both men and women are susceptible to the last two types of uncleanness that we have examined, but there are two types of impurity — those from menstruation and childbirth — to which only Israelite women are susceptible. In the passage below, the framers address one of these and explicitly show that the bondwoman is subject to the same rules about impurity after childbirth as is an Israelite woman. Before attempting to analyze the Mishnah passage, let us first discuss how this type of impurity operates. Again, sages base theIsraelite religion arguments on Scripture:

> And when the days of her purifying are complete, whether for a son or for a daughter, she shall bring to the door of the tent of meeting a lamb a year old for a burnt offering and a young pigeon or a turtledove for a sin offering.
>
> Lev. 12:2-6

As we can see from the reference to the "tent of meeting," this passage refers to the situation of wandering in the desert. Sages interpret this passage, however, as applying to a Temple ritual. The point is that Israelite women who are unclean after childbirth purify themselves by sacrificing a lamb and a bird. In the following Mishnah passages, sages reveal that the bondwoman is susceptible to the same type of impurity and must therefore bring the sacrifice. At issue for the framers is what type of birth constitutes a son or daughter and thus requires an offering.

> A. These [are the women who] must bring an offering [of a lamb and a bird] and it is consumed [in the flame of the altar].
> B. "A woman who bears [an abortion] that is like a beast, a wild animal or a bird." The words of Rabbi Meir.
> C. But sages say, "Only if it has the form of a man."

D. "A woman who bears [an abortion] that is like a sandal, or an afterbirth or fully-formed foetus, or a young that needed to be cut up [during delivery]."

E. So too, a bondwoman who bears [an abortion] must bring an offering [of a lamb and a bird] and it will be consumed [by the fire on the altar].

M. Ker. 1:3

Here we see that the bondwoman is susceptible to the uncleanness of childbirth because she must bring the offering of purification (E). This means that sages treat her just like an Israelite woman and hence show that they place the bondwoman at the same level of sanctity as the Israelite woman.

It is now clear that the purity system treats the bondman and the bondwoman as full Israelites, for they stand subject to the entire purity system just like free Israelites. This point becomes further evident when we recall that, in the Mishnah's system, the bondman can attain the highest level of purity available to an Israelite, that of the status of Nazirite. M. Naz. 9:1 states "[When] women and bondmen [vow to become Nazirites, they] are subject to [their] Nazirite-vow." In comparison to the above passages, this provides a positive indication of the bondman's place in the system of cultic purity. That is to say, the previous passages described the bondman in the negative aspect of contracting impurity and then having to purify himself. The Nazirite must start in a totally pure state and then — through a vow — enter a state of sanctity to Yahweh. Corresponding to this state of sanctity is a higher level of purity. A Nazirite becomes more susceptible to impurity than a normal Israelite while, at the same time, it is more important to avoid all impurity. The bondman's capacity to enter this state shows that the Mishnah's authorities consider him to be subject to the purity system to the same extent as native Israelites.

The status of Nazirite provides an intersection between participation in cultic activities and the system of cultic purity. Like sacrificial slaughter, it requires the participant to possess the capacity of reason so that he can make a binding vow. Since the minor lacks reason, he cannot make a vow (M. Nid. 5:6) and then enter into the status of Nazirite. This is the only area of the purity system in which the minor differs from the other categories of Israelite society. That the bondman remains able to become a Nazirite, even when an ethnic Israelite may not, indicates the strength of the slave's identity as an Israelite in the purity system.

In sum, with regard to the system of the cultic purity, sages view bondmen and bondwomen as Israelites. Slaves are subject to the system of cultic purity in that they are susceptible to uncleanness in the same way as native Israelites and must attain purification through the same means. Furthermore, they can enter into the higher state of Nazirite purity and while there are subject to the stringent purity regulations that it requires. From both perspectives, therefore, the Mishnah's framers consider bondmen as Israelites.

Conclusion

The important result of our study of the bondman's place in the Temple cult is that on three social scales — each one governing participation in a different type of cultic observance — the Mishnah's framers assign the bondman a different rank. First, sages place the bondman outside the scale of kinship ties. Second, on the scale of the household, sages grant the bondman a secondary caste status which enables him, but does not require him, to take part in cultic observances. Third, on the scale of the purity system, the framers position the bondman along with all other Israelites. They make no distinction between the bondman and the householder, between the bondwoman and the free woman. It is not accidental that the bondman ranks so differently on these scales; indeed, the differences stem from a single principle. That is, the bondman's rank on a particular scale results from a direct correspondence between the type of activity the scale measures and his capacity to exercise the personal power required for that activity. This principle explains why the framers assign the bondman to a particular status on each scale, and also accounts for the variation in his status from scale to scale.

First, since the scale of kinship ties regulates the establishment and maintenance of kinship links, the type of personal power that qualifies one for inclusion is that exercised through relationships. As we saw in Chapter Three, the bondman has no such power; the Mishnah's authorities therefore do not grant him a place on the scale of kinship ties.

Second, the activity governed by the household-based division of the caste system — that is, the division into the primary level of householders who are assigned cultic duties and the secondary level of other categories who are not — is that of participation in cultic worship. All acts of cultic participation fall into the class of acts that require reason. The bondman has the full power to perform such deeds, we recall, but his master controls the efficacy of those deeds. This level of personal power corresponds exactly with the position the framers assign the bondman on this scale of cultic participation; they do not require the bondman to take part, but they do permit his participation according to his master's wishes.

Third, the purity system functions to identify people who enter a state of impurity and to prescribe the means by which those people remove that impurity and restore themselves to a pure state. The bondman, as we saw, participates fully in this system. This is because the form of personal power corresponding to this system is that of merely physical acts and bodily conditions. The bondman can freely exercise this type of power, we recall, so sages grant him full status in the system of cultic purity. The only exception to his freedom is the state of Nazirite, which depends on the bondman's uttering a vow. This utterance is an act requiring reason and hence subject to his master's control. Thus, on each scale, the bondman's status derives from his personal capacity to perform the activity being measured.

If we ask how this principle governing the bondman's social rank relates to the taxonomic criterion by which the framers distinguish the category of bondman, we discover another significant fact. On each scale, the criterion by which sages differentiate the bondman from the householder accurately predicts the difference between a bondman's status and the status of a householder. The taxonomic distinction between the bondman and the householder, we recall from Chapter Two, is that the bondman stands under a householder's total control. By definition, the householder does not. Therefore, on scales where the two categories differ in rank — the scales of kinship ties and cultic participation — the difference derives from the the bondman's subjugation to a householder's control. By contrast, where the bondman and the householder have the same rank — such as in the purity system — the bondman is not subject to the householder's control. Thus the taxonomic criterion distinguishing the category of bondman from the category of householder — that is, the householder's control — determines the bondman's position on each of the three social scales.

This formulation likewise describes how the Mishnah's authorities rank the minor son on these three scales. On each scale, the difference between the minor's status and that of a householder derives from the taxonomic criterion by which sages distinguish the category of minor son from that of householder. This criterion is the minor's lack of reason. Taxonomically speaking, the minor son is like a householder except for his incapacity to exercise reason, which in turn means that the minor son's status is identical with that of the householder except where reason is involved. On the scale of kinship ties and cultic purity, then, the minor son and the householder have the same rank, because the factor of reason is irrelevant. By contrast, on the scale measuring the capacity of minor sons and householders to participate in cultic worship — which are acts requiring reason — sages assign to the two categories different ranks. The taxonomic criterion distinguishing the category of minor son from that of householders — his lack of reason — therefore dictates the minor's position on the three social scales of the Temple cult.

When we turn to the category of women, we again find the same principle functioning to describe their standing on the three different scales. On each scale, the taxonomic criterion of gender determines the difference between the rank of women and that of the householder. Since gender has no effect on a woman's place in the system of kinship ties or in the system of cultic purity, women have the same status as householders. But on the scale that measures participation in the cult, sages assign women only a secondary status. This is because the Mishnah's framers assign caste-based cultic duties only to adult males, not to adult women.[29] The standing of women on these three social

29 The status of Nazirite does not fall into this category. It is neither caste-based nor assigned.

scales thus derives from the taxonomic criterion that distinguishes them as a distinct category in the Mishnah's system of people.

This discussion shows that the status of each category — bondmen as well as women and minor sons — on these three social scales derives directly from the taxonomic criterion that distinguishes it from the category of householder. For bondmen, this factor is the householder's control over the bondman's power to produce legal effects. For the minor son, this criterion is his lack of the capacity to reason. And for women, this criterion is their gender. In this way, the Mishnah's framers use the classificatory system — the most basic and fundamental organization of people in the Mishnah — to dictate the details of each category's social rank.

Chapter Five

The Freedman

A slave's subjugation to his master's control constitutes the taxonomic criterion for the category bondman, as we saw in Chapter Two. When a householder removes that control, the slave enters a new category, that of the freedman. The general description of this new classification is straightforward: the freedman constitutes a free Israelite who is limited by his past as a bondman. There are thus two sides to the freedman's description. On the one hand, the freedman belongs to the same social categories as other Israelites: an adult male freedman enters the Israelite category of householder, a freedwoman enters one of the classes of Israelite women, and the minor ex-slave enters the appropriate category of minors. From this perspective, then, the freedman is like a native, freeborn Israelite. On the other hand, within those categories, the freedman is set apart by a permanent after-effect of slavery. He possesses no kinship ties from the period prior to manumission. His enslavement has robbed him of all ancestral and marital links. The interplay of these two contradictory traits — status as a free Israelite without any ancestral ties — defines the category of freedman for the Mishnah's system.[1] The goal of this chapter is to analyze the

---

[1] The freedman is not the only category that fits this description; the proselyte likewise matches it. We shall explore the similarities between the two categories at different points in this chapter. However, the important point is that bondmen and proselytes arrive at that status through different processes and for different purposes. In the Mishnah's system, the freedman is not a converted foreigner who happens to have been enslaved; he is an ex-slave, who has no ethnic identity now and had none when he was a bondman (as we showed in Chapter Three). True, later rabbinic literature transforms the ex-slave into a proselyte, but this does not happen in the Mishnah. In fact, the whole process of conversion and manumission described in later texts differs in significant ways from these processes in the Mishnah's system. For example, Maimonides states that with regard to kinship ties the proselyte and the freedman are like newborn children. (See *Mishneh Torah*, Forbidden Intercourse, 14:11, which is based, in part, on BT Yeb. 48b.) This analogy, which works in Maimonides' system, does not work in the Mishnah. The reason apparently lies in the difference in the way children acquire kinship ties. In the *Mishneh Torah*, offspring apparently do not attain relationships at conception. But in the Mishnah, newborn children of a valid marriage enter at conception into a network of kinship ties (see Chapter Three). They are related to both parents and to any siblings that may have been born

interaction of both aspects and to ascertain how they delineate the characteristics of the freedman and determine his status in Israelite society.

Manumission: Release from the Master's Power

The act of manumission breaks all links between the slave and the householder. The householder no longer controls any aspect of the (now) ex-slave. Two points reveal this severing of ties. The former master cannot exert power over the freedman either, first, to force him to do something or, second, to dictate his status in the Israelite community. The first point becomes clear in a passage demonstrating that even if a freedman begins a task while enslaved, the householder cannot require him to finish it after manumission. Indeed, when necessary, the courts actually enforce the freedman's new independence. The following case exemplifies this point; in it a householder takes out a loan and gives his bondman to the lender as collateral. Since the bondman constitutes valuable property, such use is routine. After receiving the loan, however, the debtor frees his slave. Since the debtor does not own the ex-slave, the framers rule that the ex-slave can no longer serve as collateral for the loan.

A. [In the case of a] bondman whose master used him as a pledge (אפותיקי) [for a debt] to another [i.e., the lender] and then [the debtor] freed him.

B. [According to] strict law, the bondman [now an ex-slave] is not liable for anything. [That is to say, the debtor, not the bondman, is liable for the loan. But there is a problem here. As surety for the loan, the ex-slave remains in effect a slave under the lender's control. Why should he recognize the manumission performed by the debtor and release his hold on the slave?]

C. But for the sake of the public good, they [i.e., the courts] pressure his master [that is, the lender who now possesses the sole control over the slave] and he makes [the bondman] a free man and [the bondman] writes a bond [of indebtedness] for his value [to the lender]. [In other words, since the bondman himself is the security for the loan, he gains his freedom from the lender by guaranteeing that if the debtor fails to repay the loan, he himself will pay it.]

D. Rabban Simeon ben Gamaliel says, "No one writes [a bond of indebtedness] except for [the man] who frees [the bondman]. [That is, if the debtor frees the slave he used as collateral, he must formally take responsibility for the loan by writing out a new agreement.]

M. Git. 4:4b

---

prior to them, to say nothing of more distant relatives. Neither the proselyte nor the freedman have any kinship ties whatsoever at the moment they enter that category. For the Mishnah, then, the important question about the freedman and the proselyte is: what does the fact that the freedman is like the proselyte tell us about the process of manumission from slavery?

Both the anonymous ruling at A-C and Simeon at D recognize that by freeing the bondman, the debtor cuts all links to him. The bondman's problem at A-C comes not from the manumission but from his status as collateral. The clue to understanding the matter appears at B. There sages state that the bondman, "according to strict law," is free. As a freedman, he possesses no liability for his master's debts. But despite the master's action (that is, the debtor), the lender retains a lien on the ex-bondman. The agreement governing the lien states that the ex-slave is guarantee for the loan with his person; that is, his body *is* the payment. But in the framers' view, the slave, now a freedman, cannot be kept as collateral. To solve this problem, sages rule at C that the courts should persuade the lender to confirm the manumission by freeing the ex-slave from the possibility of being re-enslaved. In return, the ex-slave himself undertakes to pay the loan in the event that the debtor fails to pay it. He agrees to pay an amount equivalent to his former value as a slave. Thus, A-C attempts to resolve the rights of the lender with those of the freedman without involving the debtor. Simeon's position at D, by contrast, resolves the issue by focusing on the lender and the debtor only, neither of which — in his opinion — retains any claim on the freed slave. The debtor owes the money, not the ex-slave. Both rulings in this passage therefore take care to ensure that the freedman is treated as a free man. In this way, they show that the bondman's tie to his master is cut at manumission.

The second important effect of manumission, as we mentioned, is that afterwards the Mishnah's framers determine the freedman's status according to his own characteristics and not those of his ex-master. That is to say, the freedman loses the secondary status in his master's caste that allowed him to participate in that caste's privileges. Sages reveal this point in a passage that compares manumission to other means by which a bondman's tie to his master becomes severed, such as the sale of the slave or the death of the master. In this case, sages discuss how a priest's bondman — who, as a secondary member of the priestly caste, has the right to priestly rations — loses his caste privileges when the tie to his master is severed.[2]

> A. [In the case of a priest's] bondman who was eating priestly rations and [messengers] came and said to him
> (1) "Your master has died," or,
> (2) "He has sold you to an Israelite [i.e., a non-priest]," or,
> (3) "He has given you as a gift [to a non-priest]," or,
> (4) "He has freed you." [In each case, the bondman's tie to his priestly master, and thus to the priestly caste, is severed, hence rendering him no longer qualified to eat holy food.]...
> B. Rabbi Eliezer [holds that once the bondman's ownership has changed — whether or not the bondman knows it — he is liable

---

2 Notes concerning my interpretation of this passage can be found in the previous discussion of it in Chapter Two.

for misuse of priestly rations and therefore] requires [the bondman to pay] the principal and the added fifth. [Eliezer holds that the bondman was ineligible to eat priestly rations at the time in question and so must pay.]

C. And Rabbi Joshua exempts [the bondman from the fine of the added fifth but requires him to repay the principal]. [In other words, the bondman was not allowed to eat the priestly rations and therefore must restore the principal, but since he did not do so wantonly, Joshua rules that he does not have to pay the fine.]

M. Ter. 8:1

A lists different ways, including manumission, that bondmen become severed from their masters' control. At A1, a bondman's master dies, thereby removing himself as the source of control. At A2 and A3, the master cuts off his own power by transferring the bondman to the control of a second householder. Finally, at A4, the bondman has been freed by his master. In all four cases, the bondman's release from his master's power abruptly cancels his secondary caste position and removes his right to eat priestly rations. This becomes clear in the dispute at B-C. Eliezer's position (B) is straightforward; he holds that the bondman is no longer attached to the priestly caste. Since at the time he was eating, he had no right to consume priestly rations, he must restore the amount eaten and pay a fine. Joshua (C) agrees with Eliezer in principle, but he adds a second consideration, namely, that of knowledge. Joshua holds that the bondman's ignorance of his true status affects his liability for the fine of the added fifth. In doing so, he follows a literal view of Lev. 22:14, which states "If a man [that is, a non-priest] eats holy produces by mistake" he must pay the fine. The bondman knew he was eating holy produce and so did not eat "by mistake." It was his own status that he did not know. Thus his act does not fit the description in this verse. But since he did eat food to which he had no right, he must replace it. Thus, both Joshua and Eliezer agree that manumission severs the bondman from his master and the master's caste. Clearly, then, manumission releases freedmen from the control of their former masters. Since the freedman can no longer be defined by his relationship to an Israelite householder, the Mishnah's framers define him according to his own characteristics.

After Manumission: The Personal Power of Ex-Slaves

As a free Israelite, the freedman possesses the same capacity to exercise the three forms of personal power held by all other free members of Israelite society. First, he can perform acts requiring reason that bear immediate and irrevocable legal ramifications. Second, he can produce legal effects through merely physical acts and bodily conditions. Third, he can form and maintain relationships with other Israelites and exert power over them through those relationships. Nothing restricts the freedman's exercise of the first two forms of power — those of acts requiring reason and merely physical acts and bodily conditions. But the freedman's past enslavement hinders his exercise of power through relationships. This hindrance results from the freedman's lack of kinship ties from the period prior to his manumission. While the freedman has the full potential to exercise power through relationships, he has no ancestry or marital ties at manumission and therefore has no means by which to exercise this form of power. Let me show how the Mishnah's framers address this problem.

The freedman's power to form and maintain kinship ties becomes clear from a passage describing the conditions under which a freedwoman and a proselyte woman can marry a priest. As a general rule, members of neither class can marry into the priesthood; only people belonging to the pure native castes of Israelite society — the castes of priests, levites, and Israelites — may do so. According to Eliezer ben Jacob, however, if one parent belongs to a native caste, then the offspring — even though still a freedwoman or a proselyte — may marry a priest. Eliezer develops his principle by focusing on the proselyte and then at the end states that the principle applies to the freedwoman as well.

A. Rabbi Eliezer ben Jacob says, "An Israelite who married a female proselyte, his daughter is acceptable to [a member of] the priesthood [for marriage]. [This is because the father provides the Israelite ancestry necessary for marriage into the priesthood.]

B. "And a proselyte who married the daughter of an Israelite, his daughter is acceptable to [a member of] the priesthood [for marriage]. [This is because the mother provides the Israelite ancestry necessary for marriage into the priesthood.]

C. "But a proselyte who married a female proselyte, his daughter is forbidden to [a member of] the priesthood. [Neither parent provides Israelite ancestry.]

D. "Proselytes and freedmen are the same — even for ten generations [their descendents are forbidden to marry a member of the priesthood] unless the mother [of a descendent] is an Israelite."

M. Qid. 4:7

If we read A-C's discussion of the proselyte as applying to the class of freedmen, as D instructs us to do, we discover that freedmen possess the capacity to form all types of kinship ties. First, A-C assume that freedmen can marry and form marital ties. Second, C indicates that the offspring of a freedman and a freedwoman are related to them. Since the offspring take their parents' caste, the descendent clearly has kinship ties to them. Third, both C and D reveal the opposite point, that the offspring of freedmen have ancestral ties to their parents and to their ancestors "even for ten generations." Furthermore, C makes it clear that freedman parents exert control through the relationship to their daughter and thereby determine her status. In this way, we clearly see that the class of freedmen can exercise the power to form and maintain relationships and can exert through them the power to control others.

The case of a newly freed bondwoman shows how the exercise of this power is limited by lack of kinship ties: for the ex-slave, no relationships persist from the time before or during her slavery, not even to her own offspring. This point is revealed by a passage focusing on the question of whether the sons of a newly freed slave are related to each other. To determine the answer, the Mishnah's framers discuss whether the freedwoman's sons must fulfill the law of levirate marriage. This law, we recall, requires an adult male to marry his brother's wife if his brother should die childless. As in the previous passages, sages treat the freedman as an appendage to a discussion about the sons of a proselyte.

A. [Concerning a] female proselyte whose sons converted with her —
B. they are not [required to undergo] the rite of removing the shoe (אין הן חולצין) and they are not [required to marry] the wife of their dead brother [because they are not considered to be brothers],
C. even if the first was not conceived in holiness [i.e, before conversion] but was born in holiness [i.e., after conversion] and the second was conceived and born in holiness. [That is, the first is not related to his mother because at conception she was a gentile, not a proselyte. Thus, even though the second child is related to his mother — because he was conceived after she converted, he still is not related to the other son.]
D. And the same [applies] to a bondwoman whose sons were freed with her. [The points made concerning the proselyte and her sons at A-C apply mutatis mutandis to the freedwoman and her offspring.]

M. Yeb. 11:2

If we again read A-C as referring to the freedwoman, in line with D, we see that in the Mishnah's system the freedwoman's sons, like the proselyte's sons, are not related to her. The point is emphasized by the two cases at A and C. At A, the sons are not related to each other because neither is related to the mother. C shows that conception constitutes the crucial point for determining whether kinship ties are established between mother and offspring. The son "conceived and born in holiness" is related to the freedwoman — thus indicating that the freedwoman can form kinship ties after manumission. But the son who was conceived during her enslavement is not related to her, even though born in freedom, and so has no kinship ties with the other son. This lack of kinship tie between mother and son prevents the mother from exercising power over that son through a relationship with him. We can see, then, that the freedman possesses no kinship ties from the period prior to his manumission.

The point that newly freed slaves, by definition, have no kinship ties is further supported by a passage concerning pregnant women who are accidently injured while standing near a fight. Here sages focus on the payment of compensation for injury; they attempt to determine the amount of damages and to whom it is paid. Simeon holds that women recently freed from slavery lack kinship ties and hence receive no payment.

A. And a man who intends to [strike] his fellow, but [misses and instead] strikes a [pregnant] woman and [thereby causes] the offspring to come forth —

B. he must pay the value of the offspring.

C. How do they [calculate] the amount of payment?

D. They determine how much she was worth before the birth and how much she is worth after the birth [and subtract the second from the first to ascertain the amount of the fine].

E. Said Rabban Simeon ben Gamaliel, "If so, then after the birth, she rejoices. [Simeon's point is that this way of determining the fine will not work because the woman is worth more after the birth than before and thus there would be no fine.].

F. "Rather they determine the value of the offspring, and give [the money] to her husband.

G. "And if she has no husband, he gives it to [the dead man's] heirs.

H. "And [if she was] a bondwoman who had been freed or a proselyte, [the tortfeasor] is exempt [from paying any fine at all]."

M. BQ 5:4

The crux of the matter is that the compensation, however it is determined, must be paid to the injured woman's husband or to his heirs (F-G). The strict application of this principle to a newly freed slave woman results in no compensation being paid. Sages thus indicate that the freedwoman, like a female proselyte, has no male kin. That is to say, she formed no kinship ties to any males — whether offspring or consorts — while she was enslaved. Furthermore, it is clear that the framers do not hold that she has formed any links to free males. According to H, the woman was first impregnated and then freed. Thus she has not yet produced any free offspring since manumission and is unlikely to have acquired a free husband. This passage confirms that manumission leaves the freedman without any kinship ties from the period prior to manumission. This lack prevents him from exercising any power through relationships at first, but it does not prevent him from forming new relationships and then exercising his power.

After Manumission: Acts Requiring Reason and Merely Physical Acts

The freedman possesses the unfettered capacity to exercise power through acts requiring reason. Since no householder's control interferes with the freedman's exercise of power, each act irrevocably causes legal effects for which he bears liability. In fact, a freedman may even become liable for the legal effects of deeds he performed while enslaved. As we saw in Chapter Three, this shows that during his enslavement, the (now-)freedman could perform acts requiring reason, although his master prevented the legal effects of those acts. The framers recognized the slave's capacity to act as a human being, even while he was an Israelite's property. The case of a bondman who injured a free Israelite shows that at manumission the freedman becomes liable for the effects of certain acts he performed while a slave. In the present case, if the bondman who caused the injury had been a free Israelite himself, sages would have required him to pay compensation. But since he was a slave, the framers hold that the householder suspends the bondman's liability and thus no damages are paid. We want to know what happens once the bondman is freed.

A. The bondman and the wife — coming into contact with them is bad:
B. He who injures them is liable [to pay compensation].
C. But should they injure others, they are exempt [from paying compensation].
D. But [under the following conditions] they may pay compensation at a later time.
E. [If] a wife becomes divorced,
F. [or if] a bondman becomes free,
G. they are liable to make compensation.

M. BQ 8:4

At D-G, the freedman becomes liable for the injury he caused while a bondman. While he was enslaved, his master's power over him protected him from the legal consequences of injuring another person (C).[3] But at the moment he gains his freedom, D-G, his master's control is lifted from him and he becomes liable to pay damages to the person he injured. Thus manumission restores to the freedman the duties he incurred through acts requiring reason during slavery. He attains the full capacity to exercise his power of acts requiring reason and to bear the responsibilities for its legal effects, even for deeds performed prior to manumission.

As with acts requiring reason, the freedman has the full capacity to exert power through merely physical acts and bodily conditions. Manumission causes no change in this form of power between the bondman and the freedman because the slavery never affected the bondman's capacity to cause effects through this power. The bondman and the freedman possess the same capacity to exert this power as the freeborn Israelite. This fact becomes clear from the following passage that focuses on the bondman but also specifies his situation if he should gain freedom. At issue here is the bondman's capacity to fulfill a Nazirite vow

---

[3] Albeck, following earlier commentators (see Albeck, *Mishnah*, vol. 4, p. 41), holds that the reason bondmen and wives do not pay is because they control no resources from which they could make payment. This is a misreading of the framers' point. M. BQ 8:4 and the preceding three passages (8:1-3) focus on the issue of the tortfeasor's liability to pay, not on the question of whether he (or she) has the means to fulfill that liability. For example, M. BQ 8:2 states that an ox's actions bring on liability to pay for injury, even though he surely lacks the means (mental and monetary) to pay such a fine! Thus the issue of M. BQ 8:4 is clearly liability for one's actions. See my discussion of this issue and this passage in Chapter Three, "Reason and Action."

he has taken. This fulfillment, we recall, requires the individual to exercise the power of acts requiring reason and the power of merely physical acts and bodily conditions. To enter the status of Nazirite, one must take a vow, which is an act requiring reason. But the vow is fulfilled by maintaining a special state of cultic purity, which is a bodily condition. We saw previously that the bondman can take the vow but his master can prevent him from fulfilling its terms. After manumission, however, the householder's control no longer affects the ex-slave and he must fulfill the vow he took by entering and maintaining the pure state of Naziritehood.

A. [When] women and bondmen [vow to become Nazirites, they] are subject to [their] Nazirite-vow....

B. [The Nazirite-vow] is more strict for bondmen than wives [with regard to a second consideration],

C. for [a householder] may [permanently] revoke his wife's vows,

D. but he may not [permanently] revoke his bondman's vows.

E. [How so?] [If] he revokes his wife['s vows] — they are revoked forever.

F. [If] he revokes his bondman['s vows] — when [the bondman] is freed, [the bondman] must complete his Nazirite-vow.

M. Naz. 9:1

The freedman, at F, must fulfill the vows he made while enslaved. Thus, like the bondman, he can attain the higher level of purity necessary for their fulfillment. Since the bondman was like the free Israelite householder in this matter, the freedman likewise has the same place in the system of purity as any other Israelite householder. In this way, we see that the freedman has the unfettered capacity to exert his power of merely physical acts and bodily conditions.

Ex-Slaves and their Descendents: Freedmen as a Caste

The freedman's capacity to exercise his personal power constitutes the basis for determining his status within Israelite society. This is particularly true for the freedman's position in the caste system's hierarchy of Israelite society. The Mishnah's framers determine status in the caste system on the basis of a person's power to form relationships. That is to say, the capacity of a caste's members to marry members of other castes determines the rank of that caste. The freedman's capacity to marry into other castes derives from the distinctive nature of his ancestry, namely, that he has none. This trait gives him an interstitial position at the center of the caste system, for sages locate him between two groups of castes, those with pure Israelite ancestry and those with defective ancestry. That position enables him to marry members of both groups. To understand why the framers place him here, let us first examine the hierarchy of the caste system and the freedman's position in it, and then show how that position stems ultimately from his lack of ancestry.

A. Ten castes came up [to Jerusalem] from Babylonia:
B. (1) the priests,
   (2) the Levites,
   (3) the Israelites,
C. (4) the impaired priests [who have transgressed the rules of Lev. 21:7,13,14 and married women who are divorcees, or, in the case of a High Priest, a nonvirgin],
D. (5) the proselytes [foreigners who have chosen to worship Yahweh] and
   (6) the freedmen,
E. (7) the *mamzers* [who are the offspring of incestuous marriages, (Lev. 20:17-21)],
F. (8) the *netins* [foreigners who once were servants to the Israelites],
G. (9) the *shetuqs* [people who know who their mother is, but not their father (M. Qid. 4:2)] and
   (10) the foundlings [who know neither their mother nor their father (M. Qid. 4:2)].

M. Qid. 4:1a[4]

The hierarchy of the caste system centers on the castes that possess pure, native, Israelite ancestry and those that do not. The first three castes — priests, Levites and Israelites — form this central focus, because they possess the necessary ancestry. The members of the fourth caste, that of defective priests, also possess native ancestry, as we have mentioned, but they comprise the descendents of priests who married women with improper marital statuses. Momentarily passing over the proselyte and the freedman, the next caste, that of *mamzers*, consists of children born to incestuous unions. Next, the *netins* are the descendents of a people, not originally Israelite, who at one time agreed to act as Temple servants. The last two castes consist of people whose ancestry is not fully known. The status of the freedman in the caste system, along with the proselyte, therefore lies between those castes whose members possess pure, Israelite ancestry, and those castes whose members' ancestry is impure, whether invalid, non-Israelite, or simply unknown.

The freedman and the proselyte have similar positions in the caste system because they both lack ancestry. The freedman lost his ancestry through slavery, while the proselyte lost his by entering Israelite society. Despite this similarity, there are two important differences between freedmen and proselytes that cause the Mishnah's framers to rank proselytes higher in the caste system than freedmen. Proselytes enter Israelite society through a public process —

---

[4] For further information, see the discussion of this passage in Chapter Four (in the section "Cultic Worship and the Caste System"), and its accompanying footnotes. There I make the point that M. Hor. 3:8 contains a similar list and that the differences in the list stem from the different purposes which the rankings serve.

involving a Temple sacrifice — and by their own free choice. Freedmen, by contrast, enter Israelite society through the private actions of their masters which are not subject to control by any public institution. Furthermore, the bondman never chooses to become an Israelite; the passages on the sale of the bondman clearly present him as having no say in the matter.[5] Freedmen and proselytes are thus equivalent in that they both lack ancestry, but the framers rank proselytes higher in the caste system because of the difference in the way they lose their ancestry.

The freedman's interstitial position in the caste system — a result of his lack of ancestry — permits him to marry into the two main groups of castes. He can marry members of the castes whose members have pure, native ancestry, and he can marry members of the castes of defective ancestry, a total of nine of the ten castes. Only members of the priesthood stand beyond his grasp.

A. (1) Priests, (2) Levites and (3) Israelites are permitted to marry each other (לבוא זה בזה).

B. (2) Levites, (3) Israelites, (4) impaired priests, (5) proselytes and (6) freedmen are permitted to marry each other.

C. (5) Proselytes, (6) freedmen, (7) *mamzer*s, (8) *netin*s, (9) *shetuq*s, and (10) foundlings -- all of them are permitted to marry each other.

M. Qid. 4:1b

Freedmen can intermarry with the groups of castes listed at B and C, but not with the group at A.[6] To understand why, we start with A, the list that excludes freedmen. This list comprises the original castes of the Israelite community. These are native Israelites who possess pure descent from those who made the covenant with Yahweh at Sinai. Since freedmen have no ancestry at all, the framers do not include them. By contrast, C lists those castes conforming to the opposite definition. That is, it comprises those castes of Israelite society who lack pure descent from the original Israelites. *Mamzer*s possess impure Israelite ancestry, the ancestry of *shetuq*s and foundlings is unknown, while freedmen, proselytes and *netin*s lack native-Israelite ancestry altogether. Despite being

---

[5] BT Yeb. 48b, as well as other passages, assumes that slaves can choose not to be circumcised when they are purchased by an Israelite. This concept is not held by the Mishnah's framers. The framers do not even address the issue of circumcising slaves, let alone discuss whether the bondman has a choice in the matter. I will say, however, that the idea of giving the bondman a choice in the matter goes against everything else that we have learned about the Mishnah's system of slavery in this study.

[6] Of course, the lists at A and B overlap, which means that the only caste into which the freedman cannot marry is the caste of priests. However, the explanation for the freedman's ability to marry members of different castes lies in studying the Mishnah's three groupings. Thus, instead of focusing directly on the fact that freedmen cannot marry priests, I first need to explicate the rationale behind each group.

placed together, there are really two subgroupings in this list. The main subgroup consists of those castes whose ancestry sages consider invalid: *mamzers*, *netins*, *shetuqs* and foundlings. No one belonging to these castes may marry a native Israelite of pure descent. The second subgroup consists of freedmen and proselytes. The framers do not forbid freedmen and proselytes, as we shall see, from marrying native Israelites and so they differ from the first subgroup. However, sages permit freedmen and proselytes to marry members of the first group because they lack native ancestry. Thus the freedman's ability to marry members of the defective castes stems from his lack of Israelite ancestry.

The list at B comprises the opposite of those castes whose ancestry is invalid, namely, those castes whose ancestry is not invalid. In other words, it contains both native and non-native castes whose ancestry is not considered impure. Freedmen, like proselytes, can marry Israelites and Levites. This is because their ancestry is valid, or more accurately, not invalid. Since they lack any ancestry prior to becoming a freedman, they have no invalid ancestry. Thus, the framers treat them as valid marital partners for native castes.[7]

The same lack of ancestry that makes freedmen valid partners for Israelites makes them invalid partners for members of the priesthood (B). The framers, following Scripture, hold that priests can marry only native Israelites. There are two reasons for this. First, priests possess a higher level of holiness than other native Israelites. They are sanctified and set apart from the rest of the people Israel. As Yahweh says in Lev. 21:8, "for he [that is, the priest] is holy to his God. Thou shalt sanctify him therefore;...he shall be holy to thee." Thus, the framers forbid freedmen to marry priests because they do not want non-Israelite ancestry mingling directly with that of the priesthood. Second, another explanation is possible. Scripture expressly commands High Priests to select their brides only from native Israelites. The High Priest "shall take a virgin of his own people [meaning native Israelites] to wife (Lev. 21:14)." The framers apparently extend the requirement to marry only a native Israelite to all priests (even though they do not likewise extend the requirement to marry a virgin). The priests' special position makes him an unsuitable marriage partner for a freedman because the freedman lacks Israelite ancestry.

---

[7] The problem of the impaired priests is slightly more difficult. These are the offspring of priests who have violated the special marital restrictions for priests found in Lev. 21:1-15. These rules state that priests should not marry harlots or divorcees and that the high priest should marry only a virgin. By violating these precepts, priests remove themselves from their priestly duties. But, apparently, since these are special restrictions for the priests, he is not expelled from the society but simply enters a caste just below that of Israelites, who are not subject to such restrictions anyway. There they are not banned from the Temple altogether, just from the priestly duties. See my discussion of this issue in Chapter Four, in the footnotes of "Caste Status and Cultic Worship."

Just as the freedman's lack of native, Israelite ancestry bars him from marrying into the priesthood, it enables him to marry into a class of defective priests. These priests no longer belong to the caste because their sexual organs have been permanently damaged, an injury which causes them to lose the special, holy status held by physically perfect priests. According to Deut. 23:2, these priests may not enter the community. "He [that is, a priest] that is wounded in the stones, or has his privy member cut off, shall not enter into the congregation (קהל) of the Lord." Although Scripture is unclear about what is meant by "enter into the congregation," the Mishnah's framers decide that it means marrying native Israelites. Since a freedwomen is not a native Israelite, sages permit them to marry defective priests.

A. [A priest who is] *wounded in the stones or whose penis is cut off* is permitted [to marry] a female proselyte or a freedwoman.
B. [because these women] are not forbidden [to him], but only entering into the congregation (קהל) [is forbidden to him (Deut. 23:2, see also Lev. 21:16ff)]. [In other words, all women who are descendents of the original Israelites are forbidden marriage partners for a priest whose sexual organs are damaged.]

M. Yeb 8:2b[8]

Sages implicitly contrast freedwomen and proselytes with native Israelite women. The latter category belong to the congregation while the former do not. Since freedwomen and proselytes do not descend from the three original castes, they constitute suitable marriage partners for priests whose sexual organs are damaged. Thus the freedwoman's capacity to marry these priests stems from her lack of Israelite ancestry. In sum, the rank of the freedman in the caste system stems from his free and unfettered capacity to form and maintain relationships and to exercise power through those relationships combined with his lack of relationships prior to his manumission.

Ex-Slaves and their Descendents: The Freedman's Role in the Temple Cult

The ultimate purpose of the caste system, we recall, is to assign cultic duties to the male members of each caste. The caste of freedmen is no exception. In fact, the freedman's cultic role is nearly equivalent to that held by members of the Israelite caste; the framers require him to perform every duty required of Israelites, so long as the duty is not explicitly predicated on being a direct descendent of Abraham, Isaac and Jacob. Sages treat freedmen like members of the Israelite caste with regard to payment of the annual half-sheqel

---

[8] Deut. 23:2 is not specific to priests, but refers to all Israelites in general. However, the context of M. Yeb. 8:2 makes it clear that priests are under discussion. M. Yeb. 8:2 constitutes an extension of 8:1 which focuses on the issue of priests eating priestly rations.

tax, which goes for upkeep of the Temple. According to M. Sheq. 1:3, this tax must be paid by the twenty-fifth day of the month of Adar. However, if a person cannot pay by that day, he pledges that he will pay it later. In the following passage, we see that freedmen must make this pledge:

A. From whom do [the money-changers] exact a pledge [that they will pay the yet-unpaid Temple-tax]?

B. [They exact a pledge] from Levites, Israelites, proselytes and freedmen.

C. But [they do not exact a pledge] from women, bondmen, and minors [because they are not required to pay the Temple-tax.]....

D. And these [types of people] are liable [to pay] the surcharge [to pay the money-changers for the cost of converting the standard currency into Temple coinage]:

E. Levites, Israelites, proselytes and freedmen,

F. but not priests, women, bondmen or minors. [This is because they do not have to pay it in the first place.]

M. Sheq. 1:3,6

A-C state that freedmen, like Israelites, must pledge that they will pay the tax, thus indicating that they must initially pay the tax. This becomes clear from the contrast between B and C. At B, the framers list four castes whose members must pay the half-sheqel or pledge that they will do so. The freedman is thus treated like an Israelite and a Levite, that is, as a full participant in the Temple cult. At C, by contrast, the authorities list secondary caste members — bondmen, women and minors — who lack this duty. Sages make the same point at D-F, where they require a surcharge to reimburse the money-changers for their work. E, like B, contains a list of castes required to pay it while F, like C, lists those who do not. In the matter of Temple support, then, sages treat the caste of freedmen just like those of Israelites and Levites.

Freedmen must also take part in festivals and their accompanying sacrifices as if they belonged to the Israelite caste. At Passover, they possess the duty to slaughter and eat their own Passover sacrifice.[9] The Mishnah's framers do not allow them automatically to participate in another householder's sacrifice, as did bondmen. To demonstrate this point, the Mishnah's authorities present an unusual case. Instead of discussing a simple freedman, they examine the situation of a bondman who was once owned by two masters. One master has now freed him but the other has not. This person is considered to be half bondman and half freedman.

---

[9] Freedman, like other Israelites, may fulfill this duty in a number of ways. If their household is small, they may — in accordance with Ex. 12:4 — join their household in celebration with another and therefore slaughter only one animal. This must be arranged between the householders and is not automatic. See the following discussion.

A. He who is a half bondman and half freedman does not eat from [the Passover sacrifice] of his master [but must slaughter and prepare his own sacrifice].

M. Pes. 8:1[10]

The point here is straightforward. Sages require this man, who is half slave and half free, to slaughter his own Passover sacrifice. The fact that this person who is only half free possesses the duty to slaughter the Passover offering shows that a total freedman certainly possesses that duty. In other words, if a person who is partially enslaved and thus still subject to the control of a master must slaughter, how much the more must a freedman, who is free from the control of his former master, slaughter the Paschal lamb. The fact that the freedman possesses this duty has two further implications on his assigned role in cultic observances. First, since the animal can only be slaughtered in the Temple, the freedman is required to make the journey to Jerusalem that the Passover festival requires. Second, since the animal is slaughtered in the Temple court we see that the freedman can enter into this holy building. Thus, once again we see that the freedman's role in the cult is the same as an Israelite's.

The freedman's duty to separate the agricultural gifts due the Temple further reveals that he possesses the same cultic role as a member of the Israelite caste. The specific tithe under investigation here is called the Second Tithe. This is quite helpful to our study of freedmen; since the framers require the freedman to bring this offering, we know that he must separate all the other offerings as well. In certain years of the sabbatical cycle, householders of the Israelite caste must separate Second Tithe. This is the last item of holy produce to be separated and is set aside only after all other tithes, offerings and poor support have been removed (M. MS 5:10-11). The householder then brings this tithe to Jerusalem and there eats it "before the Lord." The eating of this tithe is accompanied by the reciting of a vow. Part of the text of this vow is important to our study:

Look down from thy holy habitation, from heaven, and bless thy people Israel, and the land that thou has given us, as thou did swear to our fathers, a land flowing with milk and honey.

Deut. 26:15

The Mishnah's framers focus on whether the freedman may recite this oath.

A. From this [passage in Deut 23:15] they say, "Israelites and *mamzers* may make the avowal [of the Second Tithe],

---

[10] The context of the passage within the tractate of Pesahim makes it clear that this man who is half slave and half free must slaughter his own sacrifice. He is not banned from celebrating Passover, as the passage might imply when taken out of context.

B. but not proselytes or freedmen,
C. because they possess no portion in the Land.

M. MS 5:14

The framers assume that freedmen must bring the Second Tithe. But they do not allow freedmen or proselytes to say the oath. C attributes this to the fact that they have "no portion in the Land." This phrase refers to part of the Scriptural vow, "the land that thou hast given us (Deut. 23:15)." The next part of the vow identifies this land further by saying, "as thou did swear to our fathers." Thus, the land under discussion is that which God swore to give to Israel's forefathers. Since freedmen, like proselytes, cannot claim descent from the Israelite forefathers, the land has not been given to them. Only the native castes who can claim Abraham, Isaac and Jacob as their ancestors are part of the inheritance of the land. Freedmen bring Second Tithe and eat it in the same manner as Israelites; they cannot truthfully say the vow. Furthermore, the fact that they bring this tithe implies that they have made the other offerings to the Temple and the poor. Thus we know that with regard to agricultural tithes, freedmen by and large possess the same duties as Israelites. They differ only in cases where their lack of Israelite ancestry interferes with specific rites.

In general, then, freedmen participate in the Temple cult like members of the Israelite caste, for they possess the same duties and tasks. There is one exception to this rule: when a task requires native Israelite ancestry, sages do not allow the freedman to perform it. Since freedmen lack any ancestry prior to their manumission, they have no Israelite ancestry and hence cannot truthfully fulfill such a task.

Ex-Slaves and their Descendents: Freedmen and the System of Purity

The purity system treats freedmen just like other members of Israelite society. In fact, it treats all members of Israelite society alike — householders, women, minors and bondmen. Since freedmen belong to one of the first three categories, depending on their age and sex, they fully take part in the system of purity. The freedmen's lack of Israelite ancestry therefore makes no difference to their position in the system of cultic purity. Like all other Israelites, they are susceptible to impurity and must take the proper steps to attain purification. There is no difference between freedmen, bondmen and native Israelites with regard to the level of purity they can achieve or the types of impurity to which they are susceptible.

The following passage demonstrates this point by portraying the freedman as subject to uncleanness from an abnormal flux of liquid from his sexual organs.

A. Everyone becomes unclean on account of a flux [and thus become
   a *zab*], even proselytes, even bondmen, whether free or not free, a
   deaf-mute an idiot, or a minor...

M. Zab. 2:1

Here it is clear that freedmen, like proselytes and slaves, are susceptible to
uncleanness from a flux. Since "everyone" refers to free Israelites —
householders and women — the passage makes it clear that freedmen are also
subject to impurity. With regard to the uncleanness of the *zab*, then, the purity
system governs the freedman's personal condition in the same way as it does that
of free Israelites and of bondmen.

The freedman, as we saw above, can also attain the higher level of purity
held by those in the status of a Nazirite. He can become a Nazirite and must
fulfill the terms of his initial vow in this higher state of purity. In this way, the
freedman takes part not only in the negative aspects of the purity system —
those of becoming unclean — but he also participates in the positive aspect of
naziritehood. The freedman is clearly a full participant in the purity system.

Freedmen and the Reclassification of People

The category of freedman provides the strongest evidence of the power of
slavery to obliterate a person's ethnic origins. It shows that the ex-bondman —
who may have been of any ethnic or caste origins — can enter Israelite society
as a full participant. The freedman has a caste status of his own, an assigned
role in the Temple cult, and takes part in the purity system. Thus the freedman
constitutes a way for foreigners and their descendents to enter Israelite society.
Similarly, enslavement enables an Israelite to change his caste status. According
to the logic of the system of slavery — but never stated — it is possible for a
member of one of the lower castes of defective ancestry to become a slave and
thereby remove all the kinship ties that link him to that caste. Then at
manumission he would enter the higher caste of freedman, which would give
him a broader capacity to take part in Israelite society; he would be able to marry
a member of a pure, native caste, and he would be allowed to enter the Temple
and participate in worship there.[11]

The possible use of the system of slavery for this type of maneuver is
discussed by two of the Mishnah's authorities. Although the subterfuge is not
the one just described, it accomplishes a change of status by making use of the
same principle.

---

[11] Indeed, this type of subterfuge has been done with slavery in other societies.
In Rome, for instance, people occasionally sold their sons to a friend who
possessed a higher level of citizenship than their own. The friend would then free
the son, who would take on the citizenship of his "ex-master."

A. Rabbi Tarfon said, "It is possible to purify *mamzers* [from their defective ancestry]. How so?
B. "[Take the case of] a *mamzer* who 'marries' a bondwoman, [their] offspring is a bondman.
C. "If [the offspring] is freed, the son [*sic*] becomes a freedman."
D. Rabbi Eliezer said, "Lo, the [offspring] is a bondman-*mamzer*."

M. Qid. 3:13[12]

Tarfon obviously sees a systemic possibility similar to the one we observed, namely, that a member of the Israelite community, a *mamzer* in this case, could improve his offspring's caste status by having that offspring pass through slavery. Eliezer also sees the possibility but wishes to prevent it from happening. The significant point about this passage is that it shows two of the Mishnah's tradents consciously standing back from the system and commenting on the implications of its systemic logic. In this way, the Mishnah's framers provide further evidence of the power of the category of the bondman — and by extension that of the freedman — to redefine a person's ethnic and caste background.

We should not forget, however, that the categories of bondman and freedman were not designed to accomplish the feat of bringing a person into Israelite society or of changing the status of a member of that society. The latter point is clear from Eliezer's comment above. He sees the capacity of slavery to change an Israelite's caste status as an undesirable side-effect. Similarly, the framers did not design the two categories for the purpose of bringing foreigners into the Israelite community. For that purpose, they designed the category of proselyte, which enables a non-Israelite to enter Israelite society in a much more direct manner. Thus, the capacity of slavery to bring outsiders in and to change the caste origins of those already in is, from the system's point of view, a side-effect and not the main purpose of the scheme of slavery. The ultimate purpose of the category of bondman, as we saw, is to ensure that a slave's master has the greatest degree of control possible over his slave, while the purpose of the category of freedman is to ensure that the ex-slave is free from his former master's control and has a position of his own in Israelite society.

---

[12] Later writers approve this maneuver. See for example Maimonides, *Mishneh Torah*, Forbidden Intercourse, 15:4.

Part Three

The Mishnah's System of Slavery

Chapter Six

Freedom and Slavery

The overall purpose of the Mishnah's bondman — the purpose to which all his attributes point — is to be his master's human tool. This statement has two important implications. First, since the bondman belongs to his master, he is the master's tool to use. He cannot be controlled by other individuals, by social institutions, or even by the bondman himself. Second, if he is a "tool," the householder must use him to perform specified tasks. When the framers discuss the labor the bondman does for his master, they describe particular tasks assigned to him by his master that he carries out at definite periods of time. These jobs have a clear beginning and end; they are not a general form of ongoing labor. To say that the bondman is a tool, then, is to say he is like a hammer. When a householder decides to use a hammer for a certain task, he picks up the hammer and uses it. When he completes the task, he puts the hammer away until the next time he needs it. The Mishnah's framers view the householder's use of his bondman in a similar manner. A householder decides that a particular task should be done by his bondman and then "uses" him. He informs his slave of the required task and the bondman then performs it. Once the job is completed, the bondman has nothing more to do. Like the hammer, the householder "sets aside" the bondman until the next task. Thus the bondman is not merely a rung on a social scale, the framers design him to be used by his master.

The Mishnah of course recognizes a difference between hammers and human beings that causes difficulties in treating them alike as tools. In fact, the very feature that makes the bondman a useful tool — his humanity — also makes him a dangerous one. The bondman has the capacity to act on his own cognizance, for the master can set his slave to a task and then leave him to execute it. But this capacity also enables the bondman to act on his own without his master's instructions. He can potentially perform deeds that his master does not wish, even deeds that can cause the master serious harm. To avoid this, the Mishnah's framers enable the master to restrict the bondman's exercise of his own powers. This tension between the householder's capacity to use the bondman's powers and to restrict the bondman's own use of his powers comprises the picture of slavery presented by the system of the Mishnah. Let us take a moment to examine the elements of this tension, beginning with the restrictions.

The restrictions the householder places on his bondman take two forms, the individual and the social. On the level of the individual, as we have seen, the restrictions focus on the bondman's capacity to exercise his personal power. These restrictions become clear in comparison to the householder, who has none. The householder provides a clear example of the powers possessed by free human beings. He possesses the capacity to use the three forms of personal power: power exercised through acts requiring reason, power transmitted through relationships, and power expressed by merely physical acts and bodily conditions.[1] By contrast, two of the bondman's powers lie under the control of his master, the power of acts requiring reason and the power based on relationships. The bondman thus lacks the capacity freely to use either one. He can cause legal effects through just one form of power, that of merely physical acts and bodily conditions.

When we change our focus from the individual by himself to the individual in society, we discover that the framers acknowledge only the bondman's physical presence in Israelite society. Like a cow, the bondman's existence is recognized by the framers, but he lacks the legal capacity to participate in the social life of the community. We can appreciate this aspect of slavery when we compare the bondman's position to the householder's. The householder has the capacity to exercise his personal power as he chooses, but he can also be required to exercise his power by other individuals or by social institutions. In this way, sages balance one individual's power against the same powers held by other Israelites and against the power of social institutions. In slavery, by contrast, the framers do not balance the bondman's personal power against that of other members of society but instead altogether deny him the capacity to exercise his power. In fact, each of the two features just mentioned — the capacity to exercise power freely and the requirement to exercise it as demanded by others — corresponds to a different type of the bondman's personal power that his master controls. First, acts requiring reason constitute the only power that can be exercised by choice. Since the master controls the bondman's use of this form of power, the slave cannot exercise freely any of his powers. Second, as I shall explain in a moment, the power of relationships provides a means by which one individual can require another to do what he wants. By denying the bondman the capacity to have relationships, the master prevents others from controlling him. In this way, the master's domination of his bondman renders the bondman incapable of acting on his own in a social context and thus transforms him into a suitable object for use as a tool.

This brings us finally to the most important aspect of slavery, a master's capacity to have his bondman perform his wishes. The master accomplishes this feat through his faculty of will — that is, his own capacity to plan his actions

---

[1] See the discussion of these powers in Chapter Three.

in advance and to act in accordance with those plans. In effect, the Mishnah's authorities imagine that the master's will replaces that of the bondman. The bondman can thus effectively perform only his master's dictates, not his own inclinations. Indeed, the bondman constitutes an extension of his master's will. Furthermore, since the actions performed by both the master's own body and the bondman ultimately stem from the master's decisions, the bondman can be likened to his master's body, specifically, his hand. Take the example of a householder who wishes to slaughter a Passover lamb.[2] The householder can decide to slaughter a Passover sacrifice. When he does it, the Temple cult grants full recognition to his action. If a bondman chooses, on his own cognizance, to slaughter a Passover sacrifice, the Temple cult does not recognize that act of worship. If a master assigns his slave the task of slaughtering the lamb, however, the cult treats the slave's act as valid. But the cult recognizes the act as effective for the master, not for the bondman. In both instances, the householder's will brings about the same result — the cult accrediting the householder with the sacrifice. By having the master supply the power of will for both, the actions of the bondman become the actions of the master. The framers thus identify the bondman with his master on both mental and physical levels. This identification constitutes the Mishnah's ultimate distinction between slavery and freedom; slavery alters the constituent elements of human freedom — will and action — by sharing some of the bondman's abilities with his master and by denying the bondman the rest. In this way, the framers portray slavery in terms of their concept of freedom. To comprehend slavery as a whole, therefore, we must conclude our study by analyzing freedom.[3]

Freedom

For the Mishnah's system, we can define freedom in terms of the householder's power of will. Freedom constitutes the householder's capacity to exercise his will as he chooses, offset by his responsibility to exercise his will

---

[2] See the discussions of M. Pes. 8:2 in Chapters Three and Four.

[3] It is necessary to investigate the concepts of slavery and freedom by focusing on the abstract ideas rather than by doing a philological investigation of the Mishnah's terms for them. This is because, first, they occur in only two passages and, second, the Hebrew terms as used by the Mishnah do not constitute generalizations about the states of beings enslaved or of being free. First, the Hebrew word translated into english as slavery, avdut (עבדות), refers in the Mishnah only to the people Israel when they were in slavery in Egypt. (See M. Pes. 10:4.) It never refers to the bondman or his condition. Similarly, the Mishnah's word which is usually translated into English as freedom, herut (חרות), refers either to the status of the freedman just after manumission or to the people Israel after going out from Egypt. (See M. Pes. 10:4, M. Naz. 9:1.) It never indicates Israelites who have never themselves been enslaved. The concepts of slavery and freedom in the Mishnah are a matter of unexpressed ideology rather than of philologically explicit terminology.

as required by other individuals or by social institutions. This definition permits the framers to balance the power of the individual against the power of society. The first element of freedom emphasizes the power of the individual. Specifically, the householder has the free capacity to exercise his will according to his wishes. He can do what he wants and Israelite society recognizes his actions as effective.[4] The second element of freedom focuses on the power of society over the individual. That is, people and institutions within the community can require a householder to exercise his will to perform a particular action. For example, one householder can require another to repay a loan (M. BM 5:8-9); the Temple cult can require a householder to bring a certain sacrifice at a particular time (M. Pes. 5:1-10). The individual is not powerless in the face of Israelite society, however, for the framers hold that the householder must use his power of will to perform the actions required of him. That is, he must freely choose to exercise his will to fulfill his obligations; the other parties may not use physical coercion to enforce their demands. They can channel his exercise of will in particular directions, but they cannot override it.[5] The Mishnah's authorities thus balance the power of Israelite society with the power of its individual members.

As to the slave, the Mishnah's authorities deny him both the free capacity to exercise his will and the capacity to be controlled by social institutions or individuals other than his master. This denial is significant, for it removes the bondman in and of himself from participation in Israelite society; he cannot interact with others and others cannot interact with him. To appreciate the contrast between slavery and freedom, we must explore the full meaning of both elements of freedom to the householder.

The Mishnah's framers base the householder's power of will on his capacity to reason. Reason constitutes the mind's ability to understand information and ideas. A person's will, by contrast, comprises his capacity to use reason to deliberate and to make decisions regarding his future actions.[6] The householder's

---

[4] In Mortimer J. Adler's classification of different concepts of freedom, this element of the Mishnah's idea of freedom falls into his category of "the freedom of Self-Determination." See Adler, pp. 400-584.

[5] Of course, there are social pressures on the householder to carry out his required duties, but in the Mishnah's system such pressures do not interfere with the householder's exercise of his will.

[6] Beginning with Augustine, western thought has treated the will as a separate faculty of mind. It is often set in opposition to the "intellect." See the important study of Albrecht Dihle, *The Concept of Will in Antiquity* and R. Kane's *Free Will and Values* (pp. 15-20). The idea of will as a "faculty" has come under strong attack, most notably by Gilbert Ryle in his *The Concept of Mind*. Ryle's book has had significant influence on subsequent discussions of the issue, as exemplified by Kane's explicit rejection of the term "faculty" in preference for "power" and "set" (pp. 19-20). By contrast, the concept of will held by the

power of will thus enables him to consider possible courses of action and their ramifications so that he can arrive at a reasoned judgment about what he wants to do. Judgments of will fall into two categories, the overall goal that the householder wishes to achieve and the plan of action by which he intends to achieve it.[7] The simple case of a carpenter provides a clear example of this distinction. Using his power of will, the carpenter forms the goal of building a table and then plans a course of action to accomplish that goal. For this plan, he may decide first to obtain lumber, then cut it to size, and then join the pieces. The householder then performs his plan, which, if he does it correctly, results in a table. In this way, the Mishnah's sages imagine a direct progression from the householder's will to his actions.[8]

Will ==> Goal ==> Plan ==> Actions

The householder's capacity to exercise his will to perform actions is important, because his exercise brings about changes in the world around him; that is, it causes results. If the householder could not cause results in this way, then his free capacity to exercise his will would be meaningless; he could effectively do nothing. The householder's capacity to achieve goals and effect changes makes his power of will significant. The Mishnah's system recognizes two types of results, material and legal, both of which stem from acts of will. Material results constitute the physical changes that take place in an object as the outcome of person's actions. For example, if a man pushes a barrel, the barrel moves. If he cuts a cow's throat, the cow dies. The link between goal, action and result is straightforward. A householder uses his power of will to determine a goal and then again to formulate a plan to achieve that goal. He then puts that plan into action, which brings about a palpable alteration in the object worked upon. Thus for material results there is a direct path from willed goal to its achievement, as we can see from this diagram.

Goal ==> Plan ==> Actions ==> Material Results

Mishnah's framers treats the will as part of the power of reason, not as a distinct entity.

[7] My portrayal of goal and plan appear similar to the terms "plan" and "purpose" as used by Howard Eilberg-Schwartz in his depiction of the Mishnah's scheme of intention. In fact, my scheme derives in part from his study. (See Eilberg-Schwartz.) However, there is an important difference that must be noted. Specifically, my concept of plan has no corresponding notion in Eilberg-Schwartz' scheme; both his concepts of "plan" and "purpose" fit into my concept of goal. The distinction between his two terms, so far as I can tell, is that "plan" indicates a goal that a householder intends to carry out but has not yet done so, while a "purpose" comprises the goal that accompanied a person's action.

[8] I do not mean to imply that there is a cause-effect link between the householder's will and his action; the Mishnah's framers provide no clear evidence with regard to that issue.

Legal results, or legal effects as we have been calling them, consist of the changes in legal status that derive from an individual's deeds. These results stem from the combination of the material results of a person's acts and the goal with which he performed them.[9] In this scheme, the householder's goal plays a double role, it first determines his actions and then afterwards helps to dictate the legal effects of those actions. The following diagram shows this double role.

1.   Goal ==> Plan ==> Actions ==> Material Results

2.   Material Results + Goal ==> Legal Results

We can illustrate this scheme with the example of a priest who slaughters a lamb as an animal offering. From this type of sacrifice, the priest may eat some of the meat, provided he consumes it within the Temple precincts and during a specified time period. When the priest performs the sacrifice, the material result is that the lamb is dead and cut up into different sections (M. Zeb. 2:5).[10] But do his actions produce the legal effect of a valid sacrifice? That depends on the priest's intention — his goal — with regard to using his portion of the animal. If his intention was to eat the animal according to the cultic rules — that is, he formed the goal of treating it as a sacrifice — then the sacrifice is valid. If the priest intends to break the rules by eating the meat outside the Temple court or after the proper time — his goal does not treat it as a sacrifice — then the sacrifice is invalid.   The priest's willed goal is thus a crucial factor for determining the effects of his actions. In both cases the material outcome of his deeds are the same, but the legal result depends on the householder's willed goal in conjunction with the material result. In this way, then, the householder can freely use his power of will to produce both material and legal results.

This brings us to the second element of freedom, the capacity of individuals and social institutions to require a householder to exercise his will at a particular moment and for a particular purpose.[11] At first glance, this creates a problem,

---

[9] See Howard Eilberg-Schwartz's study for an analysis of the Mishnah's portrayal of the relation between a person's intention, his action, and their legal results. Let me note a difference in the area where our studies overlap. Eilberg-Schwartz shows that in the Mishnah mere intention can cause legal effects; the scheme I present in this chapter does not entertain this possibility. The apparent difference is merely one of focus.   Eilberg-Schwartz investigates all results of a householder's intentions, while I restrict my analysis to the question of whether a person fulfills his or her intended goal. Although I suppose that it is possible, I know of no case in the Mishnah where an intended goal achieves fulfillment through mere intention.

[10] See Eilberg-Schwartz's discussion of this passage on pp. 149-152.

[11] Why do individuals and institutions have the capacity to require deeds of a householder in the first place? The answer is, to balance the individual's power of will with other individuals' power of will and with the power of social

for the power to require a householder to perform certain deeds appears to override the householder's free exercise of will. The framers resolve this apparent contradiction by holding that the householder must not merely do the required task, but must want to do it. That is, he must choose of his own will to perform the expected act by internalizing the requirement, making it his own, and then performing it.[12] If he simply performs the deed, without willing it, then the deed does not bear the necessary legal effects. In fact, in terms of the required action, it is as if the householder had done nothing. In the state of freedom, therefore, a householder freely exercises his will, whether on his own or as expected by others. Let me describe how the individual's free capacity to exercise his will is compatible with the ability of others to require him to perform certain actions.

The capacity to dictate the deeds of others that affect their will comes about through a mechanism I call a "relationship of control" (or a "control relationship"). This type of relationship constitutes a link between two people or between a person and a social institution, which gives one party the power to require the other to exercise his will towards a certain goal. The second party is expected to adopt that goal as his own and execute it. What is important is that this process does not interfere with the householder's unfettered use of his will, but simply adds a prior step.

1. Goal (Outside party's) ==> Goal (Householder's)

2. Goal (Householder's) ==> Plan (Householder's) ==>

   Actions (Householder's) ==> Material Results

3. Material Results + Goal (Householder's) ==> Legal Results

The significant point is that the householder's will determines every part of this process except the original goal. At step one, the householder takes the required goal and, by choice, makes it his own. Then, at step two, he plans a course of action to achieve that goal and carries it out. At step three, the householder's goal combines with the material result to determine the legal effects. If he does not will the proper results, then they do not happen and the outside party's

---

institutions. When a number of householders get together and exercise their wills, as frequently happens in a community, the possibility of conflict between them arises. The Mishnah's authorities avoid such conflict by enabling householders to require others to do particular acts and by permitting Israelite social institutions — such as the Temple, the market place, or the courts — to likewise require specific deeds of householders. By performing the actions required of him, each householder helps to maintain good relations with the other members of the community and to further the goals of Israelite society, such as worship at the Temple cult.

[12] Eilberg-Schwartz describes in detail how this transfer of intention takes place between householders and priests. The priest who offers a householder's sacrifice must take on the householder's intention regarding that animal. See pp. 145-180.

requirement is not fulfilled. For relationships of control, then, even though an outside party — another member of Israelite society or a social institution — can require a householder to perform a certain goal, the householder must choose to fulfill that goal. He cannot be forced against his will.

Now that we understand how the householder can be required to perform particular acts and still retain his freedom of will, let me describe the control relationships in concrete detail. These details are important to understanding the difference between freedom and slavery because they are present in freedom and lacking in slavery. Control relationships fall into two classes, temporary and permanent. First, in a temporary control relationship, the controlling party requires the householder to perform one particular act. Once the householder performs the act, the relationship ceases. For example, a temporary relationship of control between a householder and another individual arises when a householder injures that person. This sets up a relationship in which the injured party requires the householder to pay damages (M. BQ 8:1). The link exists as long as the money remains unpaid; when the perpetrator pays the required amount, the relationship ceases. Temporary control relationships between householders and the institution of the Temple cult function in a similar manner. If a householder contracts uncleanness, for example, he enters a control relationship with the Temple cult that requires him to attain purity. While he remains in an unclean state, the Temple can demand that he purify himself and can even enforce its demands by barring him from the Temple precincts. Once the householder purifies himself, the Temple loses its power over him in this matter.

Second, two key differences exist between permanent relationships of control and temporary relationships. First, in permanent relationships, the dominant party obligates the other to perform many different deeds and, second, none of these deeds ever causes the relationship to cease. In a permanent control relationship between a householder and another individual, the householder must perform different activities on a continual or periodic basis. This is the case in a marriage, where husband and wife each stand in a control relationship to the other. Each must regularly perform certain activities for the other, which are usually defined on a daily or weekly basis. The wife must cook and sew for her husband, for instance, while the husband must maintain his wife by providing food and clothing (M. Ket. 5:5, 8-9). In a permanent control relationship between a householder and the Temple cult, by contrast, the required actions are linked to a cyclical calendar of years, months, and weeks. Tasks must be performed at particular moments or within certain time periods. Once a householder performs a required task, he becomes free from that duty until the next calendar cycle. For instance, at the time of harvest, the householder must separate tithes for the Temple cult and deliver them to Jerusalem. This task becomes required the moment he brings his grain in from the field and it must be accomplished before he consumes it. Once he does this, the householder has fulfilled his duty and does not have to perform the task until the following year's harvest. Although the householder's requirement to perform that specific task is over, his control relationship with the Temple cult remains. In these ways, then, individuals and social institutions such as the Temple cult can require a householder to exercise his will to perform tasks for them. Freedom thus provides the householder with the right to exercise his will as he chooses and the responsibility to exercise it, when necessary, on behalf of other Israelites and the community institutions.

When we look beyond the householder to the other categories of persons in Israelite society, we discover an important point about freedom. The extent to which the members of a category can freely exercise their will correlates with the extent to which they can enter a relationship of control. That is to say, the more latitude with which people can exercise their will, the broader the variety of ways by which individuals and institutions can require them to exercise their will. The standard is of course set by the householder, as we have just observed. For the category of the wife, there is also a correspondence between her capacity to exercise will and her capacity to enter relationships of control. In both cases, this capacity is less than that of the householder. A husband, for example, can cancel the vows that his wife took of her own will. Correspondingly, the wife cannot enter many of the relationships of control that her husband can enter. She does not enter a relationship of control by injuring someone, nor does she have a required cultic role.

This brings us to our starting point, the bondman. For the category of the bondman, a correspondence likewise exists between the ability to exercise will and the ability to enter relationships of control. But it is a negative one. He possesses neither the free capacity to exercise his will nor the ability to enter relationships of control. Thus, we discern a correspondence between the two elements of freedom. The capacity to exercise will and the capacity to enter relationships of control not only define freedom, but also indicate the degree of freedom possessed by various categories of persons. The householder constitutes the most free category, the wife a slightly less free category, and the bondman comprises a category totally lacking in freedom. That is why, to understand slavery, we need to determine its full effects on the bondman's will.

Slavery

The correlation between the two elements of freedom explains why slavery is more than the mere lack of freedom. It is the transformation of a person into a human tool. This transformation comes about when the master brings his bondman's power of will under his own control. In doing so, the master changes the bondman's power of will — which, if the bondman were free, would comprise the essential component of his freedom — into the operative element of his slavery. By controlling his bondman's will, the master can use the slave's will as if it were his own. He can send the slave to exercise the slave's own will in performing a task, but the legal effects of that performance are the same as if the householder himself had done it. Therefore, the householder can use the bondman's will as a tool for accomplishing his own goals and the bondman cannot use his will independently of his master. That is why we must now return to our opening comparison, the bondman and the common hammer. A householder can use a hammer to help him build a table. When not in use, however, the hammer lies where it was placed, doing nothing. It obviously has no capacity to build a table by itself. The state of slavery imposes upon the bondman the human equivalent of the status of the inert hammer. On the one hand, when the master uses his slave, the slave exercises his will solely to help accomplish the master's goals. In this way, the bondman and his will become an extension of the master's will. On the other hand, when the master does not use the slave, the slave becomes as inert as the hammer. When the bondman is not performing a task for his master, the master's control renders him incapable of using his will to cause legal effects. This, then, is the human equivalent of being inert. The slave lacks both aspects of freedom, not only the capacity to exercise his will effectively, but also the capacity to enter relationships of control.

Let me first consider the bondman as a tool in use. By reverting to the terms of our analysis of freedom, we can see how the bondman's will constitutes the central component of slavery. Although both hammers and bondmen can be considered as tools, they differ considerably in how they help a householder accomplish his goals. This difference lies in the distinction between material results and legal results. Material results, we recall, comprise the physical changes a person's actions bring about in material objects; legal results constitute the changes in the legal status of objects effected by a person's deeds. The householder can use the hammer to cause material results, while the master's control over his slave enables him to use the bondman to effect legal results. When we understand how both tools — hammer and human — fit into a householder's exercise of will, we shall grasp how the bondman and his power of will serve as his master's tool.

The case of the hammer is straightforward; it has no capacity to interact with the householder's will at all. The householder can use it to help him only at the stage of actions, as shown by this diagram.

Goal ==> Plan ==> Actions (Householder using hammer) ==>Material
    Results

This diagram reveals two points that are important for the comparison between the hammer and the slave. First, the hammer's role in producing the material results is passive. It only helps the householder to accomplish his goal when the householder himself wields it. Second, the hammer clearly has no effect on the householder's exercise of will; the action for which the householder uses the hammer stems directly from his own will. Thus the direct line from the householder's will to the material results is unaffected by the householder's use of a hammer.

The householder's capacity to use his bondman as a tool is similar to his capacity to use the hammer, but is complicated by the bondman's power of will. For the master to use his bondman as a tool, he must control the bondman's exercise of will, but the bondman must be able to use his will in order to act and thereby be a useful tool. The Mishnah's authorities resolve this dilemma by permitting the bondman to use his will to bring about material results while having the master's will determine the deed's ultimate legal results. We can diagram this in a three-stage process.

1. Goal (Master's) ==> Goal (Bondman's)

2. Goal (Bondman's) ==>Plan (Bondman's) ==>

    Actions (Bondman's) ==>Material Results (Bondman's)

3. Material Results + Goal (Master's at time of bondman's actions) ==>

    Legal Results (Master's)

Three points make clear the master's domination of his bondman's will. First, the bondman takes on his master's goal (Step 1). This process is similar to a free householder becoming an agent. The differences are that the master can force the bondman to perform the task, the bondman is always available for such jobs and that in most cases the bondman's actions are effective only when he acts as an agent for his master. Second, the bondman then uses his own power of will to plan and carry out a course of action to achieve that goal (Step 2). But in the end, it is the master's willed goal, not the bondman's, that determines the legal results of the bondman's deeds (Step 3). Third, the legal results are credited to the master, not to the slave (Step 3). It is as if the master himself and not his slave performed the actions.

The case of the householder who assigns his slave to separate priestly rations from his harvested crop (M. Ter. 3:4) demonstrates these points. The bondman makes the master's willed goal his own and then performs it. The slave uses his will to choose which part of the crop to sanctify and then physically separates that produce from the rest. Through this physical act, the bondman fulfills his master's goal. The important point here is that the master's goal is fulfilled, not the bondman's. This becomes more clear if the householder changes his mind after giving the bondman the assignment. If the householder decides that he does not want the bondman to separate priestly rations before the bondman performs the deed, then the bondman's act bears no legal effects. The householder's goal at the point of action determines the deed's legal effects. Since the householder's goal at the time of the bondman's act was that the bondman should not sanctify the produce, that is the legal result —

despite the bondman's actions and his exercise of his will. Thus, in the legal realm, the master's will dominates and overrides the will of the bondman. The bondman can use his own will to achieve the necessary material result, but the master's will dictates the legal results. In this way, the master uses his bondman's will as a tool.

The other aspect of being a tool, as we argued, is the capacity to lie inert when not in use. The bondman can neither exercise his will freely nor enter into relationships of control. That is the bondman's inertia. To begin with, the Mishnah's framers strip the bondman of the free capacity to exercise his will; the bondman, like a hammer, thus lacks the ability to "use himself." Sages accomplish this not by denying the bondman's humanity — his power of will — but rather by affirming the master's power over this human characteristic. In sages' view, the bondman possesses the power of will and potentially can exercise it, but the bondman's master can cancel the legal effects of that exercise. Thus, the bondman can exercise his will, but he cannot do so effectively, which from the perspective of the law, means that he cannot exercise his will. The case of the bondman taking a Nazirite vow illustrates this point clearly. The bondman can take the vow to become a Nazirite and the cult treats that vow as effective. But the bondman's master can cancel that vow, rendering it and its effects null and void. In this way, the master deprives his bondman of the first element of freedom.

The Mishnah's framers extend the bondman's inert status beyond even the hammer's inertia. Anyone can pick a hammer and use it, but a bondman can be used only by his master. No social institution or individual other than a bondman's owner can force the bondman to perform a deed. (With one exception to be discussed in a moment.) The householder preserves his exclusive right of use by denying his bondman the second element of freedom. I refer to the capacity of social institutions and individual members of Israelite society to require him to exercise his will. The master's control over his bondman prevents the bondman from entering both permanent and temporary relationships of control with others. First, the bondman cannot enter any permanent relationship of control because his master has cancelled his power to hold relationships of any kind. Second, since the master controls his bondman's exercise of acts requiring reason, the bondman cannot enter any temporary relationships of control that have their origin in an act requiring reason. The case of the bondman injuring another Israelite — an act requiring reason — provides a good example of this point. When the bondman injures another person, he does not enter a relationship of control that requires him to pay damages, as would a free Israelite.[13]   The bondman thus cannot enter a relationship of control with anyone.

---

[13] See Chapter Three for a detailed discussion of these cases.

This brings into sharp contrast the distinction between freedom and slavery. In freedom, the sign of the householder's liberty was his broad capacity to enter into relationships of control in many different ways with many different people and social institutions. The sign of slavery, by contrast, is the bondman's inability to enter a relationship of control with anyone. The bondman possesses only one relationship, namely, to his master. But even that bond is not a relationship of control, for the master in no way recognizes the bondman's right freely to exercise his own will. Not only is the bondman incapable of exercising his will on his own, he cannot be required by others to exercise it.

There is one exception to the master's power to prevent the bondman entering into relationships of control with other parties. These are relationships caused by merely physical acts and bodily conditions, the most common of which is the contraction of uncleanness. The householder cannot prevent such relationships, as we recall, because these acts and conditions are simply uncontrollable. Thus when the bondman becomes impure, he enters a relationship of control with the Temple cult that requires him to purify himself just as if he were a free person. Although this constitutes an intrusion on the master's control over his slave, the master ultimately benefits from it, for it enables the master to have the bondman perform tasks for him within the Temple cult. If the bondman was not considered part of the system of purity, then, like a gentile, he could not even enter the Temple.

This brings us back to the question from which our investigation began: is the Mishnah's category of slavery, the bondman, similar to its categories of citizens, women or oxen? The answer is both yes and no. Yes, the bondman shares important characteristics with each of these categories. But no, in the end his definitive features distinguish him from them. Let us recall the similarities. First, bondmen and bondwomen are like citizens — that is, householders — in that the Mishnah's framers consider them to be Israelites. They are subject to the cultic system of purity and can enter the Temple. This is a privilege reserved only for people who clearly belong to Israelite society, not foreigners or marginal persons, such as Samaritans or those of uncertain parentage. Even if the bondman was born outside the people Israel, as we observed, his enslavement makes him into an Israelite. Second, slaves are like Israelite women in that they lack any assigned role in the Temple cult. They are not required to worship or to participate in any functions on their own. The only festivities in which women and slaves take part are those that the householder must celebrate with his household. Third, like oxen, bondmen and bondwomen are living creatures that are owned by their master. They constitute property that can be bought and sold without their consent. Slaves then have important similarities with each of these categories.

In contrast to these similarities are the differences between the bondman and each category. These differences focus on the bondman's capacity of will and hence on the fundamental distinction between slavery and freedom. In each case, the differences occur within the context of shared characteristics. First, the bondman and the ox are both living, moving creatures owned by an Israelite. But the bondman, unlike the ox, has the power of will. The issue of slavery and freedom is not even relevant to the ox. Second, the bondman, like the woman, cannot effectively exercise his will as he chooses. Both possess the capacity of will but have their ability to exercise it restricted by the householder. However, the woman's will is merely restricted, but the bondman's is taken over by his master. Third, the householder and the bondman are alike in that they participate in the Israelite community by using their will. But the householder uses his will to participate in Israelite society for himself, while the bondman uses his will to help his master participate in the Israelite community. Not only is the bondman's will restricted, but when he can use it, he uses it for the benefit of his master. This distinction then constitutes the ultimate difference between the free man and the slave. The householder uses his will to participate fully in freedom. The bondman's potential to exercise freedom — his capacity of will — is absorbed by his master in order to assist the master in exercising his own freedom.

Finally, the results of this study point beyond the category of the bondman to the system of the Mishnah as a whole. What we learn from the analysis of how the Mishnah's system deals with the slave teaches us much about how that system solves any other problem. When the Mishnah's framers confront a problem of classification, of placing an unclassified group of objects into the taxonomic system, they identify and place that group by undertaking two distinct processes. They first compare like to like, and they second contrast like to unlike. These exercises serve primarily to designate a category's definitive characteristics and also to identify the less important attributes of its members. Furthermore, by these same means, the framers set the category into the hierarchy of the Mishnah's system, that is, they place what was unknown into relationship with what was known. That is why, by way of conclusion, we point to thought about the slave — like but unlike the ox, the woman, and the citizen — as an instance of hierarchization through the taxonomic processes of comparison and contrast. For it is through a process of comparison and contrast that the framers in the aggregate work out the structure of their system. Only in this way can they work out that orderly and balanced proportion, that sense of the whole in relationship to the parts, that for them constitute structure and system.

Annotated Bibliography

In this annotated bibliography I evaluate different studies of slavery in terms of the concerns and methods of my own investigation. In this way, I attempt to place my work within the larger spectrum of the scholarly inquiry into different forms of slavery — most from the ancient world. Thus, these are not "reviews" in the strict sense of the word; they do not provide measured accounts of authors' questions, methods, or results. The selected texts fall into three categories: I point out works that share with my study important assumptions or approaches to investigating slavery, writings that contain ideas I found helpful, and important studies that have no relation at all to my work. For works in this last category, my intention is merely to make clear that we do not share the same agenda. I do not mean to criticize the authors for failing to fulfill goals that they did not have.

Moses I. Finley, "Between Slavery and Freedom," in Moses I. Finley, *Economy and Society in Ancient Greece*, Brent D. Shaw and Richard P. Saller, eds., (New York: Viking, 1982).

In this article, Professor Finley proposes a procedure for ascertaining the slave's position in society. He suggests the formation of a scale for ranking different categories of a society in relationship to each other. The scholar should take different classes of people — such as laborers, merchants, government officials, soldiers, and so on — and place them on this scale according to criteria such as legal rights, freedom of movement, economic rights, and so on. The rights of the slave in these areas can then be evaluated and his social location in relation to other categories determined.[1] This suggestion forms the nucleus for the method by which I attempt to locate the bondman in Israelite society. However, to apply it to the Mishnah's image of Israelite society, I had to make significant

---

[1] Although this suggestion found widespread acknowledgment and approval neither Finley nor any other scholar has attempted to take it up in a monograph-length study.

modifications.[2] In particular, I had to transform the scale from one dimension to two. On the horizontal axis (which corresponds to Finley's only axis, I think), the slave is not to be compared to categories of society, such as craftsmen, day laborers and so on, but to categories of the household, namely, women, minors and the head of the household. On the vertical scale, we find that the Mishnah's framers rank the free householder — and, at a secondary level, the members of his household — against other free householders. Here, the different classes of "free" householders, such as priests, levites, and so forth, become important.[3] The Mishnah's authorities do not place the slave in direct comparison to these categories, but only indirectly through the householder.

Isaac Mendelsohn, *Slavery in the Ancient Near East: A Comparative Study of Slavery in Babylonia, Assyria, Syria and Palestine; From the Middle of the Third Millennium to the End of the First Millennium*, (Oxford:Oxford University Press, 1949).

Mendelsohn's mode of comparison falls into the class of comparisons that Jonathan Z. Smith labels as "encyclopedic," a form of comparison that Smith shows to be without theoretical foundation.[4] Thus, from the vantage point of my study of slavery in the system of the Mishnah, Mendelsohn provides a classic example of how not to study slavery. First, Professor Mendelsohn lacks any concept of a society as a system at a particular point in time. When describing slavery in any of the societies on which his book focuses, he draws upon data that may be separated in time by 1500 years or more. He treats each society as a monolith whose characteristics did not change. Second, Mendelsohn makes no attempt to perform comprehensive or systematic comparisons. He simply brings up topics relevant to slavery, such as legal rights, marriage, slave marks and so on, and presents data from the different cultures about it. He makes no attempt to understand the data in the context of its own society nor, as with Patterson, does he ever present a complete picture of slavery in any of the cultures. Mendelsohn merely collects and arranges data about slaves.

Suzanne Miers and Igor Kopytoff, "African 'Slavery' as an Institution of Marginality," in Suzanne Miers and Igor Kopytoff, eds., *Slavery in Africa: Historical and Anthropological Perspectives*, (Madison: University of Wisconsin Press, 1977).

---

[2] These modifications may have been necessitated only by difference between Greek societies to which Finley refers and the Israelite society that my study investigates. I do not know whether or not they apply to any Greek society.

[3] The horizontal aspect of the scale — the household — is discussed in Chapters Two and Three, while the vertical aspect — Israelite society — is described in Chapter Four.

[4] See Smith, "Comparison."

This article constitutes a thoughtful introductory essay to an important collection of studies on slavery in different cultures. Each essay treats slavery within its own social context and attempts to show how it fits into the society. The essays are, in essence, analyses of slavery within a system. The introductory article builds on the strength of these individual studies. Its central emphasis is on the marginal status of the slave to the society in which he lives. Despite this marginality, the slave is incorporated into the community, and different steps are taken to replace his previous identity with a new one. For African societies, this incorporated marginality with the reidentification of the slave forms the central feature of slavery, not the issue of property status.[5]

R. Morrow, *Plato's Law of Slavery in its Relation to Greek Law,* (Urbana, IL: University of Illinois Press, 1939).

Professor Morrow focuses his study of slavery on Plato's *Laws.* The important methodological point for our study is that he articulates the difference between laws in a legal system and laws that were actually practiced, together with an approach for relating the two. Morrow begins by describing the *Laws* as a product of systematic thought; Plato explains his ideas of how to organize a Greek city. Morrow's aim is to discover whether any laws of Plato's imaginary city conform to laws that governed Athens during Plato's life. Thus even though Morrow recognizes Plato's *Laws* as a system, he does not attempt to explicate systematically the scheme of slavery contained in them. Instead, he focuses on those aspects of the scheme that correspond to the laws of Athens the accidents of time have preserved. The historicity of Plato's regulations is not a given, therefore, but a question. Morrow does not use Plato as a source for Athenian law but instead uses Athenian law to evaluate the relationship of Plato's thought to the social conditions of his time.

Orlando Patterson, *Slavery and Social Death: A Comparative Study,* (Cambridge, MA: Harvard University Press, 1982).

The relationship of Professor Patterson's work to my study of slavery is anomalous. On the one hand, he provides support to my work by demonstrating the inadequacy of many standard definitions of slavery. He shows that the concepts of the slave as property, as deprived of a legal personality, as a human "thing," and so on do not encompass the complexities of the subjugation of one human being to another. In opposition to this, he emphasizes the slave's position as a liminal human being incorporated into society.[6] The slave is not a

---

[5] Similar collections of studies of slavery in different societies have appeared since the publication of Miers and Kopytoff. See Watson, *Asian*; Lovejoy; Reid; and Willis. On slavery in Africa, see also Chanock.

[6] Patterson develops this concept beyond the point taken by Miers & Kopytoff.

convert or a proselyte, both of whom are outsiders that are changed into insiders. Instead, Patterson argues, society incorporates the slave as a liminal person. His liminality forms a constituent element of his nature and is not to be denied. It is this incongruity that makes the slave useful to his master.[7]

On the other hand, from the perspective of my study, the methods Patterson uses are incapable of achieving the goal he sets for his study. He wants to discover a definition of slavery that applies to all forms of slavery in all societies at any time in the history of the world. He attempts to achieve this task by a survey of what he considers to be the important attributes of slavery in all these different societies. However, at no point in the work does he systematically explicate the definition of slavery in the context of one slave-holding society. Patterson focuses so much attention on the cross-cultural comparison, that he never stops to understand in its own right any one culture and its concept of slavery.[8] So he never proves that his definition of slavery applies to even one society.

Norman Petersen, *Rediscovering Paul: Philemon and the Sociology of Paul's Narrative World*, (Philadelphia: Fortress, 1985).

This work constitutes an important methodological advance in the study of slavery in early Christianity and, indeed, of slavery in the ancient world in general. Petersen focuses on Paul's Letter to Philemon, the central character of which is Onesimus, a slave whom Paul has converted to Christianity. In the letter, Paul tries to persuade Onesimus' master, also a Christian, that Christianity alters the nature of master/slave relationships. Petersen uses literary and sociological methods to explore Paul's strategy of persuasion as well as the social and symbolic relationships to which he appeals in this strategy. From the perspective of our study of the Mishnah, we must highlight one, basic point; Petersen realizes that the world revealed in the letter — the social and symbolic relationships to which Paul refers — stems primarily from Paul's imagination. It is a "narrative world," not the real one. The idea that Paul's letter refers to a narrative world parallels our concept of the Mishnah's system. The main difference is that the Mishnah contains no narrative or story, just a system of laws. But the ramifications are the same. In both cases, the text constitutes not a link to the real world, but to the writer's/editors' imagined world.

---

[7] This is certainly the case for the bondman in the Mishnah. By emphasizing the slave as an Israelite member of Israelite society (incorporation) but denying his freedom (liminality), the Mishnah's sages enable the slave to serve his master as a living, thinking tool.

[8] Patterson's mode of comparison is also "encyclopedic." See Smith, "Comparison."

Gregory Vlastos, "Slavery in Plato's Republic," in *The Philosophical Review,* vol. 50 (1941), reprinted in Moses I. Finley, ed., *Slavery in Classical Antiquity,* (New York: Barnes and Noble, 1968).

This article constitutes the only study of slavery in Antiquity that approaches the problem of understanding a text's portrayal of slavery in the same way as mine. Professor Vlastos recognizes Plato's thought as a system and attempts to elucidate its concept of slavery in relationship to that system. He shows, in a manner similar to my study, that Plato's understanding of slavery forms a direct product of the central concern of the Platonic system. This central concern is the *logos,* which Plato uses to determine the nature of the cosmos, the state, human beings, and therefore even the lowly slave.

Alan Watson, *Roman Slave Law,* (Baltimore: Johns Hopkins, 1987).

This useful book by a premier authority on Roman Law presents a survey of the most important regulations concerning slaves in Roman Law. Professor Watson intends to provide a clear presentation of Roman slave law for the nonspecialist and he certainly achieves that goal.[9] From the perspective of our study, however, I must note that Watson does not explain the place of the slave laws within the system, or systems, of Roman Law. At no point does he examine the laws concerning the slave in comparison to those about the other social categories or to larger legal concepts. Like Mendelsohn (below), he organizes his book by identifying topics relevant to slavery and presenting laws concerning them.

William L. Westermann, *The Slave Systems of Greek and Roman Antiquity,* (Philadelphia: American Philosophical Society, 1955).

From the perspective of my study of slavery in the system of the Mishnah, Westermann's use of the term "system" is simply a misnomer. Westermann never analyzes slavery as a system nor does he ever describe a system of slavery. In fact, his work is not even synchronic but diachronic — and therefore anti-systemic. He describes different forms of slavery from the period of Homer up to that of Justinian. The descriptions take the form of social history — unsystematic discussions of the character of slavery — rather than comprehensive presentations of different systems of slavery.[10]

---

[9] For the specialist, Buckland provides a more detailed study.

[10] See the reviews mentioned in the Bibliography, under Finley, *Ideology,* pp. 52-55; Brunt; Ste. Croix; Wolff, "Westermann".

Abbreviations and Bibliography

This bibliography lists many of the works I consulted during the course of writing this book. It is not exhaustive. For a more complete listing of studies on Judaism in late antiquity, please refer to *The Study of Ancient Judaism*, 2 vols., Jacob Neusner, ed., (New York: KTAV, 1981).

Adler	Mortimer J. Adler, *The Idea of Freedom: A Dialectical Examination of the Conceptions of Freedom*, (Garden City, NY: Doubleday, 1968).
AJS	Association of Jewish Studies
AHR	*American Historical Review*
Albeck, *Mishnah*	H. Albeck, *The Six Orders of the Mishnah*, (Jerusalem and Tel Aviv: Mosad Bialik, 1957), (in Hebrew).
Anscombe	G. E. M. Anscombe, *Intention*, (Ithaca, NY: Cornell, 1957).
Anshen	Ruth Nanda Anshen, *Freedom: Its Meaning*, (New York: Harcourt, Brace, 1940).
Arak.	Arakhin
[Avery-]Peck, *Priestly Gift*	Alan J. [Avery-]Peck, *The Priestly Gift in Mishnah: A Study of Tractate Terumot*, (Chico, CA: Scholars Press, 1981).
Avery-Peck	Alan J. Avery-Peck, *Mishnah's Division of Agriculture: A History and Theology of Seder Zeraim*, (Chico, CA: Scholars Press, 1985).
Avery-Peck, "Law"	Alan J. Avery-Peck, "Law and Society in Early Judaism: Legal Evolution in the Mishnaic Division of Agriculture," in *NP I*, pp. 67-88.
AZ	Abodah Zarah
Babylonian Talmud	Israel Epstein, ed., *The Babylonian Talmud*, (London: Soncino, 1936-38).

Balch

David L. Balch, *Let Wives be Submissive: The Domestic Code in 1 Peter*, (Chico, CA: Scholars Press, 1981).

Baltzer

Klaus Baltzer, "Liberation from Debt Slavery After the Exile in Second Isaiah and Nehemiah," in *Ancient Israelite Religion: Essays in Honor of Frank Moore Cross*, Patrick D. Miller, Jr., Paul D. Hanson, & S. Dean McBride, eds., (Philadelphia: Fortress, 1987).

Bamberger

Bernard J. Bamberger, *Proselytism in the Talmudic Period*, (Cincinnati, OH: HUC, 1939), (repr. New York: KTAV, 1968).

Barrow

R. H. Barrow, *Slavery in the Roman Empire*, (London, 1928).

Barrow, "Freedmen"

R. H. Barrow, "Freedmen," *Oxford Classical Dictionary* (Oxford: Oxford, 1949), p. 371.

Bartchy

S. Scott Bartchy, *MALLON XRHSAI: First-Century Slavery and 1 Corinthians 7:21*, (Missoula, MT: Scholars Press, 1973).

Barzel

Y. Barzel, "An Economic Analysis of Slavery," *Journal of Law and Economics*, vol. 20, 1977.

BASOR

Bulletin of the American Schools of Oriental Research

Bavli

Babylonian Talmud

BB

Baba Batra

BDB

Francis Brown, S. R. Driver, and Charles A. Briggs, *A Hebrew and English Lexicon of the Old Testament*, (Oxford: Oxford, 1953).

Bek.

Bekhoroth

Ber.

Berakoth

Bernstein

Richard J. Bernstein, *Praxis and Action*, (Philadelphia: Univ. of Pennsylvania, 1971).

Berofsky

Bernard Berofsky, "Free Will and Determinism," in *Dictionary of the History of Ideas*, (New York: Scribner's, 1973), vol. 2, pp. 236-242.

Bert.

Obadiah b. Abraham of Bertinoro, *Commentary to Mishnah* (fifteenth century), reprinted in Romm edition of the Mishnah.

Bet.

Betzah

Bidney

David Bidney, ed., *The Concept of Freedom in Anthropology*, (The Hague: Mouton, 1963).

Bikk.   Bikkurim

Blair   William Blair, *An Inquiry into the State of Slavery
                         amongst the Romans; From the Earliest Period, Till
                         the Establishment of the Lombards in Italy*,
                         (Edinburgh: Thomas Clark, 1833, reprinted by Negro
                         History Press, Detroit, MI).

BM   Baba Metsia

Boecker   Hans Joche Boecker, *Law and the Administration of
                         Justice in the Old Testament and Ancient Near East*,
                         (Minneapolis: Augsburg, 1980), esp. pp. 155-183.

BQ   Baba Qamma

Bradie and Brand   Michael Bradie and Myles Brand, eds., *Action and
                         Responsibility*, (Bowling Green, OH: Philosophy,
                         Bowling Green State, 1980).

Brand   Myles Brand, ed., *The Nature of Human Action*,
                         (Glenview, IL: Scott, Foresman and Co., 1970).

Braude, "Attitude"   William Gordon Braude, "The Rabbinic Attitude Toward
                         Proselytization and the Social Position of the
                         Proselyte within Jewry in the so-called Talmudic
                         Period: A Survey of Secondary Sources," (M.A. Thesis,
                         Brown Univ., 1934).

Braude, *Proselyting*   William Gordon Braude, *Jewish Proselyting in the
                         First Five Centuries of the Common Era: The Age of
                         the Tannaim and Amoraim*, (Providence, RI: Brown
                         Univ., 1940).

Brockmeyer   Norbert Brockmeyer, *Antike Sklaverei*, (Darmstadt:
                         Wissen-schaftliche Buchgesellschaft, 1987).

Brooks, *Peah*   Roger Brooks, *Support for the Poor in the Mishnaic
                         Law of Agriculture: Tractate Peah*, (Chico, CA:
                         Scholars Press, 1983).

Brunt   P. A. Brunt, Review of Westermann, in *JRS* vol. 48,
                         1958, pp. 164-70.

BT   Babylonian Talmud

Buckland   William W. Buckland, *The Roman Law of Slavery: The
                         Condition of the Slave in Private Law from Augustus
                         to Justinian* (Cambridge: Cambridge Univ. Press,
                         1908).

Cambiano   Giuseppe Cambiano, "Aristotle and the Anonymous
                         Opponents of Slavery," *Slavery and Abolition*, vol. 8,
                         1987, pp. 21-40.

Cantarella

Eva Cantarella, *Pandora's Daughters: The Role and Status of Women in Greek & Roman Antiquity*, (Baltimore: Johns Hopkins, 1987).

Chamberlayne

John H. Chamberlayne, *Man in Society*, (London: Epworth, 1966), esp. pp. 57-59.

Chanock

Martin Chanock, *Law, Custom and Social Order: The Colonial Experience in Malawi and Zambia*, (Cambridge: Cambridge Univ. Press, 1985), esp. pp. 160-171.

Childs, *Exodus*

Brevard Springs Childs, *The Book of Exodus: A Critical Theological Commentary*, (Philadelphia: Westminster, 1974).

Cohen, "Bondage"

Boaz Cohen, "Civil Bondage in Jewish and Roman Law," in *Louis Ginzberg, Jubilee Volume*, (New York: AAJR, 1945), pp. 113-132.

Cohen, "Dowry"

Boaz Cohen, "Dowry and Jewish and Roman Law," in *Jewish and Roman Law: A Comparative Study*, 2 vols., (New York: Jewish Theological Seminary, 1966), pp. 348-376.

Cohen, "Inscriptions"

Ch. Cohen, "Studies in Extra-Biblical Hebrew Inscriptions 1 — The Semantic Range and Usage of the Terms ^{c}amah and shiphah," *Shnaton*, vols. 5-6, 1981-1982, pp. 25-53, (in Hebrew).

Cohen, "Origins"

Shaye J. D. Cohen, "The Origins of the Matrilineal Principle in Rabbinic Law," *AJS Review*, vol. 10, 1985, pp. 19-54.

Cohen, *Reason*

Hermann Cohen, *Religion of Reason out of the Sources of Judaism*, (New York: Ungar, 1972), esp. pp. 124-128.

Cohn

Haim H. Cohn, *Human Rights in Jewish Law*, (New York: KTAV, 1984), esp. pp. 56-63.

Coleman-Norton

P. R. Coleman-Norton, "The Apostle Paul and the Roman Law of Slavery," in *Studies in Roman Economic and Social History in Honor of Allan Chester Johnson*, P. R. Coleman-Norton, ed., (Princeton: Princeton, 1951).

Crook

John Crook, *Law and Life of Rome 90 B.C.—A.D. 212*, (Ithaca, NY: Cornell Univ. Press, 1967).

Dan.

Daniel

Danby, *Mishnah*

Herbert Danby, *The Mishnah*, (Oxford: Oxford Univ. Press, 1933).

Dandamaev	Muhammad A. Dandamaev, *Slavery in Babylonia*, (Dekalb, IL: Northern Illinois Univ. Press, 1984).
Daube, "Catching"	David Daube, "Slave Catching," *Juridical Review*, vol. 64, 1952, pp. 12-28.
Daube, "Causation"	David Daube, "Direct and Indirect Causation in Biblical Law," *VT*, vol. 11, 1961, pp. 246-269.
Daube, "Conversion"	David Daube, "Conversion to Judaism and Early Christianity," in *Ancient Jewish Law*, (Leiden: Brill, 1981), pp. 1-48.
David	M. David, "The Manumission of Slaves under Zedekiah," *OTS*, vol. 5, 1948, pp. 63-79.
Davis, *Culture*	David Brion Davis, *The Problem of Slavery in Western Culture*, (Ithaca, NY: Cornell, 1966).
Davis, *Revolution*	David Brion Davis, *The Problem of Slavery in the Age of Revolution, 1770-1823*, (Ithaca, NY: Cornell Univ. Press, 1975).
Dem.	Demai
Deut.	Deuteronomy
Dias	R. W. M. Dias, "Legal Concept of Freedom," in *Dictionary of the History of Ideas*, (New York: Scribner's, 1973), vol. 2, pp. 248-251.
Dihle	Albrecht Dihle, *The Theory of Will in Classical Antiquity*, (Berkeley: U.Cal. Press, 1982).
Draffkorn	Anne E. Draffkorn, "ILANI/ELOHIM," *JBL*, 76, 1957, pp. 216-224.
Driver & Miles	G. R. Driver & J. C. Miles, *The Assyrian Laws*, (Oxford: Oxford Univ. Press, 1935), esp. pp. 221-230, 306-309.
Duff	A. M. Duff, *Freedmen in the Early Roman Empire*, 2nd ed. (Cambridge: Cambridge Univ. Press, 1958).
Dumont	Louis Dumont, *Homo Hierarchicus: The Caste System and Its Implications*, (Chicago: The University of Chicago Press, 1970).
Ed.	Eduyoth
Ehrlich	E. Ehrlich, *Fundamental Principles of the Sociology of Law*, (Cambridge, MA: Harvard Univ. Press, 1936).
Eichhorn	David Max Eichhorn, ed., *Conversion to Judaism: A History and Analysis*, (New York: KTAV, 1965).

Eilberg-Schwartz

Howard Eilberg-Schwartz, *The Human Will in Judaism: The Mishnah's Philosophy of Intention*, (Atlanta: Scholars Press, 1986).

Eissfeldt

Otto Eissfeldt, *The Old Testament: An Introduction*, (New York: Harper & Row, 1976).

Elkins

Stanley M. Elkins, *Slavery: A Problem in American Institutional and Intellectual Life*, (New York: Grosset and Dunlap, 1963).

Erub.

Erubim

Ex.

Exodus

Falk

Ze'ev W. Falk, *Hebrew Law in Biblical Times: An Introduction*, (Jerusalem: Wahrmann, 1964).

Falk, "Exodus"

Ze'ev W. Falk, "Exodus xxi 6," *VT*, vol. 9, 1959, pp. 86-88.

Farrer

Austin Farrer, "Free Will in Theology," in the *Dictionary of the History of Ideas*, (New York: Scribner's, 1973), vol. 2, pp. 242-248.

Feinberg

Joel Feinberg, "Action and Responsibility," in *Philosophy of Action*, Alan White, ed., (Oxford: Oxford Univ. Press, 1968).

Finley, "Between"

Moses I. Finley, "Between Slavery and Freedom," in Finley, *Greece* .

Finley, *Economy*

Moses I. Finley, *The Ancient Economy* (Berkeley: University of California Press, 1973).

Finley, *Encyclopedia*

Moses I. Finley, "Slavery," in the *International Encyclopedia of the Social Sciences*, 1968, vol. 14, pp. 307-313.

Finley, *Greece*

Moses I. Finley, *Economy and Society in Ancient Greece*, Brent D. Shaw and Richard P. Saller, eds., (New York: Viking, 1982).

Finley, *Ideology*

Moses I. Finley, *Ancient Slavery and Modern Ideology*, (New York: Viking, 1980).

Finley, *Slavery*

Moses I. Finley, ed., *Slavery in Classical Antiquity*, (New York: Barnes and Noble, 1968).

Flesher, "Hierarchy"

Paul V. Flesher, "Hierarchy and Interstitiality: The Bondman and The Freedman in the Mishnah's Caste System," in *NP I*, pp. 103-116.

Flesher, "Name"

Paul Virgil McCracken Flesher, "What's in a Name? The Slave in Scripture and the Mishnah," in William S. Green, *AAJ*, (forthcoming).

Flesher, "Slaves"   Paul Virgil McCracken Flesher, "Slaves, Israelites and
                           the System of the Mishnah," in *NP IV*.

Flesher, "Women"   Paul Virgil McCracken Flesher, "Are Women Property
                           in the System of the Mishnah?" (forthcoming).

Forbes   C. A. Forbes "The Education and Training of Slaves in
                           Antiquity," *Transactions of the American Philological
                           Association*, vol. 86, 1955, pp. 321-360.

Fox-Genovese and Genovese

                           Elizabeth Fox-Genovese and Eugene D. Genovese,
                           *Fruits of Merchant Capital: Slavery and Bourgeois
                           Property in the Rise and Expansion of Capitalism*,
                           (Oxford: Oxford Univ. Press, 1983).

Gaius   F. de Zulueta, *The Institutes of Gaius*, 2 vols., (Oxford:
                           Oxford Univ. Press, 1946).

Geiger   Abraham Geiger, "Nationality, Slavery, Woman's
                           Position," in *Judaism and its History*, (Lanham, NC:
                           University Press of America for Brown Classics in
                           Judaic Studies, 1985).

Gen.   Genesis

Genovese, *Economy*   Eugene D. Genovese, *The Political Economy of
                           Slavery: Studies in the Economy and Society of the
                           Slave South*, (New York: Random House, 1965).

Genovese, *Roll*   Eugene D. Genovese, *Roll, Jordan, Roll: The World
                           the Slaves Made*, (New York: Random House, 1972).

Genovese, *Slaveholders*   Eugene D. Genovese, *The World the Slaveholders
                           Made*, (New York: Vintage, 1969).

Gibbs & Feldman   John G. Gibbs & Louis H. Feldman, "Josephus'
                           Vocabulary for Slavery," in *JQR*, vol. 76, 1986, pp.
                           1-11.

Gilath   Y. D. Gilath, "Intention and Action in the Teaching of
                           the Tannaim," *Annual of Bar Ilan University*, vols. 4-
                           5, 1967, pp. 104-116, (in Hebrew).

Git.   Gittin

Glover   Jonathan Glover, *Responsibility*, (London: Routledge
                           & Kegan Paul, 1970).

Goldstein   Albert S. Goldstein, "Conversion to Judaism in Bible
                           Times," in Eichhorn.

Goodspeed   Edgar J. Goodspeed, "Paul and Slavery," *JBL*, vol. 11,
                           1943, pp. 169-170.

Grant	Robert M. Grant, *Early Christianity and Society*, (New York: Harper & Row, 1977), esp. pp. 89-95.
Gray	Mary P. Gray, "The HABIRU-Hebrew Problem in the Light of the Source Material Available at Present," *HUCA*, vol. 29, 1958, pp. 135-269.
Green	William S. Green, "Redactional Techniques in the Legal Traditions of Joshua B. Hananiah," in J. Neusner, ed., *Christianity, Judaism and Other Greco-Roman Cults*, (Leiden: Brill, 1975), vol. 4, pp. 1-17.
Green, *AAJ*	William Scott Green, ed., *Approaches to Ancient Judaism*, 5 vols., vol. 1, (Missoula, MT: Scholars Press, 1978); vol. 2, (Chico, CA: Scholars Press, 1980); vol. 3, (Chico, CA: Scholars Press, 1981); vol. 4, (Chico, CA: Scholars Press, 1983); vol. 5, (Atlanta: Scholars Press, 1985).
Green, *Joshua*	William Scott Green, *The Traditions of Joshua Ben Hanaiah, Part One, The Early Legal Traditions*, (Leiden: Brill, 1981).
Griffin	Miriam T. Griffin, *Seneca: A Philsopher in Politics*, (Oxford: Oxford Univ. Press, 1976), esp. pp. 256-285.
Haas, *Second Tithe*	Peter Haas, *A History of the Mishnaic Law of Agriculture: Tractate Maaser Sheni*, (Chico, CA: Scholars Press, 1980).
Hag.	Hagigah
Hal.	Hallah
Hall, *Plato*	Robert W. Hall, *Plato*, (London: George Allen & Unwin, 1981).
Hampshire	Stuart Hampshire, *Thought and Action*, (London: Chatto and Windus, 1982).
Hart	H. L. A. Hart, *The Concept of Law*, (Oxford: Oxford Univ. Press, 1961).
Helle	Richard Helle, *Enserfment and Military Change in Muscovy*, (Chicago: The University of Chicago Press, 1971).
Hempel	Carl G. Hempel, *Aspects of Scientific Explanation and other Essays in the Philosophy of Science*, (New York: The Free Press, 1965), esp. pp. 135-172.
Higger	Michael Higger, "Intention in Talmudic Law," in E. M. Gerschfield, ed., *Studies in Jewish Jurisprudence I*, (New York: Hermon Press, 1971), pp. 234-293.

Hoenig	Sidney B. Hoenig, "Conversion During the Talmudic Period," in Eichhorn.
Hor.	Horayoth
HTR	*Harvard Theological Review*
HUCA	*Hebrew Union College Annual*
Hughes	Graham Hughes, "Concept of Law," in the *Dictionary of the History of Ideas*, Philip P. Wiener, ed., (New York: Scribner's, 1973), vol. 3, pp. 1-6.
Hul.	Hullin
Is.	Isaiah
JAAR	*Journal of the American Academy of Religion*
Jaffee, "Lists"	Martin S. Jaffee, "Deciphering Mishnaic Lists: A Form-Analytical Approach," in Green, *AAJ*, vol. 3, pp. 19-35.
Jaffee, *Maaserot*	Martin S. Jaffee, *Mishnah's Theology of Tighing: A Study of Tractate Maaserot*, (Chico, CA: Scholars Press, 1981).
JAOS	*Journal of the American Oriental Society*
Japhet	S. Japhet, "The Laws of Manumission of Slaves," in *Studies in the Bible and the Ancient Near East Presented to Samuel Loewenstamm*, Y. Avishur & J. Blau, eds., (Jerusalem: Rubinstein, 1978), vol. 1, pp. 231-49.
Jastrow	Marcus Jastrow, *A Dictionary of the Targumim, the Talmud Babli and Yerushalmi, and the Midrashic Literature*, (New York: Shalom, 1967).
JBL	*Journal of Biblical Literature*
Jepsen	A. Jepsen, "Ama^h und Shiphcha^h," *VT*, vol. 8, 1958, pp. 293-297.
Jer.	Jeremiah
Jeremias	Joachim Jeremias, *Jerusalem in the Time of Jesus*, (Philadelphia: Fortress, 1969), esp. pp. 342-351.
Jevons	W. Stanley Jevons, *The Principles of Science: A Treatise on Logic and Scientific Method*, (London: Macmillan, 1905), esp. pp. 673-734.
JNES	*Journal of Near Eastern Studies*
Josh.	Joshua
JQR	*Jewish Quarterly Review*
JRS	*Journal of Roman Studies*

Judg.	Judges
Justinian	J. A. C. Thomas, *The Institutes of Justinian: Text, Translation and Commentary*, (Capetown: JUTA, 1975).
Kane, *Anselm*	G. Stanley Kane, *Anselm's Doctrine of Freedom and the Will*, (New York: Edwin Mellen, 1981).
Kane, *Free Will*	R. Kane, *Free Will and Values*, (Albany, NY: SUNY, 1985).
Kel.	Kelim
Kellermann	D. Kellermann, "Gur," in *The Theological Dictionary of the Old Testament*, (Grand Rapids, MI: Eerdmans, 1977), pp. 439-449.
Kelson	Hans Kelson, *General Theory of Law and State*, (Cambridge, MA: Harvard, 1945).
Kenny, *Action*	Anthony Kenny, *Action, Emotion and Will*, (London: Routledge & Keegan Paul, 1963).
Kenny, "Intention"	Anthony Kenny, "Intention and Purpose in Law," in *Essays in Legal Philosophy*, Robert Summers, ed., (Berkeley: U.Cal. Press, 1968).
Ker.	Keritoth
Ket.	Ketuboth
Kiddushin	H. Freedman, *The Babylonian Talmud. Kiddushin*, I. Epstein, ed., (London: Soncino, 1936), esp. pp. 59-123 (14a-25b).
Kil.	Kilaim
Kin.	Kinnim
King	P. D. King, *Law and Society in the Visigothic Kingdom*, (Cambridge: Cambridge Univ. Press, 1972).
Klein	R. W. Klein, "A Liberated Lifestyle. Slaves and Servants in Biblical Perspective," *Currents in Theology and Mission*, vol. 9, 1982, pp. 212-221.
Kunkel	Wolfgang Kunkel, *An Introduction to Roman Legal and Constitutional History*, (Oxford: Oxford Univ. Press, 1967).
Langford	Glenn Langford, *Human Action*, (Garden City, NY: Doubleday, 1971).
Lauterbach	J. Z. Lauterbach, *Mekilta de-Rabbi Ishmael*, 3 vols., (Philadelphia: Jewish Publication Society, 1935-1949).

Lebendiger

Israel Lebendiger, "The Minor in Jewish Law," *JQR*, vol 6-7, 1915-17, pp. 459-93, 89-111, 145-174. Reprinted in *Studies in Jewish Jurisprudence*, vol. I, Edward M. Gershfield, ed., (New York: Hermon, 1971).

Lemche, "Manumission"

N. P. Lemche, "The Manumission of Slaves — The Fallow Year — The Sabbatical Year — The Jobel Year," *VT*, vol. 26, 1976, pp. 38-59.

Lemche, "Slave"

N. P. Lemche, "The 'Hebrew Slave,'" *VT*, vol. 25, 1975, pp. 130-144.

Lev.

Leviticus

Levenson

Jon D. Levenson, "The Eighth Principle of Judaism and the Literary Simultaneity of Scripture," *The Journal of Religion*, vol. 68, 1988, pp. 205-225.

Levine

Baruch A. Levine, "MULUGU/MELUG: The Origins of a Talmudic Legal Institution," *JAOS*, vol. 88, 1968, pp. 271-285.

Levinthal

Israel H. Levinthal, "The Jewish Law of Agency," in *Studies in Jewish Jurisprudence*, vol. I, pp. 231-240, ed. Edward M. Gershfield, (New York: Hermon Press, 1971).

Lévy-Bruhl

Henri Lévy-Bruhl, "Théorie de l'esclavage," in Finley, *Slavery*.

Lipinski

E. Lipinski, "L'esclave hébreu," *VT*, vol. 26, 1975, pp. 120-124.

Lovejoy

Paul E. Lovejoy, *The Ideology of Slavery in Africa*, (London: Sage, 1981).

Lyall, "Adoption"

Francis Lyall, "Roman Law in the Writings of Paul — Adoption," *JBL*, vol. 88, 1969, pp. 458-466.

Lyall, *Metaphors*

Francis Lyall, *Slaves, Citizens, Sons: Legal Metaphors in the Epistles*, (Grand Rapids, Michigan: Zondervan, 1984).

Lyall, "Slave"

Francis Lyall, "Roman Law in the Writings of Paul — The Slave and the Freedman," *NTS*, vol. 17, pp. 73-79.

M

Mishnah

Maas.

Maaseroth

Maimonides, *Holiness*

Moses Maimonides, *The Code of Maimonides. Book Five. The Book of Holiness*, Louis I. Rabinowitz & Philip Grossman, trans., (New Haven: Yale, 1965).

Maimonides, *Mishnah*   Moses Maimonides, *Mishnah with Commentary by our Rabbi Moses ben Maimon*, (Jerusalem: Mosad HaRav Kook), (in Hebrew).

Maimonides, *Mishneh Torah*

Moses Maimonides, *Mishneh Torah*, (Jerusalem: Mosad HaRav Kook), (in Hebrew).

Maimonides, *Slaves*   Moses Maimonides, *The Code of Maimonides. Book Twelve. The Book of Acquisition*, Isaac Klein, trans., (New Haven: Yale, 1951), pp. 245-282.

Maine   H. Maine, *Ancient Law*, (London: 1861 (repr. 1930)).

Mak.   Makkoth

Maks.   Makshirin

Malina   Bruce J. Malina, *The New Testament World: Insights from Cultural Anthropology*, (Atlanta, GA: John Knox, 1981).

Malinowski   Bronislaw Malinowski, *Freedom and Civilization*, (New York: Roy, 1944).

Mandelbaum, *Kilayim*   Irving Mandelbaum, *A History of the Mishnaic Law of Agriculture: Kilayim*, (Chico, CA: Scholars Press, 1982).

Meg.   Megillah

Meil.   Meilah

Meiland   Jack W. Meiland, *The Nature of Intention*, (London: Methuen & Co., 1970).

Men.   Menahoth

Mendelsohn   I. Mendelsohn, "The Canaanite Term for 'Free Proletarian,'" *BASOR*, vol. 83, 1941, pp. 36-39.

Mendelsohn, "Alalakh"   I. Mendelsohn, "On Slavery in Alalakh," *Israel Exploration Journal*, vol. 5, 1955, pp. 65-72.

Mendelsohn, "Hupsu"   I. Mendelsohn, "New Light on the Hupsu," *BASOR*, vol. 139, 1955, pp. 9-11.

Mendelsohn, "Sale"   I. Mendelsohn, "The Conditional Sale into Slavery of Free-Born Daughters in Nuzi and the Law of Ex. 21:7-11," *JAOS*, vol. 55, pp. 190-195.

Mendelsohn, *Slavery*   Isaac Mendelsohn, *Slavery in the Ancient Near East: A Comparative Study of Slavery in Babylonia, Assyria, Syria and Palestine; From the Middle of the Third Millennium to the End of the First Millennium*, (Oxford: Oxford Univ. Press, 1949).

Mendelsohn, "State"   I. Mendelsohn, "State slavery in ancient Palestine," *Bull. Sch. Orient. Afr. Stud.*, vol. 29, 1942, pp. 64-78.

Mid.   Middoth

Miers and Kopytoff   Suzanne Miers and Igor Kopytoff, eds., *Slavery in Africa: Historical and Anthropological Perspectives*, (Madison: Univ. of Wisconsin Press, 1977).

Mik.   Mikwaoth

Milgrom   J. Milgrom, "The Betrothed Slave-girl, Lev 19:20-22," *ZAW*, vol. 89, 1977. Reprinted in *Cult and Conscience*, (Leiden: Brill, 1976), pp. 129-137.

Miller, "Contributions"   Dean A. Miller, "Biblical and Rabbinic Contributions to an Understanding of the Slave," in William S. Green, *Approaches to Ancient Judaism: Theory and Practice*, vol. 1, (Missoula, MT: Scholars Press, 1978), pp. 187-200.

Miller, "Perceptions"   Dean A. Miller, "Some Psyco-Social Perceptions of Slavery," *Journal of Social History*, 1985, pp. 587-605.

Milligan   David Milligan, *Reasoning and the Explanation of Actions*, (Brighton: Harvester, 1980).

Momigliano   Arnaldo Momigliano, "Moses Finley and Slavery: A Personal Note," *Slavery and Abolition*, vol. 8, 1987, pp. 1-6.

Moore   George Foot Moore, *Judaism in the First Centuries of the Christian Era: The Age of the Tannaim*, 2 vols., (Cambridge, MA: Harvard Univ. Press, 1927), esp. vol. 2, pp. 135-139.

Morris, *Freedom*   Herbert Morris, ed., *Freedom and Responsibility: Readings in Philosophy and Law*, (Stanford: Stanford Univ. Press, 1961).

Morris, *Guilt*   Herbert Morris, *On Guilt and Innocence: Essays in Legal Philosophy and Moral Psychology*, (Berkeley: U.Cal. Press, 1976).

Morrow   G. R. Morrow, *Plato's Law of Slavery in its Relation to Greek Law*, (Urbana, IL: Univ. of Illinois Press, 1939).

Morrow, *City*   Glenn R. Morrow, *Plato's Cretan City: A Historical Interpretation of the* Laws, (Princeton: Princeton Univ. Press, 1960).

Mossé	Claude Mossé, *The Ancient World at Work*, (New York: Norton, 1969), esp. pp. 62-74.
MQ	Moed Qatan
MS	Maaser Sheni
Myrdal	Gunner Myrdal, "Women, Servants, Mules and Other Property," in *Masculine/Feminine: Readings in Sexual Mythology and the Liberation of Women*, Betty Roszak & Theodore Roszak, eds., (New York: Harper & Row, 1969), pp. 68-76.
Naz.	Nazir
Ned.	Nedarim
Neg.	Negaim
Neh.	Nehemiah
Neufeld	E. Neufeld, *Ancient Hebrew Marriage Laws*, (London, 1944).
Neusner, *Appointed Times*	Jacob Neusner, *A History of the Mishnaic Law of Appointed Times*, 5 vols., (Leiden: Brill, 1981-1983).
Neusner, "Comparison"	Jacob Neusner, "Toward a Theory of Comparison: Alike and Not Alike. A Grid for Comparison and Differentiation," in *Judaism in the American Humanities*, (Chico, CA: Scholars Press, 1981), pp. 91-100.
Neusner, *Cults*	Jacob Neusner, ed., *Christianity, Judaism and Other Greco-roman Cults: Studies for Morton Smith at Sixty*, 4 vols., (Leiden: Brill, 1975).
Neusner, *Damages*	Jacob Neusner, *A History of the Mishnaic Law of Damages*, 5 vols., (Leiden: Brill, 1983-1985).
Neusner, *Eliezer*	Jacob Neusner, *Eliezer ben Hyrcanus: The Tradition and the Man*, 2 vols., (Leiden: Brill, 1973).
Neusner, *Evidence*	Jacob Neusner, *Judaism: The Evidence of the Mishnah*, (Chicago: The University of Chicago Press, 1981).
Neusner, *Holy Things*	Jacob Neusner, *A History of the Mishnaic Law of Holy Things*, 6 vols., (Leiden: Brill, 1978-1980).
Neusner, *Method*	Jacob Neusner, *Method and Meaning in Ancient Judaism*, (Missoula, MT: Scholars Press, 1979); *Second Series*, (Chico, CA: Scholars Press, 1981); *Third Series*, (Chico, CA: Scholars Press, 1981).
Neusner, *Purities*	Jacob Neusner, *A History of the Mishnaic Law of Purities*, 22 vols., (Leiden: Brill, 1974-1977).

Neusner, *School*

Jacob Neusner, *School, Court, Public Administration: Judaism and its Institutions in Talmudic Babylonia*, (Atlanta: Scholars Press, 1987), esp. pp. 272-275.

Neusner, *Study*

Jacob Neusner, ed., *The Modern Study of the Mishnah*, (Leiden: Brill, 1973).

Neusner, *Women*

Jacob Neusner, *A History of the Mishnaic Law of Women*, 5 vols., (Leiden: Brill, 1980).

Neusner, *Yerushalmi*

Jacob Neusner, *The Talmud of the Land of Israel: A Preliminary Translation and Explanation*, 35 vols., (Chicago: The University of Chicago Press, 1983-).

Newman, *Shebiit*

Louis Newman, *The Sanctity of the Seventh Year: A Study of Mishnah Tractate Shebiit*, (Chico, CA: Scholars Press, 1983).

Nid.

Niddah

North

Robert North, *Sociology of the Biblical Jubilee*, (Rome:1954).

NP I

J. Neusner, P. Borgen, E. S. Frerichs, R. Horsley, eds., *New Perspectives on Ancient Judaism, Volume I: Religion, Literature, and Society in Ancient Israel, Formative Christianity and Judaism*, (Lanham, MD: University Press of America, 1987).

NP IV

Alan J. Avery-Peck, ed., *New Perspectives on Ancient Judaism , Volume IV, The Literature of Early Rabbinic Judaism: Issues in Talmudic Redaction and Interpretation*, (Lanham, MD: University Press of America, 1988).

NTS

New Testament Studies.

Num.

Numbers

Oh.

Oholoth

Oppenheim, *Freedom*

Felix E. Oppenheim, *Dimensions of Freedom: An Analysis*, (New York: St. Martin's, 1961).

Oppenheim, *Mesopotamia*

A. Leo Oppenheim, *Ancient Mesopotamia: Portrait of a Dead Civilization*, (Chicago: The University of Chicago Press, 1964), esp. pp. 74-77.

Or.

Orlah

OTS

Old Testament Studies

Otwell

John H. Otwell, *And Sarah Laughed: The Status of Women in the Old Testament*, (Philadelphia: Westminster, 1977).

Par.

Parah

Patrick	Dale Patrick, *Old Testament Law*, (Atlanta: John Knox Press, 1985).
Patterson, "Slavery"	Orlando Patterson, "Slavery," *Ann. Rev. Sociol.*, vol. 3, 1977, pp. 407-449.
Patterson, *Social Death*	Orlando Patterson, *Slavery and Social Death: A Comparative Study*, (Cambridge, MA: Harvard Univ. Press, 1982).
Paul	Shalom M. Paul, *Studies in the Book of the Covenant in the Light of Cuneiform and Biblical Law*, (Leiden: Brill, 1970).
Paul, "Ex. 21:10"	Shalom M. Paul, "Exod. 21:10 A Threefold Maintenance Clause," *JNES*, vol. 28, 1969, pp. 48-53.
Pears	D. F. Pears, ed., *Freedom and The Will*, (London: Macmillan, 1963).
Pes.	Pesahim
Petersen	Norman R. Petersen, *Rediscovering Paul: Philemon and the Sociology of Paul's Narrative World*, (Philadelphia: Fortress, 1985).
Plato, *Laws*	*The Laws of Plato*, Thomas L. Pangle, trans., (New York: Basic, 1980).
Plato, *Republic*	*Plato, The Republic*, Desmond Lee, trans., (New York: Penguin, 1974).
Pope	M. H. Pope, "Proselyte," in *The Interpreters Dictionary of the Bible*, vol. 3, (New York: Abingdon, 1962), pp. 921-931.
Porton, "Dispute"	Gary G. Porton, "The Artificial Dispute: Ishmael and Aqiba," in Neusner, *Cults*, vol. 4, pp. 18-29.
Prov.	Proverbs
Psalm.	Psalms
PT	Palestinian Talmud
Qehati	Pinchas Qehati, *Mishnayot*, 6 vols., (Jerusalem: Hekal Shelemah), (in Hebrew).
Qid.	Qiddushin
Rattray	Susan Rattray, "Marriage Rules, Kinship Terms and Family Structure in the Bible," in *SBL Seminar Papers*, 1987, ed. Kent Harold Richards, (Atlanta: Scholars Press, 1987), pp. 537-544.

Raymer — A. J. Raymer, "Slavery — The Graeco-Roman Defense," *Greece and Rome,* 2nd ser., vol. 10 (20), 1940, pp. 17-21.

Reid — Anthony Reid, *Slavery, Bondage and Dependency in South East Asia,* (New York: St. Martins, 1983).

Reuck and Knight — Anthony de Reuck and Julie Knight, eds., *Caste and Race: Comparative Approaches,* (Boston: Little, Brown and Co., 1967), esp. pp. 5-16, 166-222.

RH — Rosh Ha-Shannah

Robertson & Klein — Claire C. Robertson and Martin A. Klein, eds. *Women and Slavery in Africa,* (Madison, WI: Univ. Wisconsin, 1983).

Rollins — Wayne G. Rollins, "Greco-Roman Slave Terminology and Pauline Metaphors for Salvation," in *SBL Seminar Papers,* 1987, ed. Kent Harold Richards, (Atlanta: Scholars Press, 1987), pp. 100-110.

Rosenbloom — Joseph R. Rosenbloom, *Conversion to Judaism: from the Biblical Period to the Present,* (Cincinnati, OH: Hebrew Union College, 1978).

Ryle — Gilbert Ryle, *The Concept of Mind,* (London: Hutchinson House, 1949).

Saller — Richard Saller, "Slavery and the Roman Family," *Slavery and Abolition,* vol. 8, 1987, pp. 65-87.

Sam. — Samuel

San. — Sanhedrin

Sandars — Thomas Collett Sandars, *The Institutes of Justinian with English Introduction, Translation and Notes,* (London: Longmans, Green and Co, 1922), (repr. Westport, CT: Greenwood, 1970).

Sarason, *Demai* — Richard S. Sarason, *A History of the Mishnaic Law of Agriculture: A Study of Tractate Demai,* Part One, (Leiden: Brill, 1979).

Savigny — Friedrick Karl von Savigny, *History of the Roman law during the middle ages,* (Edinburgh, 1829).

Schereschewsky — Ben-Zion Schereschewsky, "Dowry," in *The Principles of Jewish Law,* Menachem Elon, ed., (Jerusalem: Keter, 1975), pp. 390-394.

Schreiner — T. R. Schreiner, "Proselyte," in *The International Standard Bible Encyclopedia,* Geoffrey W. Bromiley et

	al., eds., (Grand Rapids, MI: Eerdmans, 1986), vol. 3, pp. 1005-1011.
Schwartz	Baruch J. Schwartz, "A Literary Study of the Slave-Girl Pericope — Lev. 19:20-22," *Scripta Hierosolymitana*, vol. 31, 1986, (Jerusalem:Magnes, 1986), Sara Japhet, ed., pp. 241-255.
Scott	S. P. Scott, *The Visigothic Code (Forum Judicum)*, (Boston: Boston Book, 1910).
Searle	John Searle, *Intentionality*, (Cambridge: Cambridge Univ. Press, 1983).
Shab.	Shabbath
Shebi.	Shebiith
Shebu.	Shebuoth
Sheq.	Sheqalim
Silver	Morris Silver, *Prophets and Markets: The Political Economy of Ancient Israel*, (Boston: Kluwer-Nijhoff Publishing, 1983).
Smallwood	Mary Smallwood, *The Jews under Roman Rule*, (Leiden: Brill, 1976), esp. p. 469.
Smith, *Bondage*	Abbot Emerson Smith, *Colonists in Bondage: White Servitude and Convict Labor in America 1606-1776*, (Chapel Hill, NC: Univ. North Carolina Press, 1947).
Smith, "Comparison"	Jonathan Z. Smith, "In Comparison a Magic Dwells," in Smith, *Religion*.
Smith, *Map*	Jonathan Z. Smith, *Map is Not Territory*, (Leiden: Brill, 1978).
Smith, *Place*	Jonathan Z. Smith, *To Take Place: Jerusalem as a Focus of Ritual*, (Chicago: The University of Chicago Press, 1987).
Smith, *Religion*	Jonathan Z. Smith, *Imagining Religion: From Babylon to Jonestown*, (Chicago: The University of Chicago Press, 1982).
Sokolowski	F. Sokolowski, "The Real Meaning of Sacral Manumission," *HTR*, vol. 47, 1954, pp. 173-181.
Solodukho	Yu. A. Solodukho, "Slavery in the Hebrew Society of Iraq and Syria in the Second through Fifth Centuries A.D.," in *Soviet Views of Talmudic Judaism*, (Leiden: Brill, 1973), pp. 1-9.
Solomon	R. Solomon, *L'Esclavage en droit comparé juif et romain*, (Paris, 1931).

Sot.	Sotah
Stace	C. Stace, "The Slaves of Plautus," *Greece and Rome*, vol. 15, 1968, pp. 64-77.
Stampp	Kenneth M. Stampp, *The Peculiar Institution: Slavery in the Ante-Bellum South*, (New York: Random House, 1956).
Ste Croix	G. E. M. Ste Croix, Review of Westermann, in *Classical Review*, n.s. vol. 7, 1957, pp. 54-59.
Suk.	Sukkah
Swartley	W. M. Swartley, *Slavery, Sabbath, War and Women*, (Kitchener, Ontario: Herald, 1983).
Taa.	Taanith
Tam.	Tamid
Tem.	Temurah
Ter.	Terumoth
Thomas	See Justinian
Toh.	Tohoroth
Tos.	Tosefta
Tractate on Slavery	Maurice Simon, trans., "ᶜAbadim," in *The Minor Tractates of the Talmud*, A. Cohen, ed., 2 vols., (London: Soncino, 1965), vol. 2, pp. 623-630.
Treggiari	Susan Treggiari, *Roman Freedmen during the Late Republic*, (Oxford: Oxford Univ. Press, 1969).
Trusted	Jennifer Trusted, *Free Will and Responsibility*, (Oxford: Oxford Univ. Press, 1984).
Turnbam	Timothy John Turnbam, "Male and Female Slaves in the Sabbath Year Laws of Exodus 21:1-11," in *SBL Seminar Papers*, 1987, ed. Kent Harold Richards, (Atlanta: Scholars Press, 1987), pp. 545-549.
Turner	V. W. Turner, *Schism and Continuity in an African Society*, (Manchester, 1957), esp. pp. 189.
TY	Tebul Yom
Uk.	Uktzin
Urbach	Ephraim E. Urbach, "The Laws Regarding Slavery as a Source for Social History of the Period of the Second Temple, the Mishnah, and Talmud," in *Papers of the Institute...*, Institute of Jewish Studies, vol. 1, J. G. Weiss, ed., (Jerusalem: Magnes, 1964), repr. (Lanham, MD: University Press of America, 1988).

van der Ploeg   J. P. M. van der Ploeg, "Slavery in the Old Testament," *VT Suppl*, vol. 22, 1972, pp. 72-87.

Vaux   Roland de Vaux, *Ancient Israel: Vol. 1: Social Institutions*, (New York: 1965), esp. pp. 80-90.

Vidal-Naquet   Pierre Vidal-Naquet, *The Black Hunter: Forms of Thought and Forms of Society in the Greek World*, (Baltimore: Johns Hopkins, 1986), esp. pp. 159-223.

Vlastos   Gregory Vlastos, "Slavery in Plato's Republic," in *The Philosophical Review* 50 (1941), reprinted in Finley, *Slavery*.

Vogt   Joseph Vogt, *Ancient Slavery and the Ideal of Man*, (Cambridge, MA: Harvard, 1975).

VT   *Vetus Testamentum*

Wacholder   Ben Zion Wacholder, "The Halakah and the Proselyting of Slaves during the Gaonic Era," *Historia Judaica*, vol. 18, 1956, pp. 89-106.

Watson, *Asian*   James L. Watson, ed., *Asian and African Systems of Slavery*, (Berkeley: University of California Press, 1980).

Watson, *Free Will*   Gary Watson, ed., *Free Will*, (Oxford: Oxford Univ. Press, 1982).

Watson, *Persons*   Alan Watson, *The Law of Persons in the Later Roman Republic*, (Oxford: Oxford Univ. Press, 1967).

Watson, *Roman*   Alan Watson, *Roman Slave Law*, (Baltimore: Johns Hopkins, 1987).

Watson, "Slave Law"   Alan Watson, "Roman Slave Law and Romanist Ideology," *Phoenix*, vol. 37, 1983, pp. 53-65.

Wegner, "Dependency"   Judith Romney Wegner, "Dependency, Autonomy, and Sexuality: Woman as Chattel and Person in the Mishnah, in *NP I*, pp. 89-102.

Wegner, *Women*   Judith Romney Wegner, *Chattel or Person? The Status of Women in the Mishnah*, (Oxford: Oxford Univ. Press, forthcoming 1988).

Westermann   William L. Westermann, *The Slave Systems of Greek and Roman Antiquity*, (Philadelphia: American Philosophical Society, 1955).

Westermann, "Between"   William Lynn Westermann, "Between Slavery and Freedom," *AHR*, vol. 50, 1945, pp. 213-227.

Westermann, "Free"   William Lynn Westermann, "Enslaved Persons who are
                         Free," *American Journal of Philology*, vol. 59, 1938,
                         pp. 1-30.

Westermann, "Freedmen"   William Lynn Westermann, "The freedmen and the
                         slaves of God," *Proceedings of the American
                         Philosophical Society*, vol. 92, 1948, pp. 55-64.

Westermann, "Manumission"

                         William Lynn Westermann, "Two Studies in Athenian
                         Manumission," *JNES*, vol. 5, 1946, pp. 92-104.

Westermann, "Slavery"   William Lynn Westermann, "Slavery and the Elements
                         of Freedom in Ancient Greece," *Bulletin of the Polish
                         Institute of Arts and Sciences in America*, vol. 1,
                         1943, pp. 332-347.

Wiedemann   Thomas Wiedemann, *Greek and Roman Slavery*,
                         (Baltimore: Johns Hopkins, 1981).

White, "Interpretation" Hayden White, "Interpretation in History," in *Tropics
                         of Discourse: Essays in Cultural Criticism* (Baltimore,
                         MD: Johns Hopkins, 1978), pp. 51-80.

White, *Metahistory*   Hayden White, *Metahistory: The Historical
                         Imagination in Nineteenth-Century Europe* (Baltimore:
                         MD: Johns Hopkins, 1973).

Williams   C. O. Williams, *Thraldom in Ancient Iceland*,
                         (Chicago: The University of Chicago Press, 1937).

Willis   John Ralph Willis, *Slaves and Slavery in Muslim
                         Africa: Volume One — Islam and the Ideology of
                         Slavery*, (London: Frank Cass, 1985).

Wolff   Hans Walter Wolff, *Anthropology of the Old
                         Testament*, (Philadelphia: Fortress, 1974), esp. pp.
                         199-206.

Wolff, *Law*   Hans Julius Wolff, *Roman Law: An Historical
                         Introduction*, (Norman, OK: University of Oklahoma
                         Press, 1951).

Wolff, "Westermann"   H. J. Wolff, Review of Westermann, in *Iura*, vol. 7,
                         1956, pp. 308-315.

Wood   Ellen Meiksins Wood, "Agricultural Slavery in
                         Classical Athens," *American Journal of Ancient
                         History*, vol. 8, 1983, pp. 1-47.

Yad.   Yadaim

Yaron

Reuven Yaron, "The Goring Ox in Near Eastern Laws," in H. H. Cohn, *Jewish Law in Ancient and Modern Israel*, (New York: KTAV, 1971), pp. 50-60.

Yeb.

Yebamoth

Yehuda

Z. A. Yehuda, "The Two Mekhiltot on the Hebrew Slave," Unpublished Ph.D. dissertation, Yeshiva University, 1974.

Yerushalmi

Palestinian Talmud

YT

Yom Tob

Zab.

Zabim

ZAW

Zeitschrift für altestamentliche Wissenschaft

Zeb.

Zebahim

Zeitlin, "Proselytes"

Solomon Zeitlin, "Proselytes and Proselytism during the Second Commonwealth and The Early Tannaitic Period," in *H. A. Wolfson Jubilee Volume*, 1965, vol. 2, pp. 871-81.

Zeitlin, *Rise*

Solomon Zeitlin, *The Rise and Fall of the Judean State: A Political, Social and Religious History of the Second Commonwealth*, 3 vols., (Philadelphia: JPSA, 1969), esp. vol. 2, pp. 271-78.

Zeitlin, "Samuel"

Solomon Zeitlin, "Mar Samuel and Manumission of Slaves," in *Studies in the Early History of Judaism*, vol. 4, (New York: KTAV, 1978), pp. 259-261.

Zeitlin, "Slavery"

Solomon Zeitlin, "Slavery During the Second Commonwealth and the Tannaitic Period," in *Studies in the Early History of Judaism*, vol. 4, (New York: KTAV, 1978), pp. 225-258.

Zimmern

A. Zimmern, "Was Greek civilization based on slave labour?" *Sociol. Rev.*, vol. 2, 1909, pp. 1-19, 159-176.

Zucrow

Solomon Zucrow, *Women, Slaves and the Ignorant in Rabbinic Literature*, (Boston: The Stratford Co., 1932).

Zuluetta

See Gaius

Appendix

Mishnah Passages Mentioning Slaves

This appendix lists the 129 passages in which the Mishnah uses a word meaning "slave" (עבד, שפחה or אמה). The first 123 belong to the Mishnah's main system of slavery (I), while the last six carry forward Scripture's categories of slaves (II). I further divide the first group into two parts. The first part (IA) delineates passages that focus on the issue of whether or not a householder has control over his slave. The passages in the second part (IB) do not turn on that issue.

IA.   104 passages that focus on whether the bondman or freedman stand subject to a householder's control.

1.	Arak. 1:1		19.	BM 4:9
2.	Arak. 3:1		20.	BM 7:6
3.	Arak. 3:3		21.	BM 8:3
4.	Arak. 6:5		22.	BM 8:4
5.	BB 3:1		23.	BQ 3:10
6.	BB 4:7		24.	BQ 4:5
7.	BB 5:1		25.	BQ 5:4
8.	BB 10:7		26.	BQ 8:1
9.	Bek. 1:7		27.	BQ 8:4
10.	Bek. 8:1		28.	BQ 9:2
11.	Bek. 8:7		29.	Ed. 1:13a
12.	Bek. 8:8		30.	Ed. 1:13b
13.	Ber. 3:3		31.	Ed. 5:6
14.	Ber. 7:2		32.	Git. 1:4
15.	Bikk. 1:5a		33.	Git. 1:5
16.	Bikk. 1:5b		34.	Git. 1:6
17.	Bikk. 3:12		35.	Git. 2:3
18.	BM 1:7		36.	Git. 4:4

37.	Git. 4:5a	71.	RH 1:8
38.	Git. 4:5b	72.	San. 11:1
39.	Git. 4:6	73.	Shebi. 8:8
40.	Git. 7:4	74.	Shebu. 4:12
41.	Git. 9:2	75.	Shebu. 5:5a
42.	Hag. 1:1	76.	Shebu. 5:5b
43.	Hor. 3:8	77.	Shebu. 6:5
44.	Ker. 1:3	78.	Sheq. 1:3
45.	Ket. 1:2	79.	Sheq. 1:5
46.	Ket. 1:4	80.	Sheq. 1:6
47.	Ket. 2:9	81.	Sot. 1:6
48.	Ket. 3:1	82.	Sot. 3:8
49.	Ket. 3:2	83.	Suk. 2:1
50.	Ket. 3:7	84.	Suk. 2:8
51.	Ket. 3:9	85.	Suk. 3:10
52.	Ket. 5:5	86.	Tem. 6:2
53.	Ket. 8:5	87.	Ter. 3:4
54.	Men. 9:8	88.	Ter. 7:3
55.	MQ 2:4	89.	Ter. 8:1
56.	MS 1:7	90.	Yad. 4:7
57.	MS 5:14	91.	Yeb. 2:5
58.	Naz. 9:1	92.	Yeb. 7:1
59.	Neg. 14:12	93.	Yeb. 7:2
60.	Peah 3:8	94.	Yeb. 7:3
61.	Pes. 7:2	95.	Yeb. 7:5
62.	Pes. 8:1a	96.	Yeb. 8:1
63.	Pes. 8:1b	97.	Yeb. 8:2
64.	Pes. 8:2	98.	Yeb. 11:2
65.	Pes. 8:7	99.	Yeb. 11:5
66.	Qid. 3:12	100.	Zab. 2:1
67.	Qid. 3:13	101.	Zab. 2:3
68.	Qid. 4:1	102.	Zeb. 3:1
69.	Qid. 4:7	103.	Zeb. 5:6
70.	RH 1:7	104.	Zeb. 5:7

IB.   Nineteen passages concerning the bondman and the freedman that do not focus on the issue of the householder's control.

105.	Abot 1:3	(1.)		115.	Ker. 2:5	(11.)
106.	Abot 2:7	(2.)		116.	Ker. 2:9	(12.)
107.	Ber. 2:7	(3.)		117.	Oh. 18:7	(13.)
108.	BQ 5:6	(4.)		118.	Qid. 2:3	(14.)
109.	BQ 6:5	(5.)		119.	Sot. 6:2	(15.)
110.	Erub. 5:5	(6.)		120.	Suk. 2:9	(16.)
111.	Git. 4:9	(7.)		121.	Yeb. 2:8	(17.)
112.	Ker. 2:2	(8.)		122.	Yeb. 16:7	(18.)
113.	Ker. 2:3	(9.)		123.	Zeb. 5:5	(19.)
114.	Ker. 2:4	(10.)				

II.   Six passages that carry forward Scripture's categories of Hebrew indentured servant and Canaanite slave.

124.	Arak. 8:4-5	(1.)
125.	BM 1:5	(2.)
126.	BQ 8:3&5	(3.)
127.	Erub. 7:6	(4.)
128.	MS 4:4	(5.)
129.	Qid. 1:2-3	(6.)

Index of Texts Cited

Hebrew Scriptures

The Mishnah

General Index

Abraham   14-5, 151, 154.
Acts requiring reason   37-8, 51-3, 77-88, 105-7, 119-131, 142-3, 160.
Adler, Mortimer J.   162.
Adult Daughter   45-9, 105-7.
Agency 79-81, 127-131.
Albeck, Hanock 14, 82, 113, 115, 146.
amah   17.
Animals   85-90, 108.
Aristotle   27, 37.
avdut   161.
Avery-Peck, Alan J.   44.
Avot   15.
Babylonian Talmud   iii, 3.
Bamberger, Bernard   i.
Bertinoro   123.
Bondman   32-8, 40-5, 58-9, 62, 67-108, 109-37, 145-7, 152, 159-71.
Bondwoman   90-102, 129, 131-4, 144-5, 156. See also Bondman.
Brody, Robert   vi.
Canaan 54.
Canaanite Slave 35-6, 54-9. See also Foreign Slave.
Caste Status 22, 37, 44-5, 90-102, 112-9, 129, 135-7, 147-51.
Caste System   6, 90-102, 112-9, 135-7, 147-51.
Chamberlayne, John 21.
Children   16, 31, 94. See also Minor.
Childs, Brevard 24.
Circumcision   22, 112.
Citizen 1, 7. See also Householder.

Classification   See Taxonomy.
Cleanness   See Cultic Purity.
Cohen, Boaz   i, 32, 92.
Cohn, Haim i.
Concubine   17.
Congregation   114-5, 151.
Control See Householder's Control.
Control Relationships   165-72.
Covenant Code   12.
Cultic Purity 37, 85, 88, 111, 123-4, 131-7, 154-5.
Daube, David   24.
Daughter   iv, 92-3, 99-100. See also Minor Daughter, Adult Daughter.
Deaf-Mute   53, 83, 88, 120, 133, 155.
Deuteronomic source   12.
Dickens, Charles v.
Dihle, Albrecht   162.
Divorcee   45-50, 83, 97, 105-7, 150.
Draffkorn, Anne 20.
Dumont, Louis   34.
Ehrlich, E.   iv.
Eilberg-Schwartz, Howard   vi, 29, 60, 130, 163-5.
Eissfeldt, Otto   12.
Eliezer 44, 50, 141-2, 143.
Falk, Zeev   18, 20.
Finley, Moses I. 27, 173-4, 177.
Foreign Slave   11-8, 21-6. See also Canaanite Slave.
Foreigner   16-7, 19, 30-1, 39-40, 54, 94-5, 98, 110, 117-8, 125, 127, 148-51.
Foundling   114-5, 148-50.